A.J. Liebling

BACK WHERE I CAME FROM

With a Foreword by Philip Hamburger

1990
NORTH POINT PRESS
San Francisco

LIBRARY OF CONGRESS CATALOGING-IN-PUBLICATION DATA
Liebling, A. J. (Abbott Joseph), 1904–1963.
    Back where I came from / A. J. Liebling; with a foreword by Philip
Hamburger.
        p. cm.
    Reprint. Originally published: New York: Sheridan House, c1938.
    ISBN 0-86547-425-7
    1. New York (N.Y.)—Social life and customs. 2. New York
(N.Y.)—Popular culture—History—20th century. 3. Liebling, A. J.
(Abbott Joseph), 1904–1963. I. Title.
F128.5.L66   1990
974.7′1042—dc20   89-38678

North Point Press
850 Talbot Avenue
Berkeley, California
94706

To Ann

Why don't you go back where you came from?   OLD AMERICAN FOLK SAYING

A New Yorker doesn't have to discover New York. He knows it's there all the time.
WHITEY BIMSTEIN

CONTENTS

CONTENTS

CONTENTS

FOREWORD

By Philip Hamburger

Back Where I Came From, a masterpiece of early Liebling, is a
love letter to the City of New York. Abbott Joseph Liebling (here-
inafter referred to as Joe) conducted an ardent and public affair
with the city of his birth. There was very little about the city that
did not entrance him and stimulate his literary juices. The sights,
the sounds, the smells, the people, and perhaps more acutely than
most of his contemporaries, the native manner of speaking gave
him special pleasure. He treasured stray phrases, uttered inno-
cently and without pretension. (Joe could spot pretension nine
miles away.) Let Izzy Yereshevsky of the immortal I and Y Cigar
Store remark that "I am de most wictim on Broadway" and Joe
was happy for a week. Tinhorn entrepreneurs who called the
Club Chez Nous the Club Chestnuts sent him joyously humming,
in a state of euphoria, to his typewriter. I had the privilege for
many years at *The New Yorker* of inhabiting a series of offices near
those occupied by Joe, close enough, in fact, to hear his grunts,
chirps, giggles, and often belly laughs of self-appreciation as he
read something that had just emerged onto his copy paper. This
is not to suggest that Joe was an immodest man. The pleasure that
he took in his own work merely reflected his sound judgment in
recognizing a good thing when he saw it.

Joe's physical largeness was matched by his immense learning,
his intense and widespread reading, his friendships with just
about everybody everywhere. To this must be added a glorious
and indefinable sense of humor, what William Shawn once re-

5

ferred to as "his special humor—the Liebling humor—quickened almost everything he ever set down on paper." Readers revelled in what Liebling wrote. His generosity of spirit spilled onto the printed page, and the result was a feeling, on the part of readers, that they were fully sharing in Joe's experiences. He has been dead now for more than a quarter of a century, and every year more and more discerning people have learned to treasure his work. There is little point in even bothering to note that so-called "serious critics" did not pay him sufficient heed during his lifetime. In so-called literary circles this is accepted par for the course. The facts are that Joe wrote beautiful prose and that people loved to read him, and I have always felt that matters were pretty well summed up at Joe's funeral by words spoken by his closest friend, Joseph Mitchell, who said, "Joe is dead, but he really isn't. He is dead, but he will live again. Every time anyone anywhere in all the years to come takes down one of his books and reads or rereads one of his wonderful stories, he will live again."

And he certainly lives again in *Back Where I Came From*. Solemn literary probing of what lies ahead, be it constructionist, deconstructionist, Zen or vegetarian, would serve only to spoil the fun and destroy the human connections. Just plunge in, relax, and enjoy yourselves.

For my part, I want to talk about my friendship with Joe. Some of the memories are framed with dazzling clarity, others have become clouded, perhaps even romanticized, as the years have passed. We talked a great deal with one another in the office, or at our respective homes. We ate countless lunches and dinners together. We often went to concerts or theaters together. We discussed books and plays, mutual acquaintances, and the state of the world. I have no way of knowing how close he may have felt to me, but in my life he was always a major presence. He gave remarkable encouragement to a younger writer. (I was ten years his junior, but I had such respect for his erudition and experience that I felt much younger.)

Like the Franklin D. Roosevelt he so much admired, Joe knew how to listen. In fact, he could listen with such silent attention to what one was saying, an attention that often precluded his making any response whatsoever, that people were often shaken to their roots. Joe would sit and stare, one hand drooped in a characteristic gesture, and listen. He was really performing two functions at the same time. For one, he was actually listening, not missing a single syllable, filing away every nuance in his photographic memory. For another, he knew that by just sitting and staring he could, sooner or later, break down his listener into pouring out his or her heart. It was an unnerving tactic, but a highly skilled one. People who started out reluctant even to tell Joe the date of their birth found themselves revealing intimate facts of their lives and times.

Joe liked to entertain on the grand scale. He relished being surrounded by friends, and he enjoyed supplying them with the very best, and in the largest quantities, of food and drink. He had a passion for the purchase of expensive oriental rugs, and the rooms in which his parties were held generally had floors covered with exotic, recent acquisitions. They were soft and seductive and added to the special aura of an evening at the Lieblings. Elaborate preparations were always made when Joe was about to come to one's own home for dinner. His culinary standards were high and vast. If chicken was to be the order of the day, a chicken was ordered for all the other guests, and two chickens for Joe. The same with lobsters: one each for regulation size stomachs, and two and perhaps three doomed crustaceans for the honored guest. In a sense Joe expected this special attention. His self-esteem included great pride in his appetite. Hosts unaware of his peculiar talents in this department often were unaware of his keen disappointment if the table at which he sat was not laden to his complete satisfaction. I recall a particularly fancy dinner one evening in Washington during the war at some friends of mine who were anxious to meet Joe, and had heard legendary tales of his talent with knife and fork. These people were engaged in extremely high level, if unrevealable, activities in connection with the national effort. Present were civilian and military nabobs, justifiably filled with themselves and whatever corner of their work they felt free to discuss. Joe seemed to glory in the sumptuous repast: fish and fowl and meat, and this and that. The host, it seemed to me, outdid himself. Joe listened (missing nothing, occasionally asking a brief, pertinent, piercing question), and ate. I remember thinking, at last this fellow is being supplied with the proper amount of victuals, and in a suitable and sympathetic setting, but no sooner had we left the glittering assemblage (about ten-thirty) than Joe, standing in front of the elegant Georgetown town house, and looking abject and forlorn, said to me, "For God's sake, do you know someplace at this hour where I can find something, anything, *to eat*?" We found a seafood place down by the waterfront, where Joe indulged in several dozen oysters, and retired, I can only hope, somewhat satisfied.

Lest the above should sound either gluttonous or ungrateful, it must never be forgotten that Joe always gave back more than he took. Should he arrive at one's home for an evening he would not bring a beautifully arranged cornucopia of a dozen flowers. He would bring several dozen. He couldn't help this. He was not showing off. He was not upstaging anyone. This was merely his way of making clear to those he loved how very much he loved them. He had no children of his own, but he always showed a tender interest in the children of his friends. He treated them as equals, inquired into their work and their play, and gave them a special sense of their personal identities and potential for growth. One of my treasures is a snapshot of Joe at one of my birthday parties, an arm around the waist of my youngest son—then about ten years old. Joe is wearing the benign smile of what can best be described as The Smile of the Uncle of the World. My son's look of pride in the attention being paid to him by this great and good man once seen can never be forgotten.

I often try to think of what Joe would make of the New York of today. The city of which he wrote has in many ways disappeared. No doubt, Joe would still be fascinated by the vitality of the city, but streets filled with the homeless would sicken him. He loved vaudeville, and vaudeville is gone, replaced by the plastic comics on the tube. Joe lived through and wrote about the great depression. The presidency of Herbert Hoover offended his deepest sense of social justice. His sensitivity to the suffering of others was never far from the surface. The sight of a disabled person or a beggar, or, say, an elderly woman in rags would reduce him to tears.

Sadly, most of the midtown Italian restaurants and fish food places where he lunched with his colleagues are now gone. Times Square, every inch of which he knew with awesome intimacy, would be unrecognizable to him today—a canyon of tall and soulless glass boxes. All this lends an added aura to *Back Where I Came From*. What Joe turned out as contemporary journalism, under the inexorable pressure of deadlines, has become history.

A final note. Joe once wrote a piece titled "Harold Ross—The Impresario"—a clinical, basically appreciative, analysis of the brilliant, wild, wonderful, nonpareil founding editor of *The New Yorker*, who had died a few years earlier. It ended sadly, Joe remarking, "I wish I had told him once how much I liked him." This made a deep impression on me, and I thank whatever heavens there be that I told Joe on many occasions how deeply I admired him.

I wish I could tell him again. Perhaps I have.

BACK WHERE
I CAME FROM

APOLOGY FOR BREATHING

People I know in New York are incessantly on the point of going back where they came from to write a book, or of staying on and writing a book about back where they came from. Back where they came from, I gather, is the American scene (New York, of course, just isn't America). It is all pretty hard on me because I have no place to go back to. I was born in an apartment house at Ninety-third Street and Lexington Avenue, about three miles from where I now live. Friends often tell me of their excitement when the train on which they are riding passes from Indiana into Illinois, or back again. I am ashamed to admit that when the Jerome Avenue express rolls into Eighty-sixth Street station I have absolutely no reaction.

I always think of back where my friends came from as one place, possessing a homogeneous quality of not being New York. The thought has been well expressed by my literary adviser, Whitey Bimstein, who also trains prize-fighters. I once asked him how he liked the country. He said, "It is a nice spot." I have been to the country myself. I went to a college in New Hampshire. But I seldom mention this, because I would like to be considered quaint and regional, like Jesse Stuart or Kenneth Roberts.

The finest thing about New York City, I think, is that it is like one of those complicated Renaissance clocks where on one level an allegorical marionette pops out to mark the day of the week, on another a skeleton death bangs the quarter hour with his scythe, and on a third the Twelve

Apostles do a cakewalk. The variety of the sideshows distracts one's attention from the advance of the hour hand. I know people who say that, as in the clock, all the exhibits depend upon the same movement. This they insist is economic. But they are the sort of people who look at a fine woman and remind you that the human body is composed of one dollar and sixty-two cents worth of chemicals.*

I like to think of all the city microcosms so nicely synchronized though unaware of one another: the worlds of the weight-lifters, yodelers, tugboat captains and sideshow barkers, of the book-dutchers, sparring partners, song pluggers, sporting girls and religious painters, of the dealers in rhesus monkeys and the bishops of churches that they establish themselves under the religious corporations law. It strengthens my hold on reality to know when I awake with a brandy headache in my house which is nine blocks due south of the Chrysler Building and four blocks due east of the Empire State, that Eddie Arcaro, the jockey, is galloping a horse around the track at Belmont while Ollie Thomas, a colored clocker of my acquaintance, is holding a watch on him. I can be sure that Kit Coates, at the Aquarium, is worrying over the liverish deportment of a new tropical fish, that presently Whitey will be laying out the gloves and headguards for the fighters he trains at Stillman's gymnasium, while Miss Ira, the Harlem modiste, will be trying to talk a dark-complexioned girl out of buying herself an orange turban and Hymie the Tummler ruminates a plan for opening a new night club. It would be easier to predicate the existence of God on such recurrences than on the cracking of ice in ponds, the peeping of spring

* The author has not checked on this figure.—The Editor

peepers in their peeperies and the shy green sprigs of poison ivy so well advertised by writers like Thoreau.

There are New Yorkers so completely submerged in one environment, like the Garment Centre or Jack and Charlie's, that they live and die oblivious of the other worlds around them. Others are instinctively aware of the wonders of New York natural history, but think them hardly worthy of mention. My father was a New Yorker of the latter sort. In separate phases of his business life, he had occasion to retain Monk Eastman, a leading pre-war gangster, and the Rev. Charles Parkhurst, a notorious crusader against vice. This seemed to him no more paradoxical than going to Coward's for his shoes while he bought his hats of Knox. When Father was President of an association of furriers during a strike he hired Eastman to break up a strikers' mass meeting. His employment of Dr. Parkhurst was more subtle. In about 1910 Father bought some real estate in West Twenty-sixth Street on which he purposed to put several loft buildings. He believed that the fur industry was going to move up in that direction from below Twenty-third. But Twenty-sixth Street between Sixth and Seventh Avenues was full of brothels, and there was no hope of getting tenants for the new buildings until the block was made respectable. First Father dispossessed the hock shops from the houses which he had acquired with his building lots. But the watchmen rented the empty rooms to the drabs for fifty cents a night. Then Father made a substantial gift to Dr. Parkhurst's society, enclosing with his check a letter that called attention to the sinful conditions on West Twenty-sixth Street. Dr. Parkhurst raised Hell with the police, who made the girls move on to another block, and then Father put up his buildings.

Father always said Monk and Dr. Parkhurst gave him his money's worth, but he never liked either of them. He became labor conscious after he retired from business, and toward the end of his life often said that unions were a fine thing, but that they had doubtless changed a lot since the time he hired Eastman. He died a staunch Roosevelt man.

Even though he made his home during the second part of his life among middle-class enterprisers with horizons slimmer than a gnat's waist, Father lived in other milieus in restrospect. He liked to talk of the lower East Side in the eighties, when the carters left their wagons in the streets of nights and the small boys would roll the wains away and burn them on election day, and of how he, a workingman at ten, boxed with the other furriers' apprentices using beaver muffs for mitts. He would even tell of the gay life of London and Paris and Leipzig in the late nineties when he was a bachelor buyer, although, he always protested, he had finished with that sort of thing when he got married. And he early introduced me to those worlds into which one may escape temporarily for the payment of a fee, the race course and the baseball park. These have their own conflicts that do not follow scenarios pre-determined in Hollywood.

Since this is a regional book about people I met back where I came from, I should like to say something here about the local language. This is a regional tongue imported from the British Isles, as is the dialect spoken by the retarded inhabitants of the Great Smoky Mountains back where *they* come from. Being spoken by several million people, it has not been considered of any philological importance. Basically, New Yorkese is the common speech of early nineteenth century Cork, transplanted during the mass immigration of the South Irish a hundred years ago. Of this Cork dialect Thomas Crofton Croker in 1839 wrote: "The vernacular of this region may be regarded as the ancient cockneyism of the mixed race who held the old city—Danes, English and Irish. It is a jargon, whose principal characteristic appears in the pronunciation of *th*, as exemplified in *dis, dat, den, dey*—this, that, then, they; and in the dovetailing of words as, 'kum our rish' for 'come of this.' " New York example, "gerradahere" for "get out of here." The neo-Corkonian proved particularly suited to the later immigrants who came here from continental Europe —the *th* sound is equally impossible for French, Germans and Italians. Moreover, it was impressed upon the latecomers because it was the talk of the police and the elementary school teachers, the only Americans who would talk to them at all. Father, who was born in Austria but came here when he was seven years old, spoke New Yorkese perfectly.

It is true that since the diaspora the modern dialects of Cork and New York have diverged slightly like Italian and Provencal, both of which stem from vulgar Latin. Yet Sean O'Faolain's modern story of Cork, "A Born Genius," contains dialogue that might have come out of Eleventh Avenue: "He's after painting two swans on deh kitchen windes. Wan is facin' wan way and d'oder is facin' d'oder way.—So dat so help me God dis day you'd tink deh swans was floatin' in a garden! And deh garden was floatin' in trough deh winda! And dere was no winda!"

There are interesting things about New York besides the language. It is one of the oldest places in the United States, but doesn't live in retrospect like the professionally picturesque provinces. Any city may have one period of magnificence, like Boston or New Orleans or San Francisco, but it takes a real one to keep renewing itself until the past is perennially forgotten. There were plenty of clipper ships out of New York in the old days and privateers before them, but there are better ships out of here today. The Revolution was fought all over town, from Harlem to Red Hook and back again, but that isn't the revolution you will hear New Yorkers discussing now.

Native New Yorkers are the best mannered people in America; they never speak out of turn in saloons, because they have experience in group etiquette. Whenever you hear a drinker let a blat out of him you can be sure he is a recent immigrant from the south or middle west. New Yorkers are modest. It is a distinction for a child in New York to be the brightest on one block; he acquires no exaggerated idea of his own relative intelligence. Prairie geniuses are raced in cheap company when young. They are intoxicated by the feel of being boy wonders in Amarillo, and when they bounce off New York's skin as adults they resent it.

New York women are the most beautiful in the world. They have their teeth straightened in early youth. They get their notions of chic from S. Klein's windows instead of the movies. Really loud and funny New Yorkers, like Bruce Barton, are invariably carpetbaggers. The climate is extremely healthy. The death rate is lower in Queens and the Bronx than in any other large city in the United States, and the average life expectancy is so high that one of our morning newspapers specializes in interviewing people a hundred years old and upward. The average is slightly lowered, however, by the inlanders who come here and insist on eating in Little Southern Tea Roomes on side streets.

The natives put up with a lot back here where I came from. If the inhabitants of Kentucky are distrustful of strangers, that is duly noted as an entertaining local trait. But if a New Yorker says that he doesn't like Kentuckians he is marked a cold churl. It is perennially difficult for the New Yorker who subscribes to a circulating library to understand how the city survived destruction during the Civil War. When he reads about those regional demigods haunted by ancestral daemons and festooned in magnolia blossoms and ghosts who composed practically the whole Confederate Army, he wonders what happened to them en route. I asked Whitey Bimstein what he thought of that one. He said: "Our guys must have slapped their ears down." Whitey does not know that we have been paying a war indemnity ever since in the form of royalties.

A. J. Liebling

Block Island, 1938

BEGINNING WITH THE
UNDERTAKER

In the middle of any New York block there is likely to be one store that remains open and discreetly lighted all night. This is the undertaker's. The undertaker or an assistant is always in attendance, waiting for something to turn up. Undertakers are sociable men; they welcome company during their unavoidable periods of idleness. High school boys study for their State Regents' examinations in undertakers' offices on hot June nights. The door is always open, the electric fan soothing, the whole environment more conducive to reflective scholarship than the crowded apartment where the boy lives. Policemen going off duty sometimes drop in for a visit with the undertaker before climbing into the subway for the long trip home to another part of the city.

There is no merchandise in the front part of an undertaker's store. Usually there are a few comfortable chairs for bereaved relatives, and policemen sit in these chairs. During the day, the undertaker acts as a referee in the disputes of children. Housewives tell him their troubles; priests appeal to him to head church committees. Ten to one he becomes the biggest man in the neighborhood, like my friend Mayor Angelo Rizzo of Mulberry Street. Some New York streets have Mayors, but they are not elected. A man lives on a street until the mayoralty grows over him, like a patina. To Mayor Rizzo Elizabeth Street, although but two blocks east of Mulberry, is an alien place. For the feast of San Gennaro, who is the Mulberry Street Saint, Mayor Rizzo usually heads at least three committees and festoons his shopfront with electric lights. A celebration on Elizabeth Street leaves him unmoved. "Just one of them Sicilian saints," he says.

Once Mayor Rizzo told me he was hard put to keep track of his constituents' baths. "I think I will have to get a secretary," he said, as he improved the taste of a casket salesman's gift cigar with a swig of iced barbera wine. He sat in front of 178 Mulberry Street, enthroned upon one of the elegant portable chairs which he is prepared to furnish in any number for correct funerals. "They should call this cigar a La Palooka," he remarked on the side.

"Mrs. Aranciata is getting crazy because she don't remember whether Jimmy has been to Cooney * Island twenty-two times or twenty-three times. So she come to me and said I should tell the kid not to go no more, because maybe that will make it an even number of times and he will get rheumatism. So I said to her, 'But suppose he has been only twenty-two times? Then by keeping him home you will be preventing him getting on the odd number again, and the rheumatism will be your fault.'

" 'Oh, Madonna mia,' she says, 'and what will I do?'

"So I says, 'Why don't you forget all about it and purtend this is a new year. Start all over again and when he goes to Cooney tell me, and I will keep track of it on a piece of paper.' So she is delighted and the next thing I know she tells all her friends and now I got about fourteen

* This is the New York pronunciation of Coney Island. It seems to me as noteworthy as the Texan fashion of saying "Hughston" for Houston.

women coming in wanting me to keep score how many times the family goes swimming.

"It is like when I feed one cat sphagetti a couple of winters ago and in a week I got a waiting line of 598 cats, including a lot of Sicilian cats from Elizabeth Street."

"But what difference does it make how many times you go swimming—at Coney or any place else?" I asked.

"What difference does it make?" shouted Mr. Rizzo. "Do you mean to tell me that you, an educated man, do not know that salt water baths are only good for you if you go an odd number of times? Any old woman on Mulberry Street knows that much."

To prove his point Mayor Rizzo called the cop on the beat.

"You are an Italian," said His Honor. "Which is it lucky to take baths, an odd number or an even number?"

"Odd number," answered the officer promptly. "My mother-in-law, she keeps count on her fingers. She would never go in the water two times, or four times, in an afternoon, but always three times or five times."

The argument became a little involved here. Some of the folklore hydrotherapists held that each immersion counts as a bath, and if you go in the drink an odd number of times at each visit to the beach, your health will not suffer.

Others maintain that you must keep track of the total number of days' bathing, and be sure to wind up the season on an odd.

"I remember when I was a kid an old lady from Calabria made me go in fifty-one times one summer," said Al Gallichio, the restaurant man.

An antique and gracious lady waddling past with a bag of zucchini, was invoked as a superior authority.

"Pardon me, madame," said Mayor Rizzo, "but I would wish to request a word with you."

"Voluntarily," she replied.

"When you are accustomed to go bathing, which is the more auspicious, to go an even or an uneven number of times?"

"Childish," said the dame. "It makes no difference. But once you have begun to go you must go at least fifteen times, else your bones rot. It is for that reason I have not gone to the sea, this year, because I might not be able to afford fifteen visits."

She was an exception, because the odd-and-even belief, in one or other of its two forms, is prevalent all the way from Bleecker Street down to Park Row.

"It is very important this year," said the Mayor, "because we got no public bath in the neighborhood. There used to be a bathhouse on Center Market Place where the fellow would let you take a shower for a nickel. Of course, even the old-timers do not count whether a shower is odd or even. But now the Broome St. Tamanacle * Church has bought the building. A lot of these old houses have no bathtubs even, so the nearest place the people can get a bath is Allen Street and they figure they might just as well go out to Cooney.

"Do I believe in this odd-and-even business?" he said, "Well, I tell you. I went swimming off the Battery just once, which is an odd number, and a kid pushed my head under and nearly drowned me, so I figured if I went back that would be an even number and even worse luck and I probably would remain drowned, so now I do all my swimming in a bathtub."

* A regional pronunciation of Tabernacle.

THE SEA IN THE CITY

"Where did I go to sea from? The First Ward."
—TOM WILSON.

Before it was anything else New York was a seaport, and before anything else it still is. The immigrants who came here from Europe had a good idea of that, but most of their children have forgotten it; as for the immigrants from inland America, they apparently never knew it. New Yorkers read of London River and Liverpool. They think of Nantucket and Provincetown and Gloucester as towns with a nautical atmosphere, or of New Bedford as the home of a marine tradition. But they don't realize that the fellow next to them in the subway is just as likely a second engineer off a freighter as a certified public accountant employed by Dunkelbinner & Follywinkle in the Jacob Ruppert Building. The Manhattan waterfront is not hard to find. You start in any direction and walk. But psychic barriers block it off from the rest of the city. The foot of Wall Street is as nautical as The Nigger of the Narcissus, but a block away nobody thinks of anything more seaworthy than Warner Brothers, Preferred. The great liners dock within a few blocks of the Casa Manana. Nobody gives a damn.

As good a place as any to get the feel of the port is the office of the Kennedy Towing Line at 32 South Street. It is the last old-fashioned tugboat office left. The bigger lines have gone down to buildings like 24 State and 17 Battery Place, where they employ female stenographers and rub elbows with transatlantic steamship companies. But a potbellied iron stove still overheats the Kennedy office from early fall until late spring, and a gay blue and white portrait of the tug "Idlewild," with more paint than perspective, provides its chief adornment. Of the six Kennedy boats two were built before 1875. It is Tom Wilson's favorite office for yarning.

Tom is the senior tugboat master of the harbor, with a voice on him like the Staten Island Ferry boat and a chest like an oil drum.

"I am 74 years old," he roars, "and I can jump out of that window and jump right back again." The office is on the second floor. "When they put me together they put me together right," says Tom, heaving on a handful of snow white hair. "Every hair drove in with a nail. None of your shin plasters.

"I went tug-boatin' when I was 18, aboard of the Leonard Richards, the twin of that Idlewild in the pitcher. Where did I go to sea from? The First Ward. Tugboat captains was the cream of society in them days. They wore high hats and gold watch chains and Prince Albert coats and striped trousers, and they never touched the wheel without kid gloves. They would steal the sight out of your eyes.

"The Leonard Richards was a Hooker. What was a Hooker? Why, a tug that cruised off sandy Hook for schooners, of course. Just the same as a Gater was a tug that hanged off Hell Gate, and a lugger was a tug that lugged ships to their berths after the Hookers and the

Gaters brought them in, whether the ships was pinewooders from the South, or brickers, or whatever they might be.

"Them days there was more ships than now, and plenty of sail. The most part of them had no regular agents ashore to hire tugs, and there was no radio, anway, so the agents wouldn't a' knowed when they was coming in. The first tug that seed a ship he made up to her and the two captains paced their deck awhile and called each other this and that and at last they struck a bargain, or they didn't, and you sheered off and he run up the American flag for another tug.

"But the tug that got out first had the best chance. So sometimes at night the captain would shake you by the shoulder and say. 'Get up and cast off with no noise,' and you would try to give the other boats the shake and get out to sea before they was wise. You would go out without lights, by Rockaway or South Beach or Coney Island, where you knowed there was nothing you could hit only maybe an oyster boat, and you wouldn't stop for that.

"Sometimes when you would get out in the stream you would hear the whistles tooting if they suspicioned you, and the whole gang would be after you.

"Then, if the old man was wise, he would switch his running lights. He would put his red and green lights astern and his white light on the bow, and it would look like he was coming in instead of going out. But if the other guy was wise he wouldn't take none of that—just give her more medicine.

"We would cruise off the Hook two or three days. We would carry that much coal, but only water for twenty hours, steady steaming; but we could get water at the Hook, but not coal. How far did we go? Half way to Ireland, boy—half way to Ireland. Ten per cent of what he got was for the captain, besides what he could steal, and if he didn't get no tow he didn't get no wages.

"Thirty or forty hours at a stretch working was nothing. The first command I got, after I got my license in 1883, I asked my owner for some bedding so's the men could lay down. 'I didn't hire them men to sleep,' he says. I can work thirty hours right now without squealing, and on my hoofs, too.

"Then when you would get out there sometimes there would be a good wind and they would sail right past you, and maybe offer you a line.

"But when the wind died they had a different tune.

"Once I picked up a French bark off Fire Island, and I couldn't make a price with him. I follied him and I follied him, and at Long Beach, sure enough he goes ashore. Now I had him, I figured, and he would pay me a damn good price to pull him off. Up comes a nor'west gale, and what does the sucker do but back her off under sail! Ah, well, heartaches in every trade.

"But one time they wouldn't bargain was the war. That was the golden age. All I had to do was cruise down by the Highlands on a calm day and take my pick of the schooners and barks that was bringing supplies to New York. I would make up to the one that looked the best bet.

" 'Morning, captain,' I would tell the old man. 'Seed anything of a submarine around here?'

" 'My God!' he would say. 'So close to New York?'

" 'Shelled a ship up by Hoffman's Island this morning,' I would say.

" 'How much to take me in?'

" 'Fifteen hundred dollars.'

" 'You're a pirate. I'll not pay it.'

" 'Very good, captain. Sorry we can't do business, captain. But I ain't got no time to waste out here. I don't want to lose this little craft or the few lives I got on board.'

"I'd start off, and five minutes later he'd be signaling for me to come back and tow him at my price.

"When I'd get him up to Quarantine I'd drop him. 'If you want to go any further,' I'd say, 'get a local. This is an express.' "

It was during the war that Tom performed his greatest feat of pilotage.

The Swash Channel, between Homer Shoal and Flynn's Knoll, two treacherous shallows, is charted good for twenty feet of water.

"I took a five-masted bark, the Orleans, up there, drawing twenty-four and a half," Tom said pridefully. "When I got her through Morgan, the captain, nearly went crazy.

" 'Why the hell did you take her through there?' he asks.

" 'I knowed the tide, and I knowed the spot. You didn't bump, did you?'

" 'No, but if that hawser had parted, or if something had gone wrong with that little boat, she would have been left dry and broke her back sure.'

"The reason I done it, of course, was I saved three miles instead of going round by the Main Ship Channel, and I was running short of water."

Tom says he never *knew* a harbor thief.

"I knew some that had the name of it," he said, "but I could not give you their pedigree. There were stories of some fellows that would go out in a schooner and make a price to bring her in. Then they would wait until night, and any tug they found at the end of a pier they would just take it and do the job and get their cash, and then leave the tug at the nearest slip and think no more of it.

"But taking gear, now, that is something else again. Anything that was not nailed to the boat, in the old days, the owner was not considered entitled to it."

The cow, he roared . . .

The story of the sea cow is Captain Bob Forsythe's masterpiece—the choicest fruit of a long experience in steam navigation, and well he knows it.

Captain Forsythe is a limber and lean-faced towboater from Kingston on the Hudson, "which has produced more steamboat men than I daresay any town in the United States." ("Canawler," snorts Tom Wilson.) But he has plied the waters of the Harbor and the Sound so long that he feels at home in the office of the Kennedy Line.

"It was during prohibition," Captain Forsythe always begins, as one who would say, "it was during the civil war."

"We was lying at the foot of Sackett Street, Brooklyn, when I seed the man that owned the boat coming along with what I thought was a big Newfoundland dog, and then I made out this bull, whatever t'hell he was—a cow."

Captain Forsythe pronounced "cow" with a quality of bitterness such as towboat men generally reserve for the pilots of ferryboats, and he also got into his tone a suggestion that he had moved all his life in a different social sphere from cows, that he hardly knew what a cow was, and that he would feel himself degraded by the acquisition of such knowledge.

"We had a big open lighter that had belonged to the Navy," he said, "and we had it loaded with provisions and coal and slops that we was to take out to a rum boat at sea east of Block Island, and bring back 4,000 cases of booze.

"Well, all would have been well, but the bootlegger conceived the idea to send this cow out to the ship so he would give the boys fresh milk, and then when they wanted meat they would kill him. The minute the cow seed me he let a roar out of him, and we had a big time making him walk down a plank into the lighter. Then when we got him aboard he liked to kick our brains out, but we made his legs fast and stowed him by the rail.

"We even shipped a bale of hay, which is fuel for them damn animals.

"We cast and went out by Hell Gate, and there was a fog in the Sound that you couldn't see a hundred yards in front of you, it was perfect. She was so deep in the water with coal, and no deck onto her, just an open lighter, the sharks come swimming right up on the side to visit with the cow. If we had good sense we would have thrown him overboard. But we amused ourselves feeding loaves of bread to the sharks instead. She shipped some water, but everything would have been all right if it wasn't for this cow.

"He began to beller so we didn't need no fog horn. I bet you could hear him in Boston. And sure enough we get a hail—one of those Coast Guard four stackers out of New London. They send an officer aboard and I give him a line that I am taking provisions to an Isthmian Line boat at Boston, but he says the Isthmian does not run any boats to Boston.

" 'Turn her around and folly us into New London," he says.

" 'You're only a public servant,' I says, 'this is piracy and damn impudence, and if you want to take her into New London you can run her yourself.' So I called up my engineer and the firemen, and we sat with our arms folded on top of the canned goods, and cursed the cow who continued his impersonation of a whistle buoy. They put the crew aboard, but so much water came over the side that they couldn't keep steam on her. The steering gear locked, and she nearly rammed the destroyer.

"They had to tow her into New London, and the further they towed the madder they got, until by the time they docked her the only one in the party that was pleased with himself was the cow.

"Of course they didn't really have anything on us, because we had not been out there to get the rum yet, and there wasn't a drop aboard, but still and all nobody would acknowledge ownership, fearing some kind of a tangle with the law, and meanwhile me and my crew was stranded. The bootlegger that owned the boat wouldn't send us a penny. The Coast Guard wouldn't release the boat until some owner turned up, and we stayed aboard hoping to collect our pay.

"To keep going I sold the coal off her, and then the provisions, and at last there was nothing left but this here bull, whatever it was, a cow, and I hated him more every time I looked at him. We were tied up at a dock in the Thames River, a high dock, and it was low water, and we were way below level. I goes ashore and looks for a farmer, and sure enough, the second field I look into I find one."

Captain Forsythe pronounced "farmer" in much the same manner as "cow," but with slightly less acerbity.

" 'Do you want to buy a cow?' I asks him.

" 'Maybe,' he says. 'Where is it?'

" 'Come with me,' I says. He follies me onto the dock and I show him the cow in the lighter.

" 'How much do you want for him?' he says.

" 'Fifty dollars,' I asks him, guessing at the value.

" 'I'll give you fifty dollars for him,' he says, 'delivered on the dock.'

"I says, 'Give me the fifty and I'll have him on the dock in five minutes.' So he gives me the fifty and I went aboard and we made a couple of belly bands and put them around the cow and lifted him with the steam hoist, meaning to put him down on the dock, but when I got the cow up and started to lower away, the power stopped, and there was the cow dangling a good fifteen feet above the dock. Up comes my engineer. " 'I stopped her,' he says, 'because there's no more rope on the drum. She's block to block. How will we get rid of the cow?' he says. 'I'll show you,' I says.

"With that I grabbed an axe and cut through the cable with one wallop. The bull, whatever t'hell he was, a cow, came flying through the air and landed on his four feet like a cat, and up the hill into New London, making a good eighteen knots, and the farmer after him. And that was the last I seed of either one."

Henry Hudson warn't going nowhere . . .

New York is more than a port on the ocean. It is a great river town, and when Hudson River men stand up to a West Side bar with harbor towboat men and deep-water sailors, three marine cultures meet without mingling. So, in Minoan Crete, the barbaric Greek seamen, the native cockney stock and the Phoenician A.B.'s must have quaffed their inferior beer while indulging in a round robin of contempt. Most harbor towboat men are of native city stock. River men are born in places like Kingston and Athens up the Hudson. Kingston men usually are pilots. Engineers belong to Athens, which is pronounced Aythens. The river men are of an America which is not New York. They say "narthing" when they mean "nothing." Harbor men say "nuttin." The Mississippi is said to breed bombast, but Hudson River men have a gift of understatement which is a more effective medium for remarkable lies. This is known as the deadpan or London Times system of prevarication. The Hudson is a river where wise men spawn. Arrived at maturity they go down to the sea in towboats. Judge from this story of Captain Billy Barnett's.

"I remember when I was a lad," Captain Billy once told me—he's almost eighty now—"I shipped in the schooner Benjamin Akin, carrying bluestone from Roundout Creek to Mount Vernon. We had to pass up Eastchester Creek to deliver our cargo, and the old man had never been up there so he hove to and waited for a pilot.

"After a piece an old feller come along and 'Captain,' he says, 'are you in want of a pilot? I been taking vessels up this creek all my life and I never been on a rock yet.'

" 'I'll be damned if I believe you know where the rocks are, then,' says the old man, and he wouldn't have him. Along come another old feller. 'Ever been on the rocks?' asks the old man. 'Been on every goddam rock in the creek,' he says. 'You're the man for me,' says the old man. 'You got experience.'

"When I was a boy," Captain Barnett remarked on another occasion, "it snowed and it blowed and it hailed and it made ice. The old Norwich, of the Cornell Steamboat Company was built in 1836 and she was the greatest icebreaker on the river. She had a cross-head engine like the original Clermont and a high bow, and she would run way up on the ice and crash down on it, and sometimes she would fall over on her side.

"Then she'd sort of shake herself and get up and come down on that ice like a terrier worrying a rat and she'd clear a course through twenty inches of ice like a man would eat a buckwheat cake. Yes, sir, she was a remarkable boat." The antithesis of a remarkable boat, in Captain Billy's language, is "a boat that couldn't draw a shad out of a net," or "couldn't draw the slack out of a line."

The Hudson made New York, for after the opening of the Erie Canal in 1825* and before the completion of the railroads into the West, all the produce of the Lakes region came through the canal and down the Hudson to this port, and all the merchandise from civilization went back up that way. By the time the railroads got going New York had such a headstart on the other centres of regional culture that the city has been on the chinstrap since, tincanning a mile in front of the field and without a challenger in sight. Hudson River men even today like to remind New Yorkers that the Hudson gave our town its bust at the gate.

*   *   *   *

The longest voyage I ever made into inland America was on the Trojan of the Albany Night Line.† I got to Albany. That was far enough for Henry Hudson so I decided it was far enough for me. I came home. Captain

---

* The author is not responsible for dates. He relies upon local word-of-mouth tradition for all of them.

† This is an exaggeration, probably for effect. He visited Buffalo in January 1937.—The Editor.

George Warner was the commander of the Trojan then and he was very angry because the river was so full of lights and aids to navigation.

"Dangerous having all these lights," he said. "Fellows get used to 'em. Might go out any time. Weakens their estimation." We were up in the pilot house and there were no lights there except the one on the compass.

"From here we run almost straight across the river, to a place called Snedeker's," the Captain said. I asked what light he ran to there.

"To where we can see a hollow in the hills, and if there is fog we have the course timed; so given the tide and the speed of the boat we could run it in the dark. Estimation," remarked Captain Warner. "Three things makes up a steamboat man: estimation, calculation and judgment. You estimate where you are, you calculate how fast you are going and then you use your judgment. But soon there will be no boatmen. No boatmen and no steamboats. Only Sandy Hook pilots riding theirselves up to Albany in blamed tankers."

A long, dark dragon loomed in the middle of the stream, lights at her stern and masthead.

"They anchor at night," said Captain Warner. He meant the Sandy Hook pilots.

"When I went lookout," Captain Warner continued, "river men steered by a ball on the for'ard flagstaff. It was a big ball that slid up and down on the staff by ropes. The steersman would sight by it like a gunsight. A steersman shifts his position, of course, but the ball was steady.

"He'd get it against a church steeple, or a hill, or a sawmill, or a certain formation o'trees, and he'd set his course according. 'H'ist her up!' he'd call to the lookout, or 'H'ist her down!' according to how he wanted it. The lookout stood out there on the bows, where he could see ahead."

Night closed down on the Trojan. Twilight had remained behind in Haverstraw Bay, which all rivermen pronounce "Har-verstraw."

The quartermaster began to play the searchlight. He flashed it on residences on the Highlands. Almost every one flashed on the porch lights in response.

"There was once a divorce suit based on that light," the skipper reminisced. "Quartermaster turned it on one of those summer places. Husband was in the house and the light just hit his wife and his friend in a compromising situation. Well, they subpoenaed the quartermaster. 'Very sorry it happened,' he said. 'I wouldn't have done that to nobody for the world.' Went ashore and took to farming. He was a very tender-hearted fellow."

In 1849 ten steamboats left New York for Albany every morning and an equal number at night. Each of these steamers teamed with a boat coming down from Albany. Also there were a dozen local lines running to intermediate ports, like Poughkeepsie, Sing Sing, Kingston, Saugerties and Catskill.

Now there's one boat by day and one at night. The railroads have taken most of the passenger business.

"Some things about the river'd surprise you," says Captain Warner. "Now there's a tug, puffing like she had the asthmy, with six barges astern.

"Now take that tug. With a tow of ten barges she could make maybe five miles an hour. Well, you'd think maybe with one barge she could go ten times as fast. But she couldn't. S'prise, you, wouldn't it? It would s'prise you, if we got past this cliff. River makes a perfect S here, and if you didn't know the way out, you'd turn back."

This was at West Point. I asked, "How did Henry Hudson find his way up?"

"Because he warn't going nowhere, of course," said the skipper.

George Fox Clapp, Captain Warner's purser, had been on the river fifty years. In 1883 he was purser of the St. John, then rated a floating palace.

"The river was the fashionable route to Saratoga in those days," the purser said as the Trojan glided on past Pollopel's Island in Newburgh Bay. "Isaac Murphy, the great colored jockey, and William Whitney, the Secretary of the Navy; Snapper Garrison and John Morrissey, the old tough turned gambler; Richard Canfield and Jim Corbett and Charlie Mitchell and half of society would be aboard the night after the getaway from the New York tracks.

"The black stable boys stayed on deck and shot craps all night long and the bar stayed open until 2 in the morning. The dining saloon in those old boats was below decks. Wine parties sometimes lasted all night. The St. John had a beautiful ornate staircase of carved mahogany inlaid with white holly. How the ladies loved to walk down it—the pretty ones, especially!

"During August all the talk you heard was of racing. The air was full of tips—and the horses owe me $300 since 1887. I married then and quit betting.

"In the early spring we had the legislators travelling back and forth between Albany and New York. They all had passes in those days. I don't think we ever had professional gamblers on the Hudson boats like on the Mississippi. There wasn't time to make acquaintance and build up the victim's confidence by letting him win small sums.

"But a purser's life never was a pure delight, even then. I remember one snowy night on the Dean Richmond—I was on her after the Drew—the chief steward and I had to deliver a woman. The old man put the boat into Rhinebeck, but we couldn't find a physician at that hour. So we did the trick. It was a nice boy, and the woman named him Dean Richmond."

The purser sauntered towards his cabin on the saloon deck. Captain Warner spoke again.

"Not a sail on this river," he said. "Was a time when it was all sloops. Before my time. It cost $14 to go from Tivoli to New York. Took 'em a week, sometimes. And then later there was a rate war between steamers and the rate got down to ten cents, New York to Albany. Then old Dan'l Drew and the Peoples Line they bought out the opposition. And they made a lot of money. A mint of money. Cripes, what a lot of money they made. Good money came out of this river. They piled up the silver dollars on the table in the dining saloon every night."

Gunboat Diplomacy

The port of New York has known strong seamen, but Comrade Osterhannsen, an A.B. whom I once met at the International Seamen's Club, is the only one who ever held a 3,000-ton ship for twelve hours with his feet. The I.S.C. was an exceedingly militant organization, a forerunner of the CIO maritime union.

"Because of the size of my feet," said Comrade Osterhahnsen told me, as he got outside of a bowl of chili and rice, "I am on the capitalist blacklist; but no matter—I struck a great blow for our industry that morning in Dakar on the old Anthony Roosevelt.

"I signed articles for that voyage in New York. The captain he says 'usual articles,' and I, what knows 'em by heart, signed without reading. Then we got to sea and I found they had cut the wages $5.

"But as luck would have it, when I grabbed that ship I had one pair of shoes to my name, and they was in pretty bad shape. All cracked they was with salt water and the soles wore off on the cobbles of South Street. So a couple of weeks out I went to the slop chest to buy some new shoes. And I wear size 13. They didn't have my size in stock.

"So I knew I had 'em. The ship's officers, I mean. We unloaded our cargo in Dakar and we was just about to weigh anchor. I didn't stir a foot. 'Turn out,' says the boatswain. 'I will,' I says, 'when the slop chest stocks to fit me.'

"The old man was swearing like a black-hearted slave of the capitalist system, which he was, and he says, 'We'll miss this tide and lose twelve hours. I'll put you ashore, and let you stew with the natives,' he says.

" 'Well,' I says, 'what about the counsel?' " " 'The counsel will do nothing for you,' the old man yells, 'you sonofabitching sea lawyer.' So they put me ashore. I didn't go to the counsel direct. That does no good. I knew from experience. I just walked up to the first cop I seen and knocked him down.

"Fifteen minutes later I was in the jug.

" 'What did you do it for?' says the counsel. So I told him. 'And I am going to keep on doing it every day until you get me a ship away from here,' I told him.

"So the counsel jumps in his own motorboat and races out to the ship and he says to the old man if he leaves me there he will have him arrested for a marooner and a pirate and a menace to the peace of nations. So they hold the ship and I gets my shoes."

Professor Shill

Comrade Osterhahnsen understood the comedy of situation, but Professor Charles Edwards was my favorite sea-going character comedian. The Professor was a solemn, chubby old fellow with a round and innocent face. I called him Professor because he had spent so much time instructing undergraduates who were working their way to Europe on cattleboats. The last time I saw Professor Edwards he called at the office of the New York World-Telegram to tell me that "the call of the sea had outpulled the lure of the footlights, you might say," and that he was sailing away on the old Leviathan.

"I had numerous offers from carnival shows touring the most populous centres of Arkansas and Texas," said the professor, "but the sea after all you might say, is my element. And when a ship breaks down you get a tow to port, which, when a show busts, you might say, you are on the beach."

"As soon as you decide to do one thing you are sorry you didn't do the other," he said a little sadly. "The show business is certainly exciting. Yes, sir, the last outfit I was with we travelled down in Texas, and we had a wrestling and boxing show, a cooch show, a car of games and a balloon excension.

"I used to dress as a farmer, with a straw in my mouth, and play those thimble games and win. Then the other hicks would play and lose. Anything to earn an honest dollar.

"Also I used to go ahead of the show and meet the local boxers, and tell them to go easy with the boxer in the show and he would go easy with them. They would box a draw all fair and square the first night the show came to town, and then toward the end of the week we would have a return match and bet on it. The hick would think it was fixed again, and he would go easy and our fellow would knock him out."

The benevolent professor beamed.

"The fellow with the show was a fine boxer," he said. "But he got hurt in a balloon excension. He wasn't no good after that, but he got a job as an armless man, only his wife used to beat him up.

"She was a featherweight boxer, too. They was exactly the same size and we used to put curls on the man so you couldn't tell them apart. We would have the girl out in front of the tent and promise $50 to any man who could stay three rounds with her and then, coming into the tent, we would switch, and the husband would do the fighting.

"They both used to make balloon excensions, too, and they had a balloon hound."

"A what?"

"A balloon hound. He was built more like a dachshund with long legs like a greyhound. He would always want to go in the balloon with the woman, but they would never let him. They would hold him back and he would watch the balloon getting smaller and smaller in the sky, and then when it was three or four miles away the boss of the show would fire a shot. That was the signal for the woman to jump out with her parachute.

"When they heard the shot they would let the dog go, and he would put his nose to the ground and run straight to the place the balloon landed.

"Only once I seen him fail. The balloon got tangled in the horns of a herd of deer and scared them and they run it straight over the border into Mexico. The show people went to get it, but there was a revolution and the rebels had took it to bomb Porfirio Diaz. So we lost that balloon."

Now and then something happens to remind New Yorkers that there must be another side to the ocean. For example pilot Christopher Ahearn of the Cobh of Cork gets carried to sea in a storm and pays the town a visit. Ahearn is the pilot for the United States Lines at Cobh, and when he takes a ship out in rough weather the captain makes him stay aboard. "It's for why I always carry my bag with a good suit of clothes," Ahearn says. He doesn't mind being carried away. "Oh, God sir," he once told me, "I have a fine time in New York. It be full of people belonging to Queenstown—that is to say, Cobh." Ahearn has two American ships a week at Cobh and the rest of the time he pilots colliers up the River Lee to Cork. He is a decent man, and when I was a reporter it was always a pleasure to greet him. It was the only way I could keep up with the politics of Ireland, or "trouble" as Ahearn called it, the words being interchangeable in Queenstown, that is to say Cobh. Since I last saw the pilot I have lost track of them entirely. "We're on De Valera to a man," he said to me that time,—it was on the Manhattan—"and if there was an election tomorrow, he would walk in. I don't know O'Duffy" (General Eoin O'Duffy, the Irish Fascist) "but sure, I don't approve of him. And his Blue Shirts! We'll paint them green surely." He would never talk of politics for very long at one session. He always seemed preoccupied. "Oh, God sir," he used to say, "I have a fine time in New York."

It was in the convalescent ward at the Marine Hospital on Ellis Island that Frank Watt, a retired ship's carpenter, told me about a slave ship.

"The strangest Christmas I remember was fifty-four—no, maybe it was fifty-five—years ago," Watt said. Watt was a cardiac case, a seawise and kindly man, and probably by now he is dead.

"It was aboard the square-rigged brig Rosalie. American crew and British registry, plying between Safa in Morocco and Pernambuco in Brazil, and she was lying about a hundred miles west of the Cape Verde Islands on her westbound voyage.

"The captain, I misremember his name, but he was a Sunday school man, would call all hands aft of a Sunday and there he would preach to us for at least an hour. On Christmas Day he would preach two hours, and he would not have a man aboard that had no Bible.

"This Christmas was a fair day, and the ship loafed along, while we all stood out in the sun and the Captain preached. His text was, 'The Word shall make ye free,' and the way he jawed about it we thought we would never get to the dinner the cook had put together out of the finest selected salt pork and sourdough bread and coffee.

"And all the time he was talking the cargo was looking up through the open hatches and jabbering and smiling and wondering what the talk was for. The cargo was 300 Negro slaves, and there were we, eight men, a-freighting them across the Atlantic Ocean."

The fellow in the next bed muttered something like "How could eight men manage 300?" But the ship's carpenter was ready with his answer.

"They were like children," he said. "Mild and wide-eyed. We threw them their food in the morning and we sluiced out the hold at night, and barring one or two that died and we had to throw overboard, we had no trouble with that cargo. The Moors brought them aboard in boats, and in Dom Pedro's empire the coffee planters called for them, and that was all there was to it."

Sometimes a thing you hear in one New York world will set you thinking of another thing that you have heard in a different microcosm. This story of Watt's reminded me of a saying of Battling Norfolk's, an old colored pugilist who works at Stillman's Gymnasium where the fighters train.

"My ancestors wasn't *run* here," Bat says when he gets into an argument with a white man. "They was *brought* here. They came here *By Request.*"

Interlude: Natural History

"Fish is brain food," Fritz Strohschneider, a waiter and a friend of mine told me, "but around cities they is brainier. It is just like people, the city fish is more slicker as the country fish.

"I don't go fishing more," he went on without encouragement, "since they exploded Heinrich Heine." *

* All German dialect in this book, except in the story "Frau Weinmann and the Third Reich," was written before 1933. The fish's name used to be Beethoven, but the author changed it to Heinrich Heine so "Back Where I Came From" would not become a best-seller in Germany.

"In the old days it was so nice on Sunday to fish for tommys from the docks. Tommys and eelses. On 96th Street dock we used to sit, me and my friend Jake Poppberger, with a case of beer and our clarinets. It was the most convenient fishing.

"Each one would have four, five lines. The lines are tied to wires and on each wire there is a bell. When a fish bites, the bell rings, like an elevator. You pull him up and it is sport.

"So one Sunday we was sitting on the dock, and we had eight lines out. Suddenly, along comes Heinrich Heine.

"It seems between those bells was musical gradations, by chance of the length of the wires, and as I am sitting tuning my clarinet, so I hear played wonder good on the bells the scale. 'Do, re, mi, fa, sol,' and the rest of it. 'My God, Jake,' I says, 'what is this for a fish?'

"Back it comes the other way the scale—being a fish the scale was its specialty—and then 'dingle, dingle,'—it was trying to pick out 'Annie Laurie.'

"Jake wanted to pull up the line, but I said, 'What, you would murder a musician?'

"We looked down it shouldn't be boys in a boat under the pier, but there was nothing. The next Sunday we came to the same spot. We set the lines and soon it gave 'Ich Weiss Nicht Was Soll Es Bedeuten.' Then I named the fish Heinrich Heine. So we played on our clarinets and Heinrich Heine would accompany us.

"Every Sunday new tunes we were teaching him, and sometimes he even offered for us original compositions. So nice it was in the sunset to sit there with a case of empty beer bottles and play 'Love's Old Sweet Song.' "

Fritz sighed. He flicked listlessly at an imaginary speck of dust with his towel.

"I never saw Heinrich Heine," he said. "I don't know whether he was a tommy or whether an eel. But in a way I helped kill him. Among the tunes we taught him was 'Die Wacht Am Rhein.' We didn't mean no harm. It was before America went in the war. Scotchers, Englishers, Irishers used to come down to the pier. It made them mad to hear the fish play so nice the German antler.

"But when this country went in the war a battleship came in the river. A bright Sunday morning Heinrich Heine commenced to play. 'Ta-tum-tee-um-tee-um-Die Wacht Am Rhein.' The battleship shot a torpedo and exploded Heinrich Heine. Since then I go no more fishing."

REGIONAL COOKING

All over the country pig snouts are a favorite regional dish with people who can afford nothing better. With the snouts a Bowery epicure can get soup, potatoes, two kinds of vegetables, stewed prunes, pudding, all the slightly shopworn bread he can eat and a bowl of coffee, for fifteen cents. That is a *diner de gala*, but the quality probably would not please you. The standard Bowery meal consists of four terrifying crullers and coffee, all for a nickel. Coffee is usually served in a porridge bowl.

Still, there are viands at which the Bowery palate revolts. I remember that toward the end of President Hoover's blessed reign, Mrs. Gifford Pinchot suggested a five-and-a-half cent meal to sustain the depressed. It included cabbage rolls stuffed with salmon and rice, apple and orange salad, sticks of corn bread, breadsticks of whole wheat flour and spinach. I discussed this menu with a man named Minder who runs a Bowery restaurant. He said, "It sounds lousy. I couldn't sell no crap like that." Minder was a thinker. He wore a purple turtleneck sweater and khaki pants while he presided over his own place in the joint quality of maitre d'hotel and bouncer. He said that he thought a good many of the men on the Bowery had been driven from their homes by wives who prepared food like cabbage rolls stuffed with salmon and rice. Reluctant to go home to dinner, these men had taken to hanging around saloons, drinking on empty stomachs. Eventually they had hit the skids and been forced to abscond from the genteel communities where their wives still lingered, commiserated by their neighbors and continuing to copy recipes out of the Ladies' Home Journal.

The typical Bowery eating house is a long-high-ceilinged room with a plate-glass storewindow in front for all its light by day. There are long wooden tables varnished with gravy, which has been massaged into the grain of the wood in the course of years. Salt and pepper are in open dishes and the customers reach in with their hands. The average check is ten cents, and payment entitles the customer to sit up all night and keep out of the cold.

The Bowery restaurateur has his own problems.

"Sometimes my customers come in with one of those nickel shots under their belt," Mr. Minder says. "They order some soup. The hot soup does not go good with the alky. When the hot soup gets in their stomach they drop right off the chair. Then we got to telephone for the ambulance. The telephone call adds to the overhead."

It would be difficult to say which is the oldest school of cooking back where I came from—the Armenian or the Chinese. Both began when French cooking was a matter of a naked Gaul tearing a raw rabbit. I know an Armenian named Krikor Sousikian, who is "cooker and treasurer" of a small restaurant called the Bosporus, and who was once the chef of Derdat Babayan, Abdul Hamid's jeweler, in Constantinople. I know Babayan's son, Levon, who lives in Paris and vouches for old Krikor. I once knew a New Yorker named Sam Johnson who claimed to be an illegitimate son of Abdul Hamid's, but I never believed him and it has nothing to do with cooking anyway. I just mention it to show what quaint characters we have back here.

The cook of a great jeweler occupied a peculiarly re-

sponsible position under Abdul Hamid because the Chief
Eunuch bought the jewels for the harem. The only way to
the Chief Eunuch's affection was through his stomach.
Krikor cooked Derdat Babayan into a monopoly of the
wedding present market, which was important because the
Sultan took a new wife every year. At each wedding there
were great gifts, not only to the bride, but to the guests
and to the members of the harem who ranked her. Krikor's
cooking had no personal importance to the Sultan, who
ate nothing at all except eggs boiled in the shell and soup
out of cans because he was afraid of being poisoned.
Krikor says this. He learned his cooking from a man named
Avedis Azdikian, who was the Escoffier of the Near East.
I once asked Krikor Sousikian how many dishes were in
Azdikian's repertoire.

"Ai! From Patlijan, eggplant, he could make three
million dishes. Patlijan karniyark. Patlijan moussaka.
Patlijan dousme. Patlijan chaup kehab. Patlijan azyze—in
the style beloved of the Sultan Aziz. Patlijan"—

"That's plenty!"

Sousikan paused meekly. "In all there are three million."

Krikor cooked his first state dinner at the age of twenty.
It was the birthday of one of the jeweler's family.

"What did you serve?"

"Chirim, fish," he said. "Chirim in cream soup." So it
seems a bisque of shrimps was the first course. But the
shrimps of the Sea of Marmora are to the shrimps of
Fulton Street as the dome of St. Sophia is to the Little
Church Around the Corner, he explained. Everything
tastes better in Constantinople.

"Then," he said, "was patlijan moussaka—eggplant

stuffed with meat and tomatoes. Then bouillabaisse our style, fish stew from wonderful fish of Constantinople. Then kouzou guvej—lamb in casserole with leeks and peppers. Then mushrooms in pastry. Then"—

"What sort of wines?"

"Wait, wait, there is more eating to tell. Then, Russian salad. Then lokma—like fritters in honey. Then varti anoush, rose leaf jelly; then hanoum dour dahel, so sweet —dessert we call 'the lady's lips'—and kaymak, heavy cream, on everything, and honey—ai! That was a dinner!"

"And the wines?"

"Champanya," said Mr. Sousikian, shortly, as if to ask "and what should the Sultan's jeweler drink but champanya?"

"And after dinner," he recalled, "Derdat Babayan called upstairs and congratulated me and gave me gold."

"Where is he now?"

"He is dead."

"And what did he die from?"

"From over-eating."

The greatest Chinese cook I ever met was named Henry Hong—at least the Chinese I knew told me he was the greatest cook, for I never ate any of his handiwork.

"North China cook not much," said Henry Hong. "Shanghai cook different, not much. Nobody China people beat Canton, Hankow. Nobody Canton, Hankow, beat me.

"When we see Eulopean eat steak," he said, "we think there go one half-civilize. He know he hungry; no know make utensil for cook, burn meat on piece fire."

I thought him an arrogant fellow, like most experts on regional cooking.

Not quite gone are the days . . .

Until the end of prohibition there were certain blocks
in New York with virtually identical speakeasies in every
house. The block I remember best was west of Eighth
Avenue, in the Forties. The houses were all brownstone,
and the speakeasies all had entrances under the stoops.
They were not primarily stand-up-at-the-bar speakeasies,
although practically every one had a small bar in the
kitchen, where customers paused for a quick one on the
way back from the men's room. They were restaurants
with vaguely French table-d'hote dinners and Italian pro-
prietors, and everybody you met knew one where the cooking was the real thing. "The place doesn't look like much,"
you would be told, "but you ought to taste the food. Did
you ever have crepes Suzette?" In those basements middle-
class New Yorkers were taught that the ultimate in des-
serts was a pancake that burned with a wan flame. If you
let yourself be persuaded to try a new place, you found
yourself in a speakeasy exactly like the one three doors
down the street, where you went habitually. The only
difference would be that the proprietor was named Victor
instead of Jean, or Emilio instead of Roberto. The pro-
prietors in the block ran to names like these; never Frank,
or Joe, or Al. That was Mulberry Street stuff—not chic.
In almost all these places the dinner was a dollar and a
half until 1930, when it got down to a dollar and a quarter.
Then, in about 1932, it dropped to a dollar. Wine was a
dollar and a half a bottle white or red, during the good
days, and a dollar later. Some places charged sixty cents
for a highball, the extra dime representing pure snobbish-
ness.

Our crowd used to favor a place on this block called Aldo's. I do not remember why we started going there, but after a while it became a habit. Aldo Bulotti was in the Polyclinic Hospital with some vague ailment at the time of our first visits, and later he went back to Italy and died. His wife, a woman named Maria, ran the place while he was sick, and kept on running it after his death. She was four feet eleven inches tall and weighed a hundred and sixty pounds, and she had bobbed hair set in a series of abrupt permanent waves about half an inch apart. She was an agreeable woman. Mrs. Bulotti had two children: a boy, eight, and a girl, five. She lived with them in Corona, out in Queens. She did not think a speakeasy was any place to raise children. An Italian doctor lived somewhere in the four stories above the basement, and twice, while we were going to Aldo's, he was deported for practicing medicine without a licence. He came back both times. The doctor had needle-pointed mustaches and a skin like old, yellowed paper. He ate dinner at Aldo's most nights and was always glad to join parties of other customers, especially if they included young women. He was a real doctor, graduated from the University of Naples, he once told me, but he had never learned much English and, besides, he was so old that his medical theory might have been considered obsolete. For these, and I suppose for other reasons, he was afraid to take the Medical Board examinations.

Aldo's was a small place, even for a speakeasy of that sort. Maria had one waiter and a cook. She kept the bar herself. She changed waiters often, but Bruno, the cook, seemed to be permanent. He was an Umbrian, very fair for an Italian, with a sharp, tired face. A widower, he got on very well with Maria. When you came into Aldo's, there was a hall leading from the door straight to the kitchen, and there were two small, connecting rooms that opened off the hall. In the front room were five tables, a disused fireplace, and a mirror, and in the room between that and the kitchen were three tables and a painting of a scene on Lake Como.

Along one wall of the kitchen was a bench, with a trellis over it, and across from that a bar. Also in the kitchen were two tables with checkered cloths, and some of the customers preferred to sit there, where they could talk to Maria and Bruno while they were eating. That way they could hear all about the customers in the front rooms, since Maria and Bruno carried on a running discussion of them, with the waiter joining in from time to time. The customers included a number of married women who liked to talk to strangers about their troubles, and a beautiful girl named Ruth, who told people she was a private secretary and was always busting into other people's parties. There were also several discreet couples who chose the smallest room when they could get a table there and argued in whispers until they began to feel good, when they would come out in the kitchen and join the other parties. Several of the steadiest customers came from Reuters, the British news agency. Reuters' office is over on the other side of town, but people used to migrate into those West Side blocks from everywhere to take their dinners. One of the Reuters men was impressive because of his habit of sitting all alone in the front room, staring at the curtained windows and drinking brandy and black coffee out of a tall glass. His name was Skerry. He was a very dignified gentleman with an Old World courtliness. Occasionally, after a good many mazagrans and brandies, he would poke his head into the kitchen before he left for the night and make a little speech to the people at the bar. "By this means," he would say, swaying gently, "I disinfect myself from the American turmoil." Then he would bow and go home. We always felt that he was doing all he could to uphold the traditions of the Empire, like the legendary Englishman in the Borneo outpost who dresses every night for dinner in order to keep from going native.

Maria made her wine at home in Corona out of California grapes. Some of the customers were allergic to the wine and fell on their heads, but others, thank God, could stand a lot of it. I think it was in these speakeasies that "allergy" got started on its way to being a common word. Everybody, it seemed, was allergic to some particular kind of liquor. You never met a man in a speakeasy who was merely an incompetent drinker. He always said, "I can drink any amount of Scotch or rye, but I'm allergic to brandy." Or else, "I can hold my hard liquor, but when I drink red wine, I never remember what happens." One night a man named Jim, who Maria said was a very sweet gentleman except that he coudn't drink gin, was sitting in the kitchen with his wife. He was drinking gin. Pretty soon he threatened to tear his wife's clothes off. She said, "Go ahead!" very scornfully, not thinking that he would do it, and he did tear them off, all but a brassiere. The outraged woman rushed from the kitchen into the front room, in search of privacy. It happened, however, that Skerry, the courtliest of the Reuters men, was sitting there alone, drinking and thinking. He turned his face to the wall. "What a big surprise for Mr. Skerry!" Bruno remarked when he told me about it the next evening. Maria lent the woman a coat and put her in a taxi, and Skerry soon after went back to England and got married. In time he will tell incredulous juniors this anecdote of his life in the United States under prohibition, and they will say, among themselves, that it's a bit thick—the old boy's in his dotage.

When repeal came, I didn't bother my head much about Aldo's. I happened to walk through the block a few weeks afterward, and I noticed that a dozen of the speakeasies had secured licences, hung out signs, and opened up, but that Maria hadn't. From then on I took it for granted that she had not been able to raise the fee, and had gone out of business. Then, about a month ago, I found myself in the old neighborhood and I got to thinking with some tenderness of Maria and Bruno, and I walked around to the house where Aldo's had been. The front of the place looked as dismal and taciturn as ever, with all the shades drawn in the barred basement windows. But I thought that the recurrent Italian physician might be living in the house, and that he might be able to tell me what had become of Mrs. Bulotti. Perhaps she had opened a little cafe in a more prepossessing part of town, I thought, and it would be fun to visit her.

I therefore walked down the two steps from pavement level and rang the bell beside the basement grille. Maria herself came to the door. She was dazzled by the daylight, and peered out warily until I pressed my face against the bars. Then she grinned, and released the catch by pressing en electric button. It seemed to me that time in its flight turned backward to 1928. "Come in the kitch', Mista Lieba," she said. "Maybe you like a drink. Bruno!" she

yelled down the hall. "Itsa Mista Lieba!" I followed her.
The door to the front room was ajar, and I could see the
familiar tables laid with their white cloths. Nothing in
the kitchen had changed: the copper saucepans hanging
above the range, the trellis with its artificial yellow vine
leaves, the red-and-black lacquer bar, and on the liquor
shelf the pink lamp made out of a French cordial bottle.

Bruno, in his white cap and apron, was slicing eggplant
with a long knife, just as I remembered him in a previous
gastronomic existence. Maria bought a drink of Courvoisier
and smiled as I looked about me. "Just the same as ever,
eh?" she said. "I got the whole house now. The Doctor,
he'sa gone back to Italy for good. I got the children with
me, living on the first floor. Dino is in the third year 'igh
school. 'E's seventeen. Gilda, she's a freshman. She's
fourteen. I rent out eight rooms on the other floors. Bruno
and me, we do pretty good now."

She has never really got out of the speakeasy business,
she told me. Some of the old customers, like me, had taken
her retirement for granted and gone off to licenced restaurants. She didn't see them any more. But a few, either
from habit or because they liked personal attention while
drinking, had continued to come. Now there were a good
many new clients, introduced by the old ones. Some people
have never got used to drinking in public restaurants, it
seems. The atmosphere is too formal and grasping. Even
in reformed speakeasies that have tried to retain the old
spirit, the management takes a cold, impersonal attitude
toward disorderly conduct. The owners, Maria says with
scorn, are afraid that the Alcohol Board will revoke their
licences.

If Maria had bought a licence, she said, she would have

had to open her door to everybody. On that block, this would inevitably have meant invasion by uncouth types. "Truckadriv'!" Maria said. "They cannot mix with my people. My people would desert me. I gotta keep my place nice."

It sounded reasonable to me. I asked her if she wasn't afraid of being arrested. Maria said that she was less worried now than she had been during prohibition. About half the places on the block had opened as saloons, she told me, and the rest operated as speakeasies. They all got along amicably. The saloon-keepers didn't want any more open drinking places on the block, and so, since they knew the speakeasy trade came from outside the neighborhood, they didn't complain about the speakeasies.

Even if there was a raid, possession of legitimately bottled liquor was no offence. If inspectors remarked on the quantity, Maria could say that the men who lived upstairs boarded with her and liked a drink with their meals. She never sold to strangers. Anyway, the mere circumstance that a stranger would want to buy a drink at a private house nowadays would suffice to warn the least wary proprietor. As she is not subject to licence regulations, Maria stays open until six o'clock in the morning, while legal bars close at four. This is a great convenience to some of her customers.

Naturally, the business is on a small scale, but expenses also are low. Repeal was such a blow to brownstone rental values that she leases the entire house for one hundred and twenty-five dollars a month. She used to pay one hundred and seventy-five dollars for the basement. The eight roomers, who pay four or five dollars a week each, furnish enough money for the rent for the whole building,

including Maria's own living quarters. It is no longer necessary to invest money in liquor in large lots, or in tons of
grapes for wine-making. She can buy whiskey by the bottle
and wine by the gallon at the liquor store in the next block.
At thirty-five cents a drink for whiskey and forty-five cents
a pint for wine, there's a nice profit. The dinner is a dollar,
and of course there's a profit in that. Maria waits on the
tables herself now. It agrees with her, apparently, because
her weight has gone up to two hundred pounds. She says
that she averages about a dozen customers at dinner. There
are generally one or two afternoon clients who want seclu-
sion, and then there are usually a couple of drinkers who
stay on after four in the morning. It all amounts to twenty
or thirty dollars a day, and half of that is profit.

I stayed for dinner and we talked. Bruno likes it better
than working as assistant chef in some Italian restaurant.
When there are no customers, he plays dominoes with
one of the roomers, or reads Italian sporting papers, which
are brought to him by stewards on the Rex and the Conte
di Savoia. He used to be in the merchant marine, and the
place is not far from the piers, so he keeps up his acquaintance. Twice a week he goes to boxing shows.

Every so often, without any particular reason, an old
patron will return to the house just as I did, Maria told
me. It's like coming back to the scene of a crime, or one's
childhood. Sometimes the oldsters even pay prohibition-
time tabs. One of them, a week earlier, had paid her
seventeen dollars which he had owed since 1932.

A woman came in and sat down at the table next to me
in the kitchen. Maria introduced us; her name, as nearly
as I could make out, was Mrs. Buttercup. Soon we were
all talking, as in the good days. Mrs. Buttercup told me

that she had a daughter twenty-one years old, to whom she had presented a Boston terrier for Christmas, but the daughter, just because she wanted to go to California, had returned the terrier to her, Mrs. Buttercup, although she knew full well that the Buttercup apartment in London Terrace was no place for a dog. "No sense of responsibility," Mrs. Buttercup said. She had an irritating way of repeating herself and she was not particularly handsome, but she had an archaic charm, like a Gibson girl. She drank Old-Fashioned cocktails throughout her meal. I found that when a client, especially a lady, is approaching the saturation point, Maria still dilutes the drinks, although of course she does not reduce the prices on the check, as that would arouse suspicion. The place soothed me. Bruno's chicken *en casserole* and his *cannelloni* were really rather good. After all, one needn't eat the crepes Suzette. Before I left, Maria told Mrs. Buttercup and me about a woman in the front room the other night whose husband had got so angry at her drinking that he knocked out one of her front teeth. Then he had had to pay sixty dollars to have it put back, Maria said, because he couldn't stand her smile without it.

What do you expect for $2.00?

There never were many people in the finest restaurant I ever discovered within the city limits (it was at one of new York's bathing beaches) and most of those there were seemed unwanted. Sometimes a party of four sunburned adults and maybe three children would sit around a table uneasily for half an hour, the men in shirtsleeves, the women in cotton dresses, and no waiter would come near them. Three or four waiters, old, acrid fellows, would be standing in the farthest corner of the vast room, talking and laughing bitterly, and looking over at the people at the table. The waiters wore black alpaca coats and round tin badges with numbers on them. Once we saw a man at a table grow angry and bang on the water carafe with a knife. There was only yellow, tepid water in the carafe. A waiter shuffled to his table from the far corner. He seemed to take an interminable time getting there, and the slup, slup of his broken old shoes on the floor sounded loud in that almost silent place. The man said something to him, and then the waiter said in a loud, contemptuous voice, "We don't serve sandwiches or soft drinks here." The party went out, the men looking ashamed, the women scolding their males for subjecting them to such embarrassment.

"Some of them turf-cutters," our waiter said, flicking crumbs off our table with the end of his napkin. " 'Turf-cutter' is a word we use for cheap Irish," he said, knocking most of the crumbs into my girl's lap. He looked Irish himself. "The Beach is full of them," he said. "Let them go down to the Limerick House."

The restaurant must have been built shortly after the Columbian Exposition. It was an imitation of a cake-frosting exposition building, with seven senseless minarets on it. Most of the white paint had flaked off, or turned gray with age and sea air. The signs about specialties of the house were painted right on the building, in what had once been silver lettering, on what had once been a maroon ground. Evidently the lettering had not been changed since the restaurant was built. Most of the signs said, "Rhode Island Clambake, $1.75," or "Roast Chicken Dinner, $1.50." In the state to which the Beach has declined, these are high prices. They must have been high forty years ago, too, but then the Beach was a fashionable resort, with a clientele of hot sports. It cost a dollar just to get there from Manhattan, in a steamboat. Now the most dashing attractions are a couple of tired carrousels and a few saloons that advertise in the Irish-American newspapers; but most of the people who come to the Beach do not patronize even them. They just change into their bathing suits under the boardwalk and go swimming, and when they come out, they eat at hot-dog stands. The swimming is good.

The floor of the restaurant sloped like a ship's deck in a big sea. Like all the older buildings at the Beach, it had been built without a foundation, and it had settled in the sand unevenly. The dish covers, the soup tureens, and the rest of the tableware had an antiquarian interest. Each piece bore the name of an old, vanished restaurant: Shanley's, Churchill's, or Jack's.

The restaurant was so obviously decadent and unprosperous that we had not ventured into it the first few times that we went to the Beach to swim. It was only after investigating the possibilities of the Greek lunchrooms, the Japanese waffle shops, and the saloons that we had dared that ghostly pavilion, deciding that we had nothing to lose. The food in the old restaurant had astonished us. The steamed clams were small, clean, and accompanied by a stiff sauce of butter with tarragon vinegar and curry powder blended into it. The chicken fricassee was not smothered in a white flour paste, but yellow and succulent. The three-and-a-half-dollar steak, for two, was perfect. As long as we ordered substantially, took cocktails before dinner, and drank plenty of beer with the meal, the waiters tolerated us.

One evening I ordered a "combination" of steamed clams and a broiled lobster, with potatoes. It had seemed to me that included in this offering, on the menu, was a green salad. Having finished the lobster, I asked for this salad.

The waiter said, "What do you expect for two dollars? A *gold* watch?"

It was this same waiter, however, who on another evening began to talk to me, almost without condescension. It is true he had been drinking.

"The place is a hundred years behind the times," he said. "It's a summer home for broken-down waiters."

He put one hand on our table and leaned his weight on it.

"The cook is forty-nine million years old," he said. "Some day he'll fall into the clam chowder. At the end of every season the old man says to him, 'I never want to see you no more. You're as dead as a doornail.' And at the beginning of the next season he sends a taxicab for him. He used to cook at Burns's. The old man is in his second childhood. That's him setting up on the high stool by the bar. He ain't got no cash register, only an old wooden cash box. He sets there from ten o'clock in the morning until closing time, to see that no waiter gets away with a glass of beer."

The waiter pointed his chin angrily toward the figure on the stool, diagonally across the room from us. The old gentleman was dressed in a black broadcloth suit, such as a conservative undertaker might wear in winter. The upper part of the vest looked very big for him, but his lower abdomen ballooned out like a spider's. On top of his head he balanced an old *Panama* hat, colored like a meerschaum pipe. Even from there we could see how badly he needed a shave.

"He's had that *Panama* hat for twenty years," the waiter grumbled. "Every spring he has it cleaned, and I think painted, and he brags to everybody he knows about it. 'See,' he says, 'the *Panama* hat is good for another season.' He's in his second childhood. But try to take a dime off him," the waiter said, "and he ain't in his second childhood no more. You can't do it."

The old man came down off the stool, reluctantly, like a boy sliding into a too-cold swimming pool. He shuffled toward our end of the room, glaring suspiciously over the tops of his spectacles. He had a long, pointed nose. Fifteen feet from our table the old man stopped and stared at us for a minute. Then he turned and went away. Laboriously he climbed up on the stool.

"He was just coming over to see there wasn't too many customers in the place," the waiter explained. "The other night they was lined up two deep at the bar, for once, so he says to the bartender, 'Come out from behind that bar, Joe, and take a walk around the block until they clear out of here.' He don't like no customers. It's second childhood. Do you know what worries him the most? The fear that somebody would park at the curb here. He hates automobiles. So he puts a stepladder in front of the curb and a pot of green paint on top of it. So anybody that drives in will knock the ladder over and get paint on his car. 'Oh, he-he-he,' the old man laughs the last time that happens. 'Look at the damn fool! Too bad he didn't get it on his clothes,' the old man says."

The dining room opens onto a terrace on a level with

the sidewalk. We looked out and saw the ladder, with the paint pot perched on the top step.

Another waiter, even older than ours, who was pretty old himself, edged up to our man.

"I don't like to say nothing, Murph," he said, "but them people over at that table over there says they give you their order half an hour ago."

"Tell them it's a two-mile walk to the kitchen and back," said our waiter. The people, two men and two women, had been watching him right along, and knew he had not been to the kitchen. When they saw he was not going to do anything about it, they got up and left.

"Deaf as a post the old man is," the waiter went on. "You should hear him talk on the telephone with his sister that lives at the Plaza. 'I'm fine,' he yells as soon as he picks up the phone. He thinks she's asking him how he is. No matter what the hell she calls up to talk to him about, he just says, 'I'm fine,' and hangs up. But if you drop a dollar bill on the floor, he hears it hit."

Perhaps the old man sensed that we were talking about him. Hesitantly, he got down off his stool again and walked over toward us, then stopped, irresolute, at the same point as before, and turned and went back.

"It's on account of him that the Beach is going to hell," said our waiter. "He owns all the property for a mile around and he won't put a coat of paint on a building. Last year four blocks of his stuff burnt up, the damned old tinderboxes. 'It don't do me no good anyway,' he says. 'I couldn't get no insurance on them.' The papers says, '$500,000 Fire at the Beach,' but he couldn't get five cents for them buildings."

"Why does he keep the place open if he doesn't want any customers?" my girl asked.

"So he can lose money and take it off his income tax," Murph told her. "And now for God's sakes don't order no pie à la mode like the last time, for I have to walk down to one end of the old shack for the pie and then I have to walk to the other end to the icehouse for the ice cream. Before you can get an order together in this place, you got to get a letter from the Pope. And then before you can find a dish to serve it in, you got to go through all that heap of old tinware, like a junk shop."

My girl meekly ordered watermelon, but Murph did not start to get it. He felt like talking.

"Before his wife died sixteen years ago, it wasn't so bad," he said. "Sometimes she would buy a round of drinks for the house. She was always soused. Twenty-four seasons I've worked here, God help me, and now it's too late to get fired. He'll die next winter surely."

JUST FOLKS

Broadway Storekeeper

The I. & Y. cigar store at Forty-ninth Street and Seventh Avenue is open twenty-four hours a day every day of the year except Yom Kippur. During daylight hours it performs the same function as any other cigar store on a fairly busy corner. People coming up from the B.M.T. station or going down into it often buy cigarettes at the I. & Y. The essential character of the place is not apparent until nightfall, when it becomes the neighborhood's nearest approach to a country store. After dark the I. & Y. expands into a forum of public opinion and an arena of practical jokes. Permanent chairman of the debates is the proprietor, Izzy Yereshevsky.

Izzy has to keep his store open all night because one of the main props of his business is selling cigarettes to nearly every night club in town. The hat-check concessionaires, whose stakes in the resorts also entitle them to sell cigarettes at twenty-five cents a pack, never seem able to estimate their needs in advance. Izzy gets emergency telephone calls at all hours for cartons of cigarettes; his nephew, Little Izzy, is on the go making deliveries from dark to dawn. In addition, Izzy supplies those long-legged dolls and beribboned Teddy bears which cigarette girls hawk between the tables in night clubs. Izzy stays open because of the night-club trade and he gets the night-club trade because he stays open.

This stuffed-animal sideline of Izzy's is likely to puzzle the casual visitor to his cigar store—a fairly deep but narrow shop, about twelve feet by thirty. In the show window on Seventh Avenue sit three Cubans making cigars by hand. Clustered around the Cuban's feet in the window, are ranks of Teddy bears and dolls, some pert, some droopy, and all well cured in the aroma of tobacco leaves.

Izzy Yereshevsky is a Jewish peasant. Because he is essentially a countryman, his store has acquired a communal, bucolic atmosphere. Izzy performs all sorts of community services that pay him nothing. "On Broadway," Izzy sometimes says, "you got to be werry good, werry sweet to everybody. And even then they stick you in the back." Remaining an outlander, he feels it necessary to placate the local gods.

Most of his evening guests—their purchases are so infrequent that it would be misleading to call them customers—wear white felt hats and overcoats of a style known to them as English Drape. Short men peer up from between the wide-flung shoulders of these coats as if they had been lowered into the garments on a rope and were now trying to climb out. To Izzy his guests are the people of Broadway. They are the big talkers and, on the rare occasions when they have cash in their pockets, the big spenders. In truth the boys in the white felt hats and the English Drapes do not love money for its own sake. Each fosters a little personal legend of lost affluence; fifty grand dropped on the races in one day, twenty grand blown on a doll in a brief sojourn at Atlantic City. Never to have been in the chips marks one as a punk or a smalltimer. It precludes conversation in big figures. Continuous prosperity, to the boys, however, hints of avarice and is discreditable.

Until 1913 Izzy worked on a tobacco farm in the Ukraine, and when he first came to America he went from the boat to a place in Connecticut he calls East Windsor, Ill. His brother had a job on a tobacco farm there. Izzy worked with him for a year and saved eight hundred dollars. Then he came to New York to learn the trade of cigar-making. Eighteen years ago he opened the I. & Y. two blocks down Seventh Avenue from its present situation.

"I am the 'I.' and I am the 'Y.'," he explains. "Two initials sounds more responsible."

Izzy is famous for the power of his handshake. He pulls his right hand back level with his shoulder, holds it cocked for a moment, then crashes it against the hand of the person he is greeting. It is as if you have been hit on the palm with a nightstick. "Hol-*lo doc*-tor," Mr. Yereshevsky invariably shouts as he strikes. "Doctor" is his conventional salutation. In Izzy's store, as on the East Indian Island of Buru and among certain Australian aborigines, it is considered bad form to speak a man's real name lest one unwittingly give an enemy power over his future. It is also bad form in addressing a customer who has been away to ask him where he has been. He may have been in Hollywood or he may have been in jail. If he has been in Hollywood he will say so.

Izzy is a man of slightly less than medium height, with broad shoulders and gray, crinkly hair. The color is somewhat deceptive, because Izzy was young enough to be drafted in the World War. A generous and often bluish jowl offsets the effect of Izzy's sensitive nose and mouth.

He further masks his inner nature by clenching a large cigar of his own manufacture in the right corner of his jaw. The effort to sustain the cigar twists Izzy's mouth into a hard, jaunty smile hardly in keeping with his timid nature.

Izzy accepts more bad checks than anybody else on Broadway. To make his books balance in the face of such odds, he finds it necessary to work eighteen hours a day. He comes to the I. & Y. at noon and leaves at six o'clock the next morning. He likes to say he has been "thirty-six years on Broadway; eighteen years days, and eighteen years nights." After the midtown night clubs close, concessionaires and headwaiters foregather at the I. & Y. to discuss business conditions, and the cigarette girls drop in to buy their dolls and Teddy bears. Even then, Little Izzy, the delivery boy, is still darting out into the night with orders for late-closing places. On an ordinary night Izzy's nephew hustles up to Harlem or down to Greenwich Village at least half a dozen times.

Izzy does not drink, gamble, or patronize night spots. He works very hard, and most of the men who spend their evenings in his store find this irresistibly amusing. When Izzy announces that another check has bounced, his friends have been known to go out and roll with mirth on the sidewalk in back of the Rivoli Theatre. To them the calamities of virtue are exquisitely comic. They revel in unmerited catastrophe and sometimes cite Izzy as an example of the uselessness of honest toil.

Izzy shows no resentment. He feels that Broadway people who write bad checks are actuated not by greed but a need for self-expression. They want money to lose on the horse races. Izzy thinks horses are parasitic organisms that live on his human acquaintances. He blanches at the sight of a policeman's mount.

"Win money on a horse race?" he echoes, when asked his opinion of the sport. "How did you think them horses get feeded?"

Every fortnight or so he heads a subscription to bury some horseplayer who has died broke. There are always impromptu collections under way at the I. & Y. for the relief of various indigent nocturnal characters, and the boys subscribe freely. They take an equal pride in giving charity and bilking their creditors.

Izzy has another nephew, Max, who is a graduate of James Monroe High School and a deep student of human nature. A slender, pale young man with a scraggly mustache, he assists Izzy behind the counter. "Everybody who comes in here wants money so he can be a sucker," Max says. "You have to be in the money before you can be a sucker. Only out-of-towners think being a sucker's a disgrace."

One of the favorite amusements among the boys is improvising tall tales to bewilder strangers. A regular habitué of the I. & Y. will shout to another, as if they had just met for the first time, "Say, ain't you the feller that I seen with an animal act at the Hippodrome fifteen years ago, where the camel dived into the tank with you on his back?"

"Sure," the other will come back, calmly, "but it wasn't a camel; it was an elephant I was on."

A friendly stranger, just stopping in to make a purchase, may remark incredulously at this point, "I didn't think the Hippodrome tank was big enough to hold an elephant." Then everybody laughs like mad.

Some of the members of Izzy's cénacle have lovely names. A large, emphatic fellow who usually talks about big real-estate deals, rocking on his heels and shouting, is called Hairynose because of a clump of red hair sprouting from his nostrils. Everybody knows that in workaday life he is a necktie salesman, but Izzy likes to hear him talk of big land deals. Then there are Skyhigh Charlie and Three-to-Two Charlie. Skyhigh is a ticket speculator with an office on Forty-seventh Street, a large, florid man who buys Izzy's three-for-fifty cigars. The fortunes of the theatrical season may always be gauged by a quick glance at the little finger of Skyhigh's left hand. He wears a ring with a cluster of bulbous diamonds on it, buying larger stones when he makes money, pawning them and wearing smaller ones when things are dull. Three-to-Two Charlie is a betting man with a predilection for short odds which his more reckless intimates find detestable. One elderly lounger with a long goatee and a mane of hair is invariably addressed as "the Doctor." He used to have an office where he grew hair on bald men and is the court of last appeal in all I. & Y. disputes on scientific subjects. At present he is waiting for Izzy to find him a job as a washroom attendant.

The election of Thomas E. Dewey as District Attorney did not please all of the political observers of the I. & Y. "After all, what did he do only sperl a lot of t'ings dat gave people what to eat?" a friend of Izzy's called Monkey the Bum argues. "It's tough enough to make a living now. There's plenty of guys walking the streets today without where to flop, without who to ask for a dime. And in 1926 those same guys didn't have nothing either."

Izzy deprecates such gloom. When the hat-check concessionaires ask him about business conditions he tries to cheer them.

"Me they ask how's business," he says. "So I always tell them something nice. If good, I say'll stay good. If bad, I say it's the bad weather, people are staying home. Or the weather's too good, they're going to the country. Or it's coming Christmas, they're spending money in the stores. Or it's gone Christmas, they spent all their money."

Like all storekeepers of the old tradition, Izzy carries on a number of free public services. Among them he accepts telephone messages for workers in the neighborhood. Most of the messages are from wives, and when Izzy talks to them he indulges a healthy, earthy wit. One whose calls are cleared through the I. & Y. store is a newsdealer called Chopsie who used to be a song-and-dance man in vaudeville. Mrs. Chopsie calls up often.

"Yass, Mrs. Chopsie," Izzy will shout when he answers the telephone. "Sure I seen Chopsie this evening. He was walking down the street with a blonde weighed maybe three hundred pounds, he wouldn't say where he was going." While he talks to Mrs. Chopsie Izzy rolls his eyes, holds his right hand on his stomach as if in pain, and sometimes weeps with mirth. But he usually gets the message straight—Chopsie is to bring home half a pound of bologna or a copy of True Love Stories.

The I. & Y. is also a free employment agency for hat-check and cigarette girls who meet concessionaires there. On winter nights, too, a few bedraggled ladies without escort come in to warm their feet. Izzy lets them sit on chairs in the back of the store where, since they are always tired and usually slightly drunk, they often go to sleep. Once Izzy tied one to a chair as she slept. It was a great joke when she awoke and started to yell, but afterward Izzy felt badly because he had humiliated the girl. So he presented to her a box of Danny's Special Cigars, which she likes to smoke. Izzy names all his cigars after members of his immediate family. Danny is his five-year-old son. He has two daughters, too, Dora and Della, both in their teens. Izzy long ago combined their names to make a high-class title for a cigar—the DoraDella.

Certain essential facilities of the store are so popular that Izzy has nailed up a permanent sign, "Lavatory out of order." Only strangers are deceived. All through the evening neighborhood people buttonhole Mr. Yereshevsky, asking "Will you O.K. me, Izzy?" Izzy always nods, and the suppliants march toward the rear of the shop in successful defiance of the sign.

Fanciful signs are a feature of the I. & Y. Several steady customers feel gifts for chirography and, in gratitude for being saved from frostbites, they devote hours to lettering testimonials for the walls. A sample is:

> My name is Izzy
> I'm always busy
> Making I. & Y. cigars.

Mrs. Mollie Yereshevsky, Izzy's wife, works in the store during the day. She is a pink-fleshed, country-looking woman, plump and cheerful. They live in the Lincoln Apartments on Fifty-first Street west of Eighth Avenue, a block populated largely by theatre and night-club people. Mollie has a hard time controlling Izzy's generous impulses. When he opened his first store he readily believed his customers' stories of immense wealth gained quickly through theatrical productions or hat-check concessions in speakeasies. Anyone who bought a box of cigars appeared to Izzy an American millionaire. If the man said the cigars were good, he became on the spot Izzy's friend. When friends asked him to cash checks he always obliged. When the checks bounced, he was sorry because the friends often stayed away as long as two weeks. Reappearing, they would explain that, just before Izzy presented the check at the bank, a wonderful opportunity to buy a nightclub had come their way and to grasp it they had had to draw out all their cash. But to square everything they would offer to sell Izzy the hat-check concession in the club. All he had to do was pay from one to six thousand dollars in advance.

Every time Izzy invested in a concession, he says, one of three things would happen. "Or the nightclub wouldn't open," is the way he puts it, "or it would open and close in a couple weeks, the fellow would keep the concession money, or the club would start to make money they would sell the concession over my head to somebody else. Contracts you didn't have with speakeasies."

Izzy likes to pretend he is less ingenuous now. He adopts a knowing and secretive manner toward strangers, deliberating several seconds before answering even the most innocent question, such as "When did you move here from the Forty-seventh Street store?"

"Six years ago," he will finally whisper.

"Where were you during the War?"

"Fort Totten," Izzy will breathe faintly, after looking around carefully for concealed dictaphones. It sometimes takes as long as three minutes to secure his confidence. When he has given it, he will pull out a drawer in back of the counter to show you his collection of rubber checks.

"About fifty thousand dollars," he boasts, with the pride of a man showing a particularly impressive scar from an appendectomy. "Who shall I collect from, responsible people? I am de most wictim on Broadway." He is very proud of it.

Izzy sells wholesale to the night clubs, limiting his profit to two per cent. The cafés make his cigarette business larger in volume than his trade in cigars, but cigars are nearer to Izzy's heart. Because he has room for only three workers at a time, the cigar makers work in day and night shifts. Luis, the oldest Cuban, sometimes remains in the window making panatelas or perlas until three in the morning. The Cubans sit in a kind of cage, shut off from the rest of the shop by a metal grill. Izzy buys the leaf tobacco and pays the Cubans piecework rates for making the cigars. He keeps the cigars in a large humidor until he makes a sale. When he has an order for a box, Izzy takes it from the humidor, pastes on the revenue stamps, and hands it to the customer.

Izzy believes in cigars. He always recommends them for a hangover—probably because he has never suffered from one.

Tummler

To the boys of the I. & Y. Hymie Katz is a hero. He is a short, broad-shouldered, olive-complexioned man who looks about forty-two and is really somewhat older. In his time he has owned twenty-five night clubs.

"Hymie is a tummler," the boys at the I. & Y. say. "Hymie is a man what knows to get a dollar."

Hymie at present is running a horserace tipping service in an office building on Longacre Square. "What is a night club made of?" he sometimes asks contemptuously. "Spit and toilet paper. An upholstered joint. The attractions get the money and the boss gets a kick in the pants." His admirers understand that this is only a peevish interlude. Soon he will open another night club.

The tipping service requires no capital. Hymie reads out-of-town telephone books for the names of doctors and ministers fifty or a hundred miles from New York. Then he calls them, one by one, asking the operator to reverse the charges. Hymie tells the operator, let us say, that he is Mr. Miller whom Dr. Blank or the Rev. Mr. Doe met at Belmont Park last summer. If the man accepts the call, Hymie knows he has a prospect. The man probably hasn't been at Belmont, and certainly hasn't met a Mr. Miller there, but thinks he is the beneficiary of a case of mistaken identity. Hymie tells him about a horse that is sure to win. All the doctor or minster has to do, Hymie says, is to send him the winnings on a ten-dollar bet. Sometimes the horse does win, and the small-town man always remits Hymie's share of the profits. He wants to be in on the next sure thing. Doctors, Hymie believes, are the most credulous of mortals. Ministers never squawk.

Hymie picks his horses very carefully from the past-performance charts of the Morning Telegraph. He usually tips three or four entries in each race. Naturally, the physicians and clergymen who get bad tips send him no money, but the supply of small-town professional men is practically unlimited. Hymie says it is an ideal business for a man satisfied with a modest, steady income. Personally, he is resigned to opening another night club. "If I wasn't ashamed," he says, "I would put a couple of hundred dollars in it myself." The investment of his own money, according to Hymie's code, would be unethical.

All Hymie needs to open a night club is an idea and a loan of fifty dollars. There are fifteen or twenty basements and one-flight-up places between Forty-fifth and Fifty-fifth Streets that cannot economically be used as anything but night clubs. They have raised dance floors, ramps, numerous light outlets, kitchens, and men's and women's washrooms. Because they are dark during the day, or can be reached only by staircases, they are not adapted to ordinary restaurant use. Such a place may be worth six hundred dollars a month as a night club. Dismantled, it would bring only a hundred or so as a store. The owner of a night-club site makes out pretty well if his space is tenanted for six months of the year.

Hymie has been around Broadway since 1924. He is a good talker. In the past, some of his clubs actually have made money, although none of it has stuck to him. As a matter of ritual he always tells the owner of the spot he proposes to rent that he is going to spend forty thousand dollars to fix it up. The owner does not believe this, but the sound of the words reassures him. If Hymie said more than forty thousand dollars, the landlord would sense a certain lack of enthusiasm. It is customary to mention forty thousand dollars when talking about redecorating a night club. If the owner appears to be hooked, Hymie goes out and spends the borrowed fifty dollars. He pays it to a lawyer to draw up a lease. The lawyer Hymie patronizes is the only man in the world whom Hymie has never been able to put on the cuff. But he draws a fine lease. It contains all sorts of alluring clauses, like "party of the first part and party of the second part agree to share equally in all profits above ten thousand dollars a week, after reimbursement of party of the second part for outlays made in equipping the Dopey Club (said outlays for this purpose not to exceed forty thousand dollars)." It makes provision for profits of Aluminum Trust magnitude.

Hymie takes the lease to a hat-check concessionaire. This is the really critical phase of the enterprise. He must convince the concessionaire that the place has a chance to do business ("Look at the figures in the lease, you can see what we're expecting"). He must fill the concessionaire with enthusiasm for the entertainers, who have not yet been engaged. For it is up to the concessionaire to provide the cash that will make the enterprise go—three thousand dollars in advance, in return for the hat-check and cigarette concession for six months. Hymie is a great salesman. He does impersonations of his hypothetical acts. He tells about the Broadway columnists who eat out of his hand and will give yards of free publicity. While Hymie talks, the concessionaire distills drops of probability from his gallons of conversation. In his mind he turns Hymie's thousands of anticipated revenue into fifties and hundreds. If the club runs three months, the concessionaire knows, he will get his money back. If by some fluke it runs six months, he will double his money. If nobody financed night clubs, there would be no concession business. So the concessionaire lets Hymie have the three thousand.

Hymie goes back to the landlord, signs the lease, and pays him a month's rent in advance—say six hundred dollars. That leaves twenty-four hundred dollars for the other expenses. If possible, he saves himself from headaches by renting out the kitchen. The kitchen concessionaire provides the food, cooks up a stew on which all the night-club help feed every night, and even pays half of the cost of the table linen. (Linen is rented, not bought.) The proprietor of the club gets from twelve to twenty per cent of the gross receipts for food. Since night-club food is absurdly high, the food concessionaire, like the hat-check man, is bound to make a good profit if the place lasts a few months.

The club may contain tables, chairs, and any amount of miscellaneous equipment abandoned by a former tenant in lieu of rent. If it doesn't, Hymie goes to a man named I. Arthur Ganger, who runs a Cain's warehouse of the night club business on West Forty-fifth Street. Ganger can provide out of used stock anything from a pink-and-onyx Joseph Urban bar to a wicker smörgasbord table. Some of his silverware has been in and out of ten previous clubs. Usually Ganger will accept a twenty-five-per-cent down payment, which for one of Hymie's clubs amounts to a few hundred dollars. He takes notes payable weekly for the rest. Ganger is amenable to reason when the notes fall due. He has a favorite joke for customers like Hymie. "Your mother carried you only nine months," he says, "but I been carrying you all your life." The supply man retains title to his things until they are entirely paid for, and if the club folds he carts them back to his warehouse. Ganger decorates some clubs, but Hymie would not think of hiring him for such a job. Hymie gets a girlish young man to perform a maquillage for a hundred and fifty dollars, including paint.

Of the three thousand dollars received from the concessionaire, Hymie has now disbursed at most twelve hundred. He pays another six hundred dollars for a liquor licence good for six months, and puts the rest of the money in the bank as profit in case the club flops. The remaining preparations are on the cuff. Hymie hires acts for his new club on the understanding that he will pay off a week after the place opens. He engages a band on the same terms. If there is to be a line of girls in the show, the girls rehearse free. But Hymie is not a bad fellow. He sends out for coffee and sandwiches for the girls during rehearsals. Once or twice he has been known to lend a girl five dollars for room rent before a club opened.

Liquor is harder to buy on credit these days than before repeal. Mob credit was flexible, and if you bought from a bootlegger independent of the gangs, Hymie says, you never paid him at all. Wholesalers now are allowed to extend only twenty-one days' credit, according to the regulations of the State Liquor Authority. But matters sometimes may be arranged by paying a bill on the twenty-first day and then borrowing most of the money back from the wholesaler on the twenty-second.

A few days before the opening Hymie effects a deal that always puts him in especially good humor. He sells twenty waiters their jobs. The headwaiter pays four hundred dollars, two captains pay two hundred dollars each, and ordinary waiters fifty dollars. Waiters like to work for Hymie because he lets them take what they can get. He wastes no time watching his employees. "Most of the stealing they do is from the customers, so what do I care?" says Hymie.

Despite all his forethought, exigencies sometimes arise which demand fresh capital. Perhaps an unusually stubborn landlord demands three months' security, or a police official must be heavily greased before he will let the club stay open after hours. In some places, especially black-and-tan or crudely bawdy spots, all the money comes in during the illegal early hours of the morning, after the bigger clubs have closed. In such emergencies Hymie sometimes has to take in partners. He usually bilks his partners for the principle of the thing. He is not avaricious. Dollars, Hymie thinks, are markers in a game of wits as well as a medium of exchange. He refuses to let his partners keep any markers.

Once he had to take a partner in a roadhouse he was running near Babylon. He sold the fellow fifty per cent of the place for one season. It happened to be a very good season, so Hymie built a sliding metal roof over a garden one hundred feet square, installed a swimming pool, and presented all his employees with a large bonus out of the receipts.

"I thought I would make some improvements and build up good will for next year, when Milton would be out," he says.

Some persons may wonder why even a concessionaire would trust Hymie with his money. But concessionaires know that he will not skip before the club opens, for he is under a compulsion as strong as the drive of a spawning salmon to swim upstream. His clubs satisfy his craving for distinction.

A week before an opening Hymie gets out a mailing list of exhibitionists which he has accumulated through a decade of night-club operation, and sends out his announcements. Then he makes the entertainers write letters to their friends inviting them to buy ringside tables. He insists on the attendance of every salesman who has ever sold him anything for the club, even if it all was on credit. The costumer who has dressed the show is expected to take part of his pay in trade. Since this may be the only part of it he will ever collect, the costumer usually brings a large party. It is a nice arrangement for Hymie, because he pays off on the costume bill with Scotch at about six cents on the dollar. The band leader, if he has any considerable reputation in the trade, forces music publishers' pluggers to reserve tables. If the pluggers don't spend money, the leader slights their tunes.

A week after the opening, if it was profitable, Hymie gives his entertainers three days' pay. He tells them he is holding something back so they won't run out on him. Of course they never get it. If the opening has been bad, the entertainers and the concessionaire are likely to find the door locked the next night. In the event of a sour opening, Hymie takes the thousand or fifteen hundred dollars of concession money remaining to him out of the bank and lays it on a ten-to-one shot at some obscure race track. He shares the weakness for betting common to most night-club people, but he has it in an exaggerated form. He has never played a horse at less than eight-to-one in his life, because he is sure that every race is fixed. When a favorite wins he attributes it to a double-cross. Hymie almost always loses.

Occasionally the personality of one of Hymie's entertainers catches on, or the décor hits the fancy of the Broadway high-life crowd, and the club begins to make money legitimately. Under these circumstances Hymie sells it to a corporation called Hymie-club, Inc. As manager for the corporation he kicks out the hat-check concessionaire and sells the concession over again for a higher price. The entertainer who draws the crowd gets a manager and demands more money. Hymie pays blackmail in the form of weekly raises. He spends a great part of his receipts in competitors' clubs to show how prosperous he is. He stalls off all creditors on general principles.

"Sometimes you can hold them off for six months," he says. "Meanwhile everything that comes in is profit."

Finally the creditors close in, or the entertainer either

loses his brief vogue or goes on to a larger club. Hymie re-
turns to the horse-tipping business. He has written one more
chapter in his saga; he has been in the money again.

Hymie admits readily that it was vanity that drew him
into the night-club business in the first place, and that keeps
him at it.

"Take a fellow who is born in Brooklyn," he says, "and
he is a cloak-and-suiter or a shoe clerk, which he would feel
honored even to talk to a trumpet player in a famous or-
chestra. He goes into this business and in two years celeb-
rities like Rudy Vallée and Harry Thaw are calling him
Hymie. It makes him feel wonderful. But it don't mean
nothing."

Take, more specifically, Hymie Katz. He was born in
Brooklyn, in the Williamsburgh district. The record of his
early days is shadowy, but he says that once he was a fur
stretcher, and once he drove a taxi, and once he was married to a wealthy woman who died and cut him off with a
dollar in her will because she didn't want him to spend anything on other dolls. Hymie got his start in the night-club
world as a singing waiter in a pseudo-Bavarian joint where
people drank spiked near-beer at fifty cents a glass and sang
"Ja, das ist ein Schnitzelbank." He had not been there long
before he had invented a new technique for reaming the customers. When one of the parties he was serving asked for a
check he would delay bringing it, if possible, until he had
a similar request from another party of about the same size.
One check might be for sixteen dollars, say, the other for
twelve. Hymie would put the twelve-dollar check in the
hip pocket of his leather pants and collect the sixteen-dol-
lar check from both parties, one after the other. The customers seldom became aware of the mistake.

After he got used to late hours, Hymie decided to open a night club for himself. That was in the winter of 1924, and many buildings between Longacre Square and Sixth Avenue had a joint on every floor. There would be a shabby night club at street level, a speakeasy-restaurant on the second floor, and two or three ratty bars on the levels above. Hymie picked a second-floor loft that had a dance floor ten by ten and forty tables with pink lampshades on them, left by a former proprietor who had not paid his beer bill. Hymie put down two hundred dollars for an option on the place—he could not then afford his present scruples about using his own cash. He dropped in at the I. & Y., where he was beginning to be known, and sold twenty per cent of the club for a thousand dollars to a fellow we will call Johnny Attorney. Johnny came from Attorney Street originally, but he was quite a big beer-man by then, and had moved uptown.

Hymie and Johnny were able to sell the hat-check concession for another thousand because Johnny was in on a couple of speakeasies where the hat-check man did business. Then they took in the no-good brother of a famous night-club hostess who was the surest draw in town. They gave the brother twenty per cent, and all they asked was that he stay away from the place as much as possible. The hostess was working for a man named Denny Boylan, who had a large, elaborate club (for those days) about five doors up the block from their place. The Boylan club was on the street level, with a uniformed doorman and a marquee, and it had to close at two or three o'clock in the morning. Drawing her ermine wrap about her and jiggling her head-dress of egrets two feet long, the hostess would then suggest to the best spenders present that they accompany her to a little intimate spot down the street, where the party could continue. Down the street they would stagger, and up the stairs to the Daylight Club, as Hymie and Johnny called their stuffy loft. After the second week the hostess demanded a share for herself, so Hymie sold her half of his sixty per cent for five thousand dollars.

"The prices we got for liquor those days were brutal," Hymie recalls happily. "Twenty-five dollars for a bottle of champagne a guy made for us down on Mott Street. But the price didn't mean nothing. It was the bottles you could stab in on a customer's check that really counted. I mean the bottles you charged him for that he had never had at all. I remember a big patent-medicine man from Baltimore that used to come into the place that once paid me twenty-eight hundred dollars for one bottle of wine. He ordered the wine and then he fell asleep with his head on the table. I had the sense to have empty bottles in ice buckets put next to every table. When he woke up, I slipped him the check. 'What's this?' he says. 'Well,' I says, 'you ordered wine for everybody in the house. A hundred and twelve bottles at twenty-five a copy. The one on your table is on me.' He couldn't remember whether he had or not, but the money didn't mean nothing to him, so he paid."

After the Daylight Club was fairly launched, Hymie devoted late afternoons to the manufacturing department. Hymie doesn't mind work when it's fun.

"I made Black-and-White so good those millionaires wouldn't drink nothing else," he says. "There was a big towel man from North Carolina who would take cases of my Black-and-White home with him every time he come to town. Once a fellow in another joint gave him some of the McCoy straight from St. Pierre, and the towel man spit it out. 'You trying to poison me?' he says. 'This don't taste nothing like the genuine Black-and-White I buy from Hymie.' He would never go back to the joint."

Hymie thinks most of his customers in those days were temporarily insane. There was, for example, a wholesale whiskey exporter from Canada who, on his business trips to New York, had the quaint conceit of carrying only fifty-dollar bills. He would toss one of them on Hymie's bar and order drinks for everybody. If there were thirteen drinkers in the house, Hymie would charge him for about twenty-nine drinks at a dollar apiece. The Canadian never counted. He would leave his change for the bartender.

"When he come in," Hymie says, "I used to go behind the bar myself."

Hymie thinks that many of his former customers still have money, but have been afraid to throw it around in public since the depression. In a select spot like the Daylight Club, he says, "they knew they was among their own kind."

The end of the Daylight Club came when a squad of twenty prohibition agents raided the place and padlocked it.

"The reason you couldn't do nothing about them big raids," he says, "is that there was never twenty Feds who would trust each other. Each one would think one of the others in the squad was trying to put him in the bag, so you couldn't talk business. But when just one fellow or two or three come in, you knew they was on the shake. If you felt good-natured, you slipped them fifty. If you didn't, you kicked them down the stairs."

Hymie likes harness cops, but not detectives. He says the latter are like Feds, always on the shake.

"The cop on the block was a kind of doorman," Hymie

explains. "When you threw a drunk out, the cop picked him up and walked him down to the corner to sober up, so he wouldn't remember where he was thrown out of." Each place on the block paid the policeman on beat from two to five dollars a night, according to its volume of business. On a good block, Hymie estimates, it might have run to as much as a hundred dollars a night. He doesn't believe that the cop on beat was allowed to retain all this, but he says he never paid money to a police official higher up. His guess is that it was divided in the Department.

Hymie always enjoyed bouncing people in a nice way. When a big tough fellow heckled the hostess, Hymie would go to the cashier and get a roll of quarters. He would hold it in his right hand, with one end of the roll protruding, and he would lean over the fellow's table and slug him on the side of the jaw with it. Then a couple of waiters would carry the gentleman out and lay him on the sidewalk, where the cop would find him.

Mickey Finns, the pacifying pills slipped to obstreperous customers in many places, do not amuse Hymie. "Any fool can go into a drugstore for a dollar and buy a box of Mickeys," he says. Mickeys are purgative pills designed for horses, and act so drastically that one may kill a drunk with a weak heart. "But even with Mickeys, there is an art in the way to serve them," says Hymie. "Some fellows wait until the customer orders another drink, which may be too long, and others offer him a drink on the house, which maybe makes him suspicious. The best way is to tell the waiter, 'A little more ice in that glass, please.' The waiter has the ice on a spoon and the Mickey under the ice. He drops them in the drink together."

The Daylight Club ran fourteen months, during which,

Hymie says, the partners earned about a quarter of a million dollars. The race tracks got most of Hymie's share. He remembers days when he went out to the track and lost five thousand dollars in an afternoon, then came back and delivered a case of bathtub gin to make six dollars. "Money don't mean nothing to me," he says. "Maybe I'm crazy."

After the Daylight was padlocked, Hymie and his associates opened a far more pretentious place on Fiftieth Street, which he called the Club Chez Nous. He pronounced it the Club Chestnuts. The partners continued to make money. The place went out of existence because of the hostess's sense of humor. The adolescent son of a statesman then prominent came into the club drunk one night. She persuaded him to go out on the floor and do imitations of his father, who was flirting with a Presidential nomination. The father used his influence to have the place padlocked.

Hymie's third place, the Club Monastery, was a hard-lucker. It had been open only three weeks when a party of mobsmen dropped in and began shooting at Johnny Attorney and some friends. Two men were killed and Johnny Attorney disappeared. It is popularly supposed that his body was run through a rock-crusher and that he is now part of the roadbed of the Pulaski Skyway in New Jersey. The police, however, hadn't heard about this and thought that Hymie knew where Johnny was, so they gave him a terrific beating. Hymie was not the kind who would appeal to the American Civil Liberties Union. When the police let him go, some of the gangsters took him for a ride. Fortunately they forgot to gag him, and he talked so fast that they brought him back to his hotel and loaned him twenty dollars. It is one of his proudest memories. But the Monastery was "out on the street." Whenever there was a shooting in a speakeasy, the New York police closed it. That was the reason patrons about to shoot each other were always asked to leave.

The cares that might be expected to attend such a frenzied existence have left no mark on Hymie Katz. There are scars on his face from the beating the police gave him when they questioned him about Johnny Attorney, but no worry lines. He is not as handsome as he was twenty years ago, before he began to put on weight, but he has nice white teeth and pleasant features that wear a habitual unforced smile.

Hymie is unmarried at present. Wives, with Hymie, are symptoms of prosperity, like tailored shirts. His father is still living and owns a small jewelry shop on the Bowery near Canal Street. When Hymie visits him, the old man comes out to meet his son and locks the door from the outside. Then they talk on the sidewalk. Hymie is not offended by his parent's caution; he is flattered. Whenever he meets anybody new, he tells him about his father.

Hymie is living in a hotel on West Forty-ninth Street on a due bill. He pays the due-bill broker with due bills for entertainment at his next club, which he hasn't opened yet. When the club does open, the broker will sell the accumulated due bills for half their face value to couples who arrive via the bus lines and want to see New York night life.

Shortly before noon every day Hymie goes to his office, which he shares with a man who puts on stag shows, to see if any money has come in by mail. If there is any, Hymie spends the afternoon in a poolroom betting on races. If there is no money, he puts in a hard day at the telephone as Mr. Miller of Belmont Park. Generally he has dinner at an Italian Kitchen on Eighth Avenue, where he gets spaghetti, meat balls, and coffee for twenty-five cents. He smokes six cigars a day, five nickel ones and a fifty-center, buying them all at the I. & Y. He smokes the fifty-center after his twenty-five-cent dinner, so he will feel prosperous. Evenings he usually leans against a stack of cases in the cigar store and discusses his plans—never his real plans, of course, but vast enterprises like taking over the Paramount Theatre and turning it into a night club with a ski slide and a five-dollar minimum. With ribald arguments he maintains the feasibility of projects which he improvises on the spot. The other habitués of the I. & Y. listen with respect.

"You know who was in here?" Izzy, the proprietor, asks friends who come in after Hymie has departed. "Hymie Katz." Izzy shakes his head admiringly. "He's a real tummler, that Hymie. He knows to get a dollar."

THE MANLY ART

Battling Norfolk is at Stillman's every day. He sweeps the floors and occasionally gives a boxer a rubdown for a dollar. Prosperous boxers have trainers who rub them down every day in return for a weekly retainer or a small percentage of the boxers' purses, but the boys who get a fight only once in a while patronize old Bat. They get a rub only when they feel a definitely sore muscle, and they expect Bat to work over them a long time for his dollar. Bat used to be a pretty good heavyweight, the oldtimers say. He is a tall Negro with a small head and big hands, shoulders and feet. The boys are always playing jokes on him, like putting wet toilet paper in his pockets when he is not looking. Bat says, "There is nobody here that can discuss a question from an intelligent point of view." When he argues with one of the white boys, he warns him, "I going to whip you with words. I going to make the hair whirl on you goddam haid." Sometimes he holds out his right fist and says, jokingly, "If these five things gone hit you and you don't go down, they's some mighty funny things standing up in this world." There is an old Chilean light-weight named Stanislaus Loayza who trains a couple of fighters now, and he and old Bat have long arguments. Bat likes to point to his skull and say, "I got brains." Once Loayza asked him, "You got money, Bat?" Bat said, "No." Loayza said, "You got no money, you got no brains." But the surest way to win an argument from Bat is to yell "Sam Langford!" According to protocol you should say, "What did Sam Langford do to you?" but if you just yell "Sam Langford!" it will be enough. Bat will understand. He hears it a hundred times a day.

The boys say that Bat once fought the great Sam Langford. At the beginning of the second round Sam motioned to him to shake hands. "Why should I shake hands?" Bat asked him. "This ain't the last round." "Oh, yes it is," Sam said, and he knocked Bat stiff.

Langford himself, when I last saw him, was sitting on a bed in a furnished room in Harlem, drawing soft, disconnected tones out of an old guitar. "I'm busted and disgusted," he said, "and I'm playing the original blues." Still, he wasn't as badly off as he had been the first time I met him, in 1934. "I'm on the Harlem diet," he had said then. "When I'm hungry and I ain't got the price of a feed I drink a glass of water and pick my teeth." Now he has a job as watchman in the store room at the Municipal Lodging House, although he is virtually blind. His appointment was one of La Guardia's rare sentimental gestures.

Langford's dark umber hands look like snow shovels. The thumbs are knocked back, but the fingers are straight. "I never hit a man's elbows nor his head," he says. "I hit 'em in the body and then I hit 'em on the point of the chin, and I sent 'em home early if they wasn't good boys. Oh, I belted 'em oat." He is immensely fat, weighing two hundred and forty-two pounds. He is five feet six and a half inches tall. Sam likes to chew tobacco. When he wants to spit he lifts a big meat can off the floor and holds it just under his mouth. The can is marked Swift's Chitterlings.

"Before they operated on my eyes," he says, "I couldn't

see nothing in the sunlight, but I could see a little when the lights was dim. Now things is just viceryersered."

His style, when he talks of fights, is epigrammatic.

"First I made them lead," he says. "Then I made them miss; then I belted them oat."

He talks about his fight with Iron Hague at the National Sporting Club in London.

"I put my haid oat," he said, "and when he hit at it, I took it away." He spat with relish. "Then I put my haid oat again. And when he hit at me, I took it away." Sam spat again; he lay back on the bed and he roared with laughter. "Then I put my haid oat again," he said when he recovered. "But when he hit at it, I stayed right there. Naturally he hit right past me. I belted him oat."

Twice he stopped the Dixie Kid with body punches. After the second fight Dixie asked: "Why you always go for my body, Sam? Why you don't go for my haid?"

Sam said: "You haid got eyes."

Once he talked to me about training, which he never liked.

"You can sweat oat beer," he said, "and you can sweat oat whiskey. But you can't sweat oat women."

The Man in the Corner

Wherever Morris Bimstein goes at night he is accompanied by a bundle. It is a small affair, flat on one side and slightly raised on the other, like a Chinese laundry package containing one shirt and two pairs of socks, and is invariably held together with a rubber band. This bundle contains a roll of adhesive tape, a flat pad of gauze, a tube of petroleum jelly, a tube of a liquid cement known as carpenter's wax, and a row of phials labelled "Adrenalin chloride," "Tincture of iron," "Ammonia," and a styptic fluid called "Monsel's."

Mr. Bimstein does not have an M.D. degree. His formal education ended in 1910, when he graduated from Public School No. 62, at Hester and Essex Streets, on the lower East Side. He is the best-known prizefight second in New York. He works every day and almost every night in the week except Sunday. On Sunday, if he is not too tired, he goes to the movies at the Park Plaza Theatre on University Avenue, in the Bronx, with his wife, Mrs. Sophie Bimstein. Mrs. Bimstein does not see much of Mr. Bimstein except on Sunday.

The weekly orbit in which Mr. Bimstein moves begins at the St. Nicholas Palace on West Sixty-sixth Street on Monday night. On Tuesday he is to be found either at the New York Coliseum in the east Bronx or the Broadway Arena in Williamsburgh. Wednesday is the night for fighting at the Hippodrome, and at the Star Casino, a rough, tough club in south Harlem, the fight night is Thursday. Friday is Madison Square Garden's night. Saturday evenings have long been consecrated to the Ridgewood Grove Sporting Club in north Brooklyn. Sometimes Mr. Bimstein deviates from this schedule in order to accompany important clients out of town—to Baltimore, Boston, or Chicago.

Ever since his first day at P. S. 62, Mr. Bimstein has been called Whitey, because of his tow-colored eyebrows and hair. Now the hair grows only on the sides of his head, and the top gleams a warm rose pink. He is forty years old and five feet four inches tall. The lower half of his vest has begun to stand out like a small, comfortable pillow. When he walks, he hurries with short, quick steps, but does not lean forward. From the hips to the top of the head he holds himself very straight, and even when he has not had time to shave or put on a clean collar, you know at first sight that he is an authoritative person. When there is a red stubble on his baby-pink cheeks, it is a sign that he has not been to bed on the preceding night but has been sitting up with some of the boys. After such a night, his mouth hangs open and his eyes go glassy.

Even when his eyes are glassiest, the question "How did you make out last night, Whitey?" will start him on a spirited monologue. For example, he may say, "I win two underneath but I lose on top. I would win that, too, only that kid of Joe's wouldn't throw left hooks like I told him. He was crazy to throw rights. I give him plenty of abuse between rounds, but it was no good. Joe ought to hit him with a bottle."

"On top" with Mr. Bimstein means the feature bout—top billing on the posters. "Underneath" means one of the supporting contests. Early in acquaintance with Whitey one gathers that no fighter ever went wrong by taking his advice. His conversation abounds with instances of the horrible fate of those who wouldn't listen.

Neither the fighters nor the managers ever confuse these analyses of Mr. Bimstein's with the second guesses of ordinary spectators and sportswriters. Managers pay him to do the thinking for their boys, and his relation to a fighter, particularly a young one, is approximately that of a jockey to a horse. Few fighters ever have as many as a hundred engagements in a lifetime. Whitey, since he quit boxing *in propria persona,* in 1917, has thought his way through about fifteen thousand battles as a second. Often he seconds four bouts in an evening. He now averages about twenty fights a week. Since history constantly repeats itself in the ring, he knows the answers to most sets of circumstances before even a boxer of genius could fathom them for himself.

But it is with the stuff he brings in the bundle that Whitey does his best work. In the sixty seconds of grace between rounds he performs miracles of facial surgery for his clientele, turning gaping cuts over the eyes or cheekbones into mild abrasions which will pass unnoticed even by the tenderest-hearted referee. (Referees, with a gratuitous solicitude for a fighter's health, have been known to stop a bout, thus hurting the fighter's and Whitey's record.) After each round, Whitey must begin his repairs over again, but he has never been known to stop and lament because his last artistic masterpiece has been effaced by a well-thrown left hook. He is too busy with reconstruction to be temperamental.

To achieve his effects, Whitey uses every bottle in the bundle. The petroleum jelly and the carpenter's wax are preventatives. He examines his client's face before the bout for old lesions that may come open and then covers them with the wax, which hardens and forms a kind of synthetic callus. He then smears the jelly over the entire physiognomy, to give it a slippery surface.

Adrenalin, a gift to the prizefight industry from the gland doctors, will stop bleeding from superficial cuts. Packed into the boxer's nose before a bout, it patches up leaky veins, professionally known as "bleeders," and administered by mouth, it produces a flurry of energy confusing to the man in the opposite corner. The stuff costs $1.25 a bottle and loses its punch soon after it is opened, but Whitey is not stingy and sometimes uses it even on a preliminary boy. Whitey uses tincture of iron as an astringent in middling-deep cuts. But the sovereign elixir of his medicine chest, as of every other second's, is Monsel's. This is a styptic invented by a nineteenth-century English chemist with no sporting connections, a decoction of iron subsulphate. Applied to a cut, it will almost instantly form a heavy black crust that will stand a surprising amount of pounding. This is because the iron in the solution unites with the proteids of the blood to form an iron albuminoid, a reaction with which Whitey is familiar. A stray drop of the solution in an eye will end a fight as effectively as a knockout punch, because it will in all probability make the fighter permanently blind. Whitey has never blinded a fighter. In the words of a friend and patron, "Whitey has the habit of them cuts."

When Whitey is in his corner, he generally carries between his lips a few toothpicks tipped with cotton batting, which he uses to apply his astringents. These do not interrupt the running commentary and exhortation which he keeps up as he works over his principal. A second must at times offer medical as well as surgical service, because a good body beating often has as unsettling an effect as a Channel crossing. The distressed boxer then "bulches," Whitey says. To relieve this, Mr. Bimstein offers a solution of spirits of ammonia, and warm water. Bulky swellings sometimes arise to obscure a boxer's vision, and it is on these that the master second shows of what stuff he is made. He cuts into them with a lancet, and sucks out sufficient blood to deflate the swelling. This is a *coup de maitre*, reserved for emergencies, and Whitey will not perform it in anything less than a main bout. Through all these gruesome operations—and sometimes all of them need to be performed almost simultaneously—Whitey remains as calm as a Holstein. He begins his work at the end of every round as if he had time for a psychoanalysis, and continues at the same cold-blooded gait until the next bell. Then he climbs down just as the fighters achieve contact.

Whitey combines with his profession of second that of trainer, and this accounts for his long working hours. Returning after midnight to his home at 1760 Montgomery Avenue, in the Bronx, he arises at six and travels down to the borders of Central Park. Rooming houses in side streets off Central Park West are favored by earnest prizefighters, who take their runs around the reservoir. Headliners live at the Mayflower or the St. Moritz, or rent apartments in the neighborhood. Whitey lets the rooming-house fighters take care of themselves until afternoon, but the stars and their managers expect a certain amount of personal service before that.

He has among his present principals Lou Ambers, who was recently robbed of the world's lightweight championship, according to Whitey, and Sixto Escobar, the bantam-weight titleholder. They are both active young men, and the sun never rises upon the reservoir without seeing one of the pair running around its periphery on legs that half an hour later must be rubbed back into fluidity by Mr. Bimstein. After the rubdown, Whitey lingers for breakfast with whichever fighter is in training, eating his own portion and about half of what is served to the fighter. "Some of them lunatics put on a pound every time they take a deep breath," Whitey says. It is his responsibility to keep them down to weight, even though they beg for nourishment.

At about ten o'clock, he appears in Stillman's on Eighth Avenue between Fifty-fourth and Fifty-fifth Streets, and "lays out the stuff"—gloves, headguards, protectors, and shoes for about twenty fighters, who will work under Whitey's supervision. He is assisted in this by a satellite, a Mr. Emmet. Mr. Emmet, a Bostonian, is so called because, as he explains, "I always hanged in Emmet Street." He has forgotten his former name, which was polysyllabic. Dressing Room No. 2 at Stillman's is Whitey's office, hospital, and citadel. In it are a rubbing table, a medicine cabinet, a stool, and three rows of hooks, from which to hang boxing gloves.

The Bimstein seminar of bruising begins shortly before noon and continues until four o'clock. When Whitey enrolls a new fighter, he has him punch a heavy bag and then spar a round with one of the old clients. Whitey takes stock of the new man's natural aptitudes, if any— whether he seems to be a puncher or a boxer, a weaver or a dancer, whether he punches straight or throws hooks— and then devises a scheme of training. Even the headliners have flaws, like Joe Louis's habit of leaving the left side of his jaw unguarded after delivering a left jab, and Whitey must work as hard with his good boys as with his beginners. As an example of the minutiae that anguish Whitey, take the case of Vincent Pimpinella, a tough young welterweight from Brooklyn. Vincent, who has iron ribs, snuggles his left glove into his opponent's right armpit in clinches, allowing the other fellow to cuff him in the ribs. This cuffing does Vincent no harm, but sometimes catches the eye of an impressionable judge, who gives the opponent some points.

"Letting your left lay in there is a dirty habit," Mr. Bimstein keeps telling his pupil. "Turn his arm out, for God's sake, or else keep punching."

Between periods of counsel to his disciples, Whitey eats

THE MANLY ART 101

a few frankfurters and slabs of pie purchased at Stillman's lunch counter. When the last boxer has gone, he lays an old piece of wrapping paper on the rubbing table, goes to the medicine cabinet for his gauze and phials, and makes up the evening bundle.

With the bundle under his arm, he may stroll over to the Hotel Mayflower and go up to the suite where Jim Braddock and his manager, Joe Gould, sit for at least six hours a day playing two-handed pinochle. The place is called Gould's "office." The walls of the room are covered with photographs of Gould, inscribed "To my dear pal, Jim Braddock," and of the former heavyweight champion, autographed "To my dear pal, Joe Gould." Most of the pictures autographed by Gould show Gould posed between large game fish in Florida or signing contracts with promoters. The Braddock pictures mostly show Jim knocking somebody out, although there are a few of him shaking hands with eminent statesmen. There is a sentimental tie between Mr. Bimstein and the pinochle players. Whitey was in the big fellow's corner when he beat Baer, and again when Braddock lost to Louis.

But there is also a business tie between Whitey and the pinochle players. Braddock and Gould have a habit of discovering young heavyweights, whom they stake to meals and boxing lessons. Whitey takes on these young men as clients, accompanies them to fight clubs, and often has to pick them off the floor.

From the Mayflower, Whitey goes to Al Weill's office in the Strand Theatre Building. Mr. Weill manages Ambers and several other fighters, and the office is usually full of fight people. Here Whitey picks up an idea of business conditions, or, as Mr. Weill says, "what it's all about it."

If Whitey wants an item of intelligence not available there, he goes over to Forty-ninth Street and stands in front of the Forrest Hotel until a fight manager comes along who knows what Whitey wants to find out. He hardly ever has to wait more than fifteen minutes. At six, Whitey usually ducks into a Chink joint for dinner, and at seven he is on his way to a fight club.

Whitey's rise to his present eminence was impossible to foresee. As a fighter he was never exceptional, although he liked the work. Mediocrity was no bar to future success as a trainer. Ex-champions make poor guides for young boxers. They always insist that their pupils learn their own personal techniques. The result is a boxer with an inferiority complex, even though he is able to ape a little of his instructor's style. But it seemed unlikely that Whitey could ever train other boxers, because he had never been in training himself.

Bimstein, the boxer, had a passion for frankfurters and charlotte russes which he would indulge even a few minutes before a fight, and all his roadwork was done at a walk, selling boxing tickets to neighbors. Shortly after Whitey's graduation from public school, his father, a small cloak-and-suit manufacturer, moved the family uptown to Brook Avenue and 138th Street, in the Bronx. The idea was to remove Morris, as Whitey's parents insisted on calling him, from the raffish associations of the East Side. Morris took to hanging out in the basement of St. Jerome's Catholic Church on Alexander Avenue, where Father Ryan, the pastor, gave boxing lessons. Next thing his parents knew, he was fighting a four-rounder, underneath, at the Fairmont Athletic Club. His reward for the match was to be half the price of each dollar ticket he sold. He got three dollars. That time Whitey won, but afterward he mostly lost. He was a good puncher, for a bantamweight, but he was never in condition. As a ticket seller, though, he was superb. He fought about seventy times in the three years before the United States went to war, and several times sold over a hundred dollars' worth of tickets. It kept his boxing pretty well localized, since he could appear only in neighborhoods where he knew the potential ticket buyers. He was in the Navy in 1918, and acted as a boxing instructor, but the methods of mass instruction irritated him. "The trouble with the government was they wanted the whole Navy to be standup boxers," Whitey says when he discusses the world conflict.

He came back to the Bronx after his service and began hanging around the Fairmont again. Whitey could see that he would never get anywhere as a boxer unless he went on a diet. So he retired and began acting as a second for friends. In 1921, the boys in St. Jerome's basement began to notice an aura around the head of a spidery kid named Frankie Doherty. Calling himself Frankie Jerome, after the church, Doherty was soon knocking out tough boys in the small clubs three nights a week. Lou Brix, a local boy, was Jerome's manager, and Whitey trained Jerome and worked in his corner. Jerome soon graduated from the ticket-selling stage. Clubs as far away as Coney Island and Newark offered him guarantees to travel and fight their own local favorites on top. Jerome made a hit every time he showed, and Whitey, with his conspicuous coloration, was remembered as his second.

"Being associated with a man like that, you get known," Whitey says gratefully. "He was a regular hoodlum." This is Whitey's highest term of approbation, reserved for Lou Ambers among his present associates.

Jerome, aside from a pardonable foible for beer and feminine society, was a model fighting man. He never asked whom he was fighting or how much money he was getting. In the ring he was a pattern of combativeness. He would always take one in order to give two, and this made his corner an excellent clinic for Whitey, who laid the foundation of his present renown as a facial-repair man.

In 1924, Jerome was killed by Bud Taylor, the Terre Haute Terror, in the ring at the old Madison Square Garden.

"He died right in my arms, slipping punches," Whitey often says, wobbling his head from side to side to show how Frankie Jerome tried to "slip" death.

Sometimes, in the course of his professional practice, circumstances oblige Whitey to visit a place he calls "out-of-town." Out-of-town consists of states like Pennsylvania, New Jersey, Illinois, Maryland, and a couple known on West Forty-ninth Street as the State of Cleveland and the State of D. C. Each of these subdivisions of out-of-town insists on selling a second a second's licence. The licences cost $5 to $10—the New York one costs $5—and Whitey carries about $100 worth of them in a wallet in his inside coat pocket.

There is another region Whitey sometimes visits, which he calls "the country." "I like the country," Whitey says, speaking of this region. "It's a great spot."

Although a homogeneous area, Whitey's "country" falls into three divisions. These are Doc Bier's training camp at Pompton Lakes, New Jersey; Madam Bey's camp at Summit, New Jersey; and Gus Wilson's place at Orangeburg,

New York. When you arrive, they are all the same—a nice spot.

The purpose of going to the country is to sequestrate a fighter. He must be shielded from temptation, in its feminine or edible forms, and nagged into what his superiors consider a suitable frame of mind for homicide. "The country is away from temptations," Whitey explains, "and when you get a fighter out there, you can really work on him." Going to the country is less irksome to Whitey than going out-of-town. The two places possess certain features in common, such as that you cannot reach them on the subway, but whereas the country is merely dull, out-of-town is downright hostile.

Out-of-town seconds sometimes sneak flattened wads of wet cotton under their men's hand bandages, and scatter powdered plaster of Paris over them like talcum. When the glove is on, the fighter closes his fist, squeezing the water from the cotton through the bandage gauze. The wet plaster hardens, equipping the boxer with a stone fist. The rounds, Whitey religiously believes, are always longer when a New York boxer is getting murdered, and ridiculously short when the local talent is being tagged. You have to watch even the drinking water to see it isn't doped, and even then something terrible may happen, like the time he had a boy knocked down just before the bell in Indianapolis, and when he dragged him to the corner and put him on the stool, it busted. "And you only go there nine times out of ten to do the promoter a favor at that," he says broodingly. "For small money!"

It even seems sometimes that boxers' jaws develop weak spots out-of-town, and a punch that would pass off as a mild pleasantry in the bracing climate of Ridgewood or Sixty-sixth Street practically knocks an expeditionary's brains out. It is then that a second must do his hardest work. When a fighter is groggy between rounds, some seconds burn matches on his back, to restore the stream of consciousness, or jab him with needles. Whitey does not believe in such brutality. He throws cold water inside the fighter's pants and twists his ears back. Then he gives him plenty of smelling salts.

The farthest out-of-town Whitey ever went with a fighter was Spain. He went to that country to train and second Paolino against Carnera at Barcelona in 1930. On that trip he became addicted to crepes Suzette, which he now esteems even above charlotte russe or chow mein. He was presented to Alfonso XIII at the automobile races at Bilbao, which pleased him. His man did not win the fight, however. "There was one Spanish judge and one Italian judge," Whitey says. "The Spaniard vote for Paolino and the Italian vote for Carnera, but the referee give it to the big bum."

Women are the greatest evil to which fighters are subject, but there is nothing much a trainer can do about them except confiscate the fighter's money and keep his town clothes under lock and key.

Gluttony is the second most pernicious gladiatorial vice, according to Mr. Bimstein. When a fighter has to be reduced to a certain weight, he sometimes objects to being starved and deprived of water for long periods. In camp, Whitey always eats at the same table with a fighter who is overweight, getting the same minuscular portions of meat and greens, without butter, sugar, milk, or drinking water. A cup of tea with lemon is the only liquid permitted. After the meal, when the fighter has been bedded down for a nap, Whitey sneaks off and wolfs a couple of pies, washing them down with a quart of coffee. He likes a couple of apple pies particularly.

In emotional crises, when it is thought advisable to gratify an overweight fighter with a drink of water, the fighter is allowed to take it through a straw. If he seems to be taking too much, Whitey squeezes the straw between a thumb and forefinger. Whitey sleeps in the same room with his fighter to see that he does not sneak out for any pleasurable purpose. Even Whitey is fooled sometimes, though, as he was when he trained an English middleweight named Ted Moore for a fifteen-round bout with Harry Greb for the middleweight championship, weight to be 158 pounds on the day of the match. Two days before the fight Moore weighed 159. He retired for the night and got up weighing 167. His handlers, after some rudimentary detective work, found a dozen empty beer bottles under his cot. They sweated and starved the weight off Moore, and he made a very creditable showing, going the full distance against a great champion. "If he hadn't bribed some maid to smuggle in that beer, Ted Moore might have won the championship," Whitey mourns. "You gotta watch them lunatics every minute."

The reduction of Ted Moore was nothing compared to the job one of Whitey's colleagues, Ray Arcel, did on Charley Phil Rosenberg, an expansive little man whom Arcel reduced from 155 to 116 in two months by taking him down to Hot Springs and boiling him. Rosenberg would sometimes plead to gargle his throat. Arcel would watch the fighter's Adam's apple while he gargled, prepared to start throttling him if a drop leaked down. In the end, he had him at 116 pounds at weighing time, two o'clock on the afternoon of the fight. "We were fighting Eddie Cannonball Martin for the bantamweight title," Arcel will say. (Managers, trainers, and seconds all say "we" when speaking of a fight, if they wish to be polite to the fighter. Otherwise they say "I.") Between two and time to enter the ring, Arcel fed his man beef tea, steak, and chocolate bars, until he went through the rope practically a lightweight, and defeated the less elastic Mr. Martin. Soon after Arcel performed this monumental task, he and Whitey became partners in the training and seconding business. Arcel, a gaunt, big-boned man with the face of a young Talmudic scholar, had learned his art in south Harlem, emerging from the small clubs as second for Abe Attell Goldstein, just as Whitey had followed Frankie Jerome out of the Bronx. During the years of Tex Rickard, Ray and Whitey became as familiar to the regular Friday-night fight crowd at the Garden as Jimmy Walker or Joe Humphreys. Either Whitey or Ray, and sometimes both of them, appeared with every pair of boxers that entered the ring, it seemed. Often, so large was their clientele, two Arcel-Bimstein fighters clashed, and then the partners flipped a coin to see who would work behind whom.

For a time they split up an average of $1,000 every week. Ten per cent of the purse is the conventional fee for the trainer, and even mediocre fighters in those times drew down "a fortune of money." Plain "money" is never mentioned in Whitey's circle. In time of adversity, one received "short money," "small money," or "tough money." It is getting so that now one occasionally receives "fair money." Things are on the upbeat. But in the Rickard days it was always a "fortune of money." The partnership between Whitey and Arcel broke up in 1934. There was so little work for trainers by then that managers could afford to be difficult. They objected to having their boxers and their boxers' opponents trained by the same firm. Whitey and Arcel are just colleagues, now.

Most prewar managers knew all about training and seconding fighters, and directed their own meal tickets, paying a trainer only for such manual duties as rubbing and carrying the water bucket. But in the lush days of the cauliflower boom, the game was invaded by cloak-and-suiters, bootleggers, Wall Street men, and common gamblers, seeking to invest their surplus profits in prizefighters. These Johnny-come-latelies had to turn over their boxers to professional trainers for preparation. They still furnish a good part of Whitey's business. Almost every young fighter has a patron in the Garment Center or the saloon trade, who puts up the money for his expenses and tuition.

Whitey's evenings spent as a second are by no means as lucrative as his daytime training jobs. Seconds work on a contingent-fee basis. Any night of the week one may see Whitey and one Doc Robb, Braddock's personal trainer, combining their abilities to win a four-round fight for a green kid who will get twenty dollars for his work. Such fighters, naturally, pay a small fee. One year's twenty-dollar fighters may be the headliners of the next, however, and managers sometimes remember early favors. Headliners pay good fees.

The Bimsteins live in an unostentatious but comfortable four-room apartment. They have not regained their affluence of the boom years, but they have about everything they want and Whitey usually carries a fair-sized roll of bills in his right pants pocket. They have a daughter named Adele, eleven years old, and a son, seven, who is named Jerome in honor of Frankie Jerome, who was named, you will remember, after a church. When Whitey suggested the name, Mrs. Bimstein thought it was a nice gesture all around.

What did he do in '76?

I once heard a fight handler say: "Ted Lewis was the greatest natural fighter I ever seen without being insane." Obviously, he believed complete insanity would be an asset to a fighting man. It is true that a fighter who is a cutey, a smart one, will find a manager if he shows unmistakable talent, but the manager will never like him. I remember Ray Arcel telling me about a fighter who was too smart for his own good. "How does he show this smartness?" I asked Ray. He said: "He wants to know who he's fighting and how much is he going to get." Also a smart fighter's courage is always suspect, since intelligence and a strong instinct of self-preservation are qualities usually found in conjunction. Once I was standing with a colored welterweight named Buster Hall, watching a cutey spar with an ordinarily dull fighter. "Deep down in he heart," Buster said, "he know he ain't got no heart." There was, however, once a period of boxing when intelligence was not contemned. Boxers cultivated their vocabularies as well as their foot-work. Both departments are rather neglected now. The second best conversationalist in the United States, until he died, was Jack McAuliffe, a prizefighter who went into politics at the age of sixty-nine. That was in 1934, when he entered the Democratic primary election for Assemblyman from the Sixth District of Queens County. His headquarters were in Forest Hills.

"Politics is an education," Mr. McAuliffe told me that time.

"It is impossible how the human brain can conceive so many different channels of putting the bite on you until you run for office. When I was lightweight champion of the world—I am the only lightweight champion who ever retired undefeated—I had the pleasure of knowing all the gamblers and good thieves of my day—the salt of the earth. But none of them could think of so many ways to get money out of you as you encounter in the realm of statesmanship.

"A fellow called me up the other day and read me the following:—'In the eyes of all who come in contact with him either politically or in a business way, Jack is regarded as a capable and vigorous worker of manifest intelligence, and possessing an outlook which is both progressive and broad. In the political arena he may be trusted to stick by his principles with the same tenacity and courage which characterized his battles in the prize ring against any opponent, no matter how formidable. His selection as the Democratic candidate and his ultimate victory at the polls are therefore indicated, for Queens County voters can do no better than to rally to his support.'

" 'That seems a very moderate statement of the case, leaning backward in the interests of accuracy,' I said, 'and I thank you for your good wishes.'

" 'Just a minute,' he says, 'how many copies of our magazine will you take?' So I went for fifty dollars' worth.

"Then to-day, without any warning, they call me into the Register's office in the city to draw for positions on the primary ballot. The only other fellow that's contesting against me in the Sixth District is the one that has the job now, Frederick L. Zimmerman. They mix those slips in a wheel the like of which I never saw except in the New Orleans lottery years ago when I was training to fight Billy Myer.

"Out pops Zimmerman's slip the first. He gets the top space on the machine for the primaries.

" 'I'm in the money anyways,' I says. 'Second place, that's me. And if I started at three-and-even I lost nothing, anyway. It's a small advantage, the place on the machine. My mother in Cork said often "Once down is no battle." It will be more credit to me for licking him.' "

Mr. McAuliffe's headquarters were liberally decorated with photographs of Mr. McAuliffe completely outclassing the lightweight cream of the Sullivan era, and also with a portrait medallion of Mr. McAuliffe and his contemporaries, John L. Sullivan and the original Jack Dempsey, the Nonpareil. This medallion was entitled:—"The Three American Jacks, their country's pride."

The Assembly candidate wore a green feather in his rakish hat, and widely separated bold blue eyes looked out of his broad, mottled countenance. He wore a blue suit with black and white sport shoes.

"I went into this contest," he said, "because the taxes are too high, the wages of the little fellow are being cut, and nobody has ever went right down to the basis. I will not make any speeches until the Saturday before the primaries, and I am somewhat in doubt as to what I will say then, but it will be good and to the point.

"I remember when I was a boy in Bangor, Me., in Irishtown—my father, God rest his soul, blew the roof off the house entirely with too much hops in the ale he was brewing, but that's irrelevant—that there was a fellow always campaigning there, and he would always begin his speech, 'What did he do in '76, my friends?' and then the band would let out a blast and the next thing you would hear would be, 'And what did he do in '76?' and another blast. And so on, so nobody ever knew what the fellow done in '76, or who he was talking about anyway.

"But I will not make a speech like that. The small home-owner is taxed too much. The sanctity of the home must be protected against easy divorce laws. There are men in our Legislature today who remind me of Paddy the Pig, who would steal your eye for a breastpin."

Mr. McAuliffe was not chosen in the primary election. Consequently he was not elected to the Assembly. It was a grave loss to American statesmanship. In Dan Webster's day, when the voters appreciated a good talker, Jack would have been elected surely.

Old Silvertongue

The finest talker of the English language in the City of New York today (McAuliffe was only the second and besides, he's dead), is a man by the name of Philadelphia Jack O'Brien. O'Brien first attained celebrity as a pugilist, and at sixty is the masculine counterpart of those well-preserved showpieces Fanny Ward and Edna Wallace Hopper. He considers his youthful appearance an advertisement for his business, which is, as his letterheads proclaim, "Flesh-reducing, Body-building, and Boxing Taught Without Punishment." But his attainments as a boxer and molder of the human form pale compared to his mastery of high-toned language.

"I have always loved to hear the verbiage that flows from an Englishman, whether he be an Oxfordian or otherwise," Jack once told a friend. "It is a beautiful thing." It was while sojourning in the British Isles from 1900 to 1902 that he built his prose style. During the same period of artistic formation, O'Brien knocked out sixteen British prizefighters.

Jack never was beautiful, but he was slim and extremely rugged, and still is. His waist is narrow, his shoulders wide, his complexion like rare roast beef. He is usually clad in a wine-red silk shirt, a blue pin-stripe suit, and patent-leather shoes with gray spats.

Although, by calling himself Philadelphia Jack O'Brien, he has done more to publicize his native city than any-body else since Benjamin Franklin, he claims no credit for it. "The name, as it were, was the result of a pair of fortu-itous coincidences," Jack says. He was christened Joseph Francis Anthony Hagan, the son of a County Londonderry man who had a small contracting business in Philadelphia. Patrick Hagan, the father, owned ten dirt carts, and he wanted his son to grow into the business with him. Joe, however, wanted to be a prizefighter. Like every other long-legged stripling during the early nineties, he identified himself with the scientific, slender, gentlemanly James J. Corbett, who had just won the heavyweight championship from the wind-broken old slugger John L. Sullivan. Joe used to box with his shadow whenever he got the chance, and instead of walking he habitually ran, to develop his legs and wind. When he made an acquaintance of his own age, it was his custom to ask him over to his house "for dinner and a fight."

He used to attend amateur tournaments with a neigh-bor's boy who, by the first of the "fortuitous coincidences," was named O'Brien. Since Joe's father did not approve of his boxing, he would box under O'Brien's name, and every morning, after the boys had attended a tournament, old Patrick Hagan would read, in the Philadelphia *North American*, that "Jack O'Brien" had won a medal in the lightweight class. This worked until young Hagan came home with a black eye. "Sure," Patrick said, "you must have had your face where O'Brien's was supposed to be." By that time the boy was ready to turn professional, and the name Jack O'Brien had become an asset. He soon was known as Philadelphia Jack O'Brien, because, by a further coincidence, another Jack O'Brien was already established in New York.

Jack was a lightweight when he began to box, but he was five feet ten inches tall, so as he grew older he put on weight. During the process he fought against light-, welter-, middle-, and heavyweights. The difference between a professional and an amateur when Jack started was chiefly one of dignity. A fighter handled as little cash as a sharecropper. A trusting landlady was the first essential of a ring career. Fighters trained each other, serving as reciprocal sparring partners and then rubbing each other down. By the time a fighter earned a purse, he owed it to his landlady for board. Jack recalls a hard fifteen-round draw he fought in Baltimore before a house that totalled $52.

One of the bleakest days Philadelphia Jack remembers was December 19th, 1898. On that afternoon he fought a colored heavyweight named Hugh McWinters at the Greenpoint Athletic Club in Brooklyn. McWinters outweighed him twenty pounds, but Jack got the decision after twenty bitter rounds. When he had paid off his landlord, who had a ringside seat, he had $8 left for himself. He was living at Coney Island, and after the bout the landlord drove him home in a buckboard. On the way, O'Brien thought it was getting dark early, even for that season of the year. When they reached Coney Island, he could see nothing. Both his eyes were swollen shut.

Jack's method, like Corbett's, was to step away from an opponent's blows or parry them with his hands—"pick them off" is the professional term. Attacking, he would step in with swift, cutting left jabs to the face. When the other man, infuriated by this skirmishing, rushed wildly after him, O'Brien would have a chance to counter with his right. It was a spectacular, exasperating style, making great demands on the eyes and legs.

By 1900 Jack weighed 155 pounds and was pretty nearly a topnotcher. There were so many good men fighting in the United States at approximately this weight that their talents were at a discount. O'Brien conceived the idea of going to England, where, he heard, the competition was softer. When he went up the gangplank his prose style was as yet unformed. His clothes, while loud, were in the American manner. Nobody came to see him off except two or three of his six sisters. When he came back, in May, 1902, the Mayor of Philadelphia and ten thousand proud fellow-citizens were at the Broad Street Station to await the train that brought him from New York. "They acclaimed me," Jack likes to say. He had built himself up into the greatest drawing card in American boxing. Yet during the interlude in England he had not had one fight as hard as his $8 match in Brooklyn. The British boxers were so bad, Jack says today, that sometimes he felt guilty about meeting them at all. He knocked out Dido Plum, the British middleweight champion, in six rounds, and George Crisp, the heavyweight titleholder, in eleven. These feats were well advertised at home, because O'Brien sent accounts of them to the Associated Press, which at that time had little foreign-sports coverage of its own. "I was always a fellow who knew how to use the cables," Philadelphia Jack says now.

In England Jack acquired a top hat and a frock coat, a five-carat diamond ring and a four-carat scarf pin, all of which became elements of his personality. His first evening in London he attended a bout at the National Sporting Club. He was introduced from the ring as "Philadelphiaw Jack O'Brien from Americaw," a version of his own name which he admired so greatly that he still uses it. When depressed, he sometimes says it in a loud voice to cheer himself up.

He brought back from London eighteen trunks of clothes, including a gross of cherry-red and robin's-egg-blue silk undergarments—seventy-two sets at five guineas a set. Moreover, he could tell truthfully of a sparring match with Lord Dalmeny, son of a former British Prime Minister, and now the sixth Earl of Roseberry.

Once back in Philadelphia, Jack was in a position to dictate to the promoters. He insisted on seventy-five per cent of the gate receipts, and out of this amount would pay his opponent a couple of hundred dollars, leaving twenty-five per cent to the promoter, out of which he had to pay for the rent and the preliminaries. O'Brien favored six-round no-decision bouts, which were not tiring, and he boxed almost every week. He frequently allowed the other fellow to make a good showing, in order to encourage attendance at the inevitable return bout. By way of assuring a good performance he sometimes rehearsed his opponents in the stable in back of a home he had bought. The frequent short fights were so profitable that by 1904 Jack was said to be worth $80,000. It was the greatest fortune accumulated by a professional boxer up to that time. He had done his own managing and his own scheming, and had kept all his earnings.

Philadelphia Jack now had everything but a championship, and he saw a chance to get that when Jim Jeffries, the Boilermaker, retired as undefeated heavyweight champion of the world. Among the claimants to the abandoned title was Bob Fitzsimmons, who had lost it to Jeffries in 1899. Nobody but Jeffries had ever beaten him, the former champion argues, and since Jim had retired the title reverted to him. Fitzsimmons had won the title when he was thirty-six and lost it at thirty-eight. By 1905, when O'Brien formally challenged him, he was forty-four. This age, in a prizefighter, is the approximate equivalent of one hundred and sixty-four for a chorus girl. The old man could still hit, but Jack believed that with his speed afoot he could stay out of Bob's reach. It looked like a safer gamble than a match with a good middleweight. The men met at San Francisco in December, 1905, and after thirteen rounds Fitzsimmons collapsed. He had hit Jack only once, a glancing right uppercut to the chin, but that tore the flesh from the bone. O'Brien has a long, clean scar, as from a knife cut, to show for it.

"He was a game old man," Jack says. "He wanted me to fight winner take all, but I declined. I knew that he would need some money, so I told them to make it 75-25. My share was about $7,628.75. My memory is getting so bad lately I cannot invariably recall the odd cents.

The purse was not a primary consideration with O'Brien. As quickly as he could cross the country after the bout, he opened a vaudeville tour in Boston, the Irish-American capital of the United States, as the new heavyweight champion of the world. He got $700 a week. After Boston, he headed for New York, announcing his intention to register at the Waldorf-Astoria, with a valet, a secretary, a press agent, and twenty-five trunks. The Waldorf had never before sheltered a prizefighter, so his arrival was, per se, a story for the newspapers. But his press agent, not content with the legitimate story, decided to turn it into a hoax of the ingenuous old Anna Held milk-bath variety. He invited all the sporting press, managers, trainers, and plug-uglies in town to a reception in Philadelphia Jack's suite. When the guests began to arrive, the press agent stepped into another room and called the desk, complaining of a riot in O'Brien's rooms. The management asked Philadelphia Jack to leave. He acceded and headed up Fifth Avenue to the Hotel Netherlands, leading a caravan of hansom cabs that carried the twenty-five trunks, the valet, the secretary, and all the invited guests. O'Brien was hardly settled in the Netherlands before the management, egged on by the same anonymous complainant, urged him to depart. O'Brien had expected to be bounced from the Waldorf, but the Netherlands ouster surprised him. He didn't know how thorough the press agent was. Jack tried the Savoy next. The news of the scandals at the other hotels had preceded him and the Savoy wouldn't even let him register. After an afternoon of travel among hotels, coming nearer to apoplexy at each rebuff, the bon-ton bruiser wound up at the Marlborough, a sporting resort at Thirty-sixth and Broadway which would have welcomed Buffalo Bill's Wild West Show in full regalia.

The contretemps had no effect on Jack's social position

in Philadelphia. He was by this time allied with the Biddles. Major Anthony J. Drexel Biddle was, like President Theodore Roosevelt, an amateur boxer. He believed in muscular Christianity. With Philadelphia Jack as a foil, the Major travelled to Episcopalian Sunday schools, entertaining the pupils with boxing exhibitions. Jack was the drawing card, but the Major did most of the talking. He always made a little speech, Jack recalls, "about how Christ had been an athlete, and how He had gone into the jungle for forty days to train for a match with the Devil." Then Philadelphia Jack O'Brien and Philadelphia Anthony J. Drexel Biddle would spar a couple of fast rounds, and the little Episcopalians would go home edified.

On pleasant Sunday afternoons, Major Biddle used to indulge another sporting fancy. He gave boxing teas on the lawn behind his home, admittance by card only. A card would read, "You are invited to a tea in honor of Sailor Burke," or "Mike Schreck," as the case might be. It was up to O'Brien to provide as guest of honor a prominent pugilist who happened to be in Philadelphia on business. After tea, cake, and introductions, the guest would be expected to spar a couple of rounds with the Major. Only once did a recitalist fail to react to the high-toned atmosphere. He was a towering California heavyweight named Al Kaufmann, "a well-meaning fellow," Jack says, "but of a literal mind. When I asked him to put on the gloves with the Major, he assented readily. They got into the ring, and then what does this lowly person do but hit Major *Biddle* on the chin and knock him out for about ten minutes!"

Even though Jack had beaten Fitzsimmons, his claim on the heavyweight championship was not universally recognized. A Canadian named Tommy Burns was a rival claimant, and after a good deal of diplomatic and journalistic crossfire, they were matched to fight at Los Angeles in May, 1907. By that time O'Brien's flair for serious pugilism had been diminished by rich living.

Before the fight began, Burns announced that he had agreed to let himself be knocked out, but that he was repudiating the agreement and would fight on the level. Philadelphia Jack was in poor condition, but boxed the entire twenty rounds. The decision went to Burns, who was thenceforth, until knocked out by Jack Johnson, acknowledged as the heavyweight champion of the world.

Despite his wealth, Philadelphia Jack brooded over the Burns reverse. He thought he saw a chance to redeem himself by one spectacular victory over Stanley Ketchel, the middleweight champion. O'Brien himself, although he had been fighting heavyweights, was virtually a middleweight. He was thirty-one, ten years older than Ketchel. But he had heard about Ketchel, and thought he was just the kind of fellow he could beat.

"I had heard that Ketchel's dynamic onslaught was such it could not readily be withstood," Jack says, "but I figured I could jab his puss off."

Ketchel had never fought east of the Alleghenies, and he wanted a victim with a big name for his Eastern debut. His manager, Willus Britt, known as the best eye-gouger and shin-kicker in America, thought O'Brien was decrepit. Britt was as willing as O'Brien to sign for the match, which was to be held at the National Athletic Club of New York. Ten rounds was the limit under the New York boxing law of that date, and no decisions were allowed. The National was a new "society" athletic club, with quarters on East Twenty-fourth Street.

Philadelphia Jack, by his predilection for high-toned language, top hats, and Biddles, had antagonized the sporting public. Ketchel, handsome in a tough way, rough and reckless, was exactly the kind of a fighter the mobs adore. He was a Polish-American from Grand Rapids, né Stanislaus Kiecal. The match, on the night of March 26, 1909, packed the club. The building held only two thousand fans, but because of the high admission prices the bout drew about $20,000. The middle-class occupants of the $5 seats were wholeheartedly for Ketchel, but the ringside swells, some of whom had come rakishly in automobiles, cheered Philadelphia Jack and Major Biddle, who was in his corner as honorary chief second.

When the fighters met at two o'clock to weigh in, O'Brien weighed 162 pounds, Ketchel 160. Britt insisted that Philadelphia Jack discard the two pounds. O'Brien said, bitterly, "Shakespeare had a character like you in 'The Merchant of Venice.' " But he had to put on a mountain of sweaters and jump rope until he had sweated off two pounds.

When Ketchel entered the ring before the fight, he walked over to O'Brien's corner to shake hands. Philadelphia Jack pretended not to see him. He went on talking to his second until Ketchel turned away. This strategy was supposed to have a profound psychological effect. Working on a slightly less cerebral plane, Jack's seconds massaged the horsehair filling of his left glove away from the knuckles and up toward his wrist.

These bony knuckles, arriving in Ketchel's face twenty

times during the first minute of boxing, turned it into a red, puffy smear.

"I should have put the bum away early," Jack says regretfully when he thinks of it, "but my timing was a fraction of an iota off." For eight rounds Philadelphia Jack twirled around the ring, shooting in his left and stepping away from counters, and sometimes nailing the Westerner with straight rights to the jaw that staggered him. "A dozen times in the fifth round alone," the *Times* boxing man wrote, "it seemed that Ketchel must be knocked out." He wasn't, and Jack began to slow up. He says now that he began to feel weak from sweating off the extra weight a few hours before the fight. He still hit Ketchel at will, but he couldn't escape the counters. And in the ninth round Ketchel landed flush on his jaw with a right swing thrown from far back of the shoulder. O'Brien went down for a count of nine but he got up again and hung onto Ketchel's arms until the round ended. In the tenth, the Pole went after Jack without even trying to avoid the jabs. O'Brien was knocked down again, came up, clinched. Tim Hurst, the referee, pulled the men apart. Ketchel doubled Jack up with a left to the pit of the stomach and then crashed a right to the jaw. O'Brien fell back, out cold, with his head in the resin box in back of Ketchel's corner. Just as Hurst counted six, the gong sounded. The fight was over, and since there had not been time to count ten, Philadelphia Jack had not lost.

In the Metropole Bar on Times Square, and in the bars and restaurants of Sixth Avenue, the arguments raged far into the next morning. Thousands of dollars had been bet on Ketchel to win by a knockout. The O'Brien bettors would not pay. Nor would the Ketchel men. They protested that the round had been twenty seconds short, a charge that has never been proved.

The few remaining bouts of Jack's ring career were anti-climactic, and would have been even if they had included the battle of Gettysburg. Two months after the Ketchel fight he collected his largest single purse, $10,225.50 (if Jack's memory isn't faulty on the odd cents), for boxing six rounds to no decision with Jack Johnson at Philadelphia. Johnson was by that time heavyweight champion, and outweighed O'Brien 220 pounds to 161. He knocked O'Brien down in the first round, but most critics thought Philadelphia Jack finished the stronger of the two.

As time elapsed, the renown of the Ketchel fight blotted out all the rest of Philadelphia Jack's two hundred and twenty-five bouts, and Jack now seldom hears any reference to them. New customers in his gymnasium always ask him how it felt when Ketchel landed, and Jack has learned that it is good business to treat it all as a joke. Secretly, though, he feels that Ketchel was lucky.

O'Brien's gymnasium is situated on the seventh and top-most floor of the Roseland Building at 1658 Broadway. Connected with it by a hall and stairway are a board running track and handball courts on the roof. Enormous white letters on the fence around the running track flaunt the proprietor's alien origin in the face of the theatre district.

	FLESH REDUCING	
PHILA.		MEN
	O'BRIEN	
JACK		WOMEN

the sign says. In recognition of his loyalty, transplanted sprigs of Philadelphia aristocracy are among O'Brien's best customers. Rosamund Pinchot Gaston frequently ran on O'Brien's track behind the fence, her long legs wrapped in sweat pants, a fur coat flapping behind her. Usually she ran two miles, and she easily outfooted most of O'Brien's male customers. In earlier days, Jack taught the rudiments of boxing to Tony Biddle, now Ambassador to Poland, and Eaton Cromwell, comparatively reticent brother of the reverberant Jimmy H. R.

With the active collaboration of Mrs. O'Brien, who abandoned the practice of law to share his fortunes, Philadelphia Jack makes a pretty good living out of the gymnasium. Mrs. O'Brien manages the women's department and all fiscal arrangements.

Philadelphia Jack has no patience with health clubs where the client is constantly warned to avoid strenuous exertion. The customer in some of these places, he says, is let off with deep-breathing exercises, a massage, and a big bill.

When the O'Brien overweight customer reaches the locker room and disrobes, he is seized by a couple of O'Brien retainers and swathed in concentric layers of India rubber, until he feels like a cigar in a Sumatra wrapper. The attendants then tie him into sweat clothes and add a cardigan jacket, knitted gloves, and a wool toque such as small boys affected for belly-whopping in the late nineteenth century. They rush the wretched man to the roof, turn him loose on the running track, and bid him trot. When the customer staggers down the stairs, Philadelphia Jack alleviates his sufferings by cheerful words and hearty slaps on the back. After that Jack puts him through calisthenics as he lies recumbent on a table, since his legs can no longer support him. Then Jack encourages him to play handball or punch the bag if he has any ambition left.

A heavy man can't miss knocking off four pounds in a workout, but he gains about three back overnight if he drinks water. A determined customer carries on in this manner, like running down an escalator, until at the end of a few months he has taken off a good deal of weight. Jack once took fifty-eight pounds off a man in three months —the fellow was terribly overweight and wanted to pass a life-insurance examination. He stopped exercise as soon as the insurance company accepted him and is now just as heavy as ever. "But I hear his business is good," Jack says, "so some day he'll be wanting some more insurance and I'll get him again."

There is a florid good humor about O'Brien and his place. This extends to the Boxing Taught Without Punishment Department, in which most of the pupils are inoffensive middle-aged men. Philadelphia Jack doesn't say that boxing can be learned without punishment—just taught.

Jack is sometimes sought out by angry elderly men who demand instruction in beating up their brothers-in-law or business associates. In such cases Jack always advises a rigorous course of training. After a couple of lessons, the clients almost invariably develop sore muscles and give up their warlike projects. Jack remembers only one customer who actually had a fight, a jealous husband in his mid-fifties who insisted on punching a much younger man.

"We did our best to dissuade him," says Jack, "but one day he showed up with a black eye, and then we knew he had met with disaster."

Sometimes Jack becomes bored with the businessmen, even though they are profitable. Periodically, his flesh-reducing customers are excited by the eruption into their midst of hard-looking young men who snuffle through flattened nostrils as they pound each other inside O'Brien's regulation boxing ring. The fighters attract an audience of sportswriters, and the flesh-reducers get stagefright. No forty-seven-year-old manufacturer of ladies' underwear who has grown a fifty-inch waistline feels comfortable doing calisthenics before a gallery. When the flesh-reducers' attendance drops off, O'Brien banishes the fighting men and vows never to let another fighter train at his place. The sequence is repeated about once every two years.

The money Philadelphia Jack earned in the ring did not last long. He speculated in Philadelphia real estate. When values failed to rise, he could not pay off the mortgages and lost everything he had. By 1917 he had passed through bankruptcy and opened his first gymnasium. He moved from Philadelphia to New York three years later.

Jack and Mrs. O'Brien, a compact, red-cheeked woman, very precise in gesture and conversation, live in a four-room apartment on West Fifty-fourth Street. They have been married for twenty-four years. Every morning the O'Briens arise at eight and perform a series of calisthenics before going to work. On Sunday mornings, they attend Mass at the Church of the Holy Innocents on Thirty-seventh Street, where they were married, and on Sunday afternoons, in good weather, they like to ride the Forty-second Street ferry to Weehawken. They then walk briskly along the Jersey shore as far as the George Washington Bridge, which they cross on foot.

In his business, Jack has always displayed the same gift

for publicity that inspired his cable dispatches from England. As soon as he opened his first gymnasium, he began a practice of boxing with prominent prizefighters at their training quarters, to demonstrate his fitness. As recently as 1936, when he was fifty-nine, he got into the ring at Pompton Lakes, New Jersey, and boxed a round with Joe Louis, making the Negro look rather silly for the first minute. Even when the principals in an approaching bout will not box with him, Philadelphia Jack visits the training camps, inspects the adversaries, and usually succeeds in getting quotations into the *comptes rendus* of all the sports-writers.

Only once in his quest of publicity was Jack abashed. That was at the time when people were reading about Cal Coolidge's electric horse. O'Brien got the Representative from Nevada, whom he had met through a divorced customer, to introduce him to the President. As soon as Coolidge said, "How do you do?" Jack was prepared to make a speech offering to teach him boxing without pain. When he got to the President's desk, however, Jack says, he felt "such an aura of latent hostility that emanated from the fellow" that he choked up. He was shoved out of the way to make room for a visiting troop of Boy Scouts before he had remembered anything to say.

The Vest, the Brush, the Clutch

There is a fight manager in New York who is known as The Vest, because according to popular legend he always gets soup stains on his waistcoat, and another called The Brush because he has a moustache. The most amusing fellow around Stillman's, in the opinion of the habitués, is always referred to as The Clutch. He grabs strangers' hands and crushes them until the strangers fall to their knees and scream. He particularly likes to do this to big heavyweights and visiting boxing commissioners, because it embarrasses them. Once The Clutch was a good light heavyweight, but he had a peculiar difficulty in training. He was constantly getting shot, which was an occupational disease in the live poultry business in which he was employed. Next to breaking fingers, The Clutch enjoys showing his bullet wounds. The bullets did no real harm, he carefully explains, but they often caused him to ask for postponements, so matchmakers quit giving him work. He still works in the poultry market, loading trucks with crates of live chickens. Once a chicken offended him and he bit its head off.

The Clutch is a softhearted fellow compared to the parents of a Southern boxer who came up to New York five years ago to fight Maxey Rosenbloom. "My boy is a slow starter," the mother said before the fight, "but when he is cut up a little he goes right after the other fellow." They gave me a nice, homey, folksy interview. The highlight, I thought, was when I asked the mother (who attended all the boy's fights) whether she yelled when her son was hit. "Boy," interpolated old Pappy, "she sings right out like a mocking bird." The fight had not gone a minute that night when deep cuts over the boy's eyes opened up, sluicing blood all over him. The referee stopped the fight. No professional manager would have let a fighter go into the ring in that shape.

About as nice a woman as I ever met was Barney Ross's mother, Mrs. Sarah Rasofsky. "Rasofsky, Rasoff, Ross," she said—"names I've got more than money." I met her when she came on with Barney from Chicago, for his second bout with Tony Canzoneri. She was a short woman with a flat, cheerful face. She said that she had never in her life torn a piece of paper or lighted a match between sundown Friday and sundown Saturday. But if Barnele wanted to fight on Friday night that was all right with her, because there was nothing in the Talmud about boxing, one way or another.

"You never I suppose was a mother," she said, "so you don't know how I feel. But I think if I look at the other fellow all the time, maybe I will hypnotize him. At Barnele I don't look."

She was stopping in a small room at the Hotel Edison. Except for charities she was very abstemious. "Not a cent Barney has of the money he earned," she said. "It worries me. Of course we live good, and he has two brothers. I hope he should send them through college, but he must watch the money."

But a good boy!

"For me he would take and sell a bag of onions," Mrs. Rasofsky bragged. "When he began to fight I argued with him he should stop it. But the people saw it and they liked it, and he started in and he said, 'Momma, I'll make for you a good living.'

"So I said:—'A good living from a boy 19 years old, I don't expect. Ten dollars a week is enough.' But they got him in. I think he got this in his blood in the tough neighborhood we lived. There was a lot of kids, bums, so he organized himself a little gang they should give them back, and that is how it came in his head to be a fighter.

"I don't think he did a great thing for the world, like Lindy. But I am not sorry. Only he should not get hurt."

PEOPLE IN TROUBLE

The worst trouble a man can be in, I think, is to have one hope left, and that a hope of something so inherently improbable that he knows deep in his heart it won't happen. It has been said in favor of lotteries that they prevent a great many people from committing suicide. I think that is one of the chief arguments against them. But even more painful than a lottery ticket is a stock of goods that no one will buy. If you don't believe this re-read "The Poor Little Match Girl," which makes me weep unreservedly every time I look through it,* because like most natives back here where I came from, I have a heart of gold beneath my cold exterior. Three feeble gardenias on a vendor's tray in the rain an hour after curtain time; a cup of fly-specked jelly beans in a shop window: these are the merchant's last precarious handhold on the window ledge. The cruelest merchandise is a talent for which there is no demand.

An example that saddens me every time I think of it was the unique gift upon which Louis Van Dycke had to depend for a living. If he had had the price, he could have advertised:

"Will Exchange—Sure method of curing a sick gorilla for permanent position as zoo keeper or animal boss with circus. Louis Van Dycke, 212 E. 26th St."

Captain Van Dycke had a few other assets, although he conceded that since the four-ton elephant had stepped on

* The last time was in 1913.

his foot, necessitating a special shoe, he lacked the agility to work a cat act in the arena; and since the orang had broken two of his ribs he had difficulty jumping up onto an elephant's head as he used to do with Power.

"How many trainers today know how to feed a lion act right?" he asked me. "How many can cure an elephant with a fever? They call in a vetzionary—a horse doctor."

Mrs. Van Dycke, pinned in between a traveling trunk and a gas plate, nodded proudly. "Not many, I bet you," she said.

"And my Louis never drinks," she bragged. "He's steady, and that's more than I can say for any other trainer I ever saw."

While waiting for that improbable event, an answer to one of the letters he sent out, Captain Van Dycke (trainers receive their commissions with their first red tunics and high boots) lived among circus photographs and clippings of newspapers that filled two trunks.

"And seven onner ones in storage," he liked to say. "There is nit in the world an onner collection like it.

"That was Bonavita that the polar bear got," he said when he displayed the pictures, "and that is Prieto which makes the hippopotamus walk the tight rope, and Kaslak with the trained pigs, and Henrich Henriksen the tiger wratsler."

There was also a gay lithograph of Captain Louis Van Dycke, the young Hollander who came to the P. T. Barnum circus in 1896 with an act including a lion, a gnu, a camel and a Great Dane. The lion rode the camel and then drove the gnu in harness.

"That is Fallacita," he said turning to the ladies' department, "the best leopard act what ever was. Her best leopard killed her, what she had playing the piano.

"And Margaret Kreskopf. On 38th Street by McNally in the storehouse Yulius clawed her down the side. He were a bad lion. Once he hit me the fork out of the hand in Rocky Point, R. I."

The picture of the next dompteuse pleased him especially. "Look," he said, "Mary Ellen." Then, after a pause, "That were me. I took an act for a girl that hurted herself. The contract called for a woman trainer, so I worked in a red wig and a Oriental costume for nineteen months, twelve lions, and I got away with it."

"He brought them back alive before Frank Buck," volunteered his wife. "He was in the jungle when he was 15 years old."

In the 10,000 pictures of his collection the trainer identified as many animals as men.

"That's Consul and Betty," he said, pausing at the portraits of two chimpanzees playing billiards, "the original Consul and Betty that was Max und Moritz before the war. Then when they came here we changed the names. They was two tough customers! In San Francisco, Joanescu, my manager, and I was riding in a motorcycle with the chimps in the sidecar, and coming down a hill we skidded into a trolley. The chimps ran into a saloon and with bottles the mirrors broke up and chased the bartender and got drunk and beat up a cop, and when we woke up we was in the hospital and the chimps was in jail."

For a long time it had been tough sledding for the Van Dyckes. The insurance policies were dead—cashed in. The gold chain with the gold elephant charm had passed to a pawnbroker in permanence.

"These are hard times," said the Captain. "It seems like everybody let me in the hole.

"When I think how I fed each lion every Sunday fifteen eggs in milk I wish I had it now ourselfs. I lost in three years seventy pounds, and Booby, my wife, has nit to eat many times."

He had a good head of blond hair and looked younger than the 55 years he acknowledged, but the winged collar of his salad days was loose around his neck.

"And every six weeks kidneys," he said, reverting to the lions. "When you see with the ribs sticking out lions, they is like doped. Cheap trainers' tricks. You should have seen the great Julius Seth of Hamburg. Twelve horses and twelve gnus on a carrousel what went around, and on every horse and every gnu a fat lion, and when he waved the hand they changed."

There are no spangles on E. 26th Street. The block between Third and Second Avenues would crush the spirit of a Micawber.

The sound of the water running in the broken toilet across the hall furnished a tonal background for the roar of the passing elevated trains.

"Still," Captain Van Dycke asserted proudly, "I am the only trainer which can cure a sick gorilla. How, is my secret."

Oenologist

Those were tough days for an oenologist.

The wine got sick because it was not kept right, but it was the wine of poor people. So the wine doctor seldom had more than one barrel as a patient. Also it was hard to collect his fee after he had effected the cure.

"Prohibition," Professor Giuseppe Lapiccirilla mourned in his idiomatic Italian, "has cut off my arms. Before prohibition I earned good bread. Now," he waved his arm in a gesture that included his worn furniture, the elegant prospect of a gasoline station across Kenmare Street, and the yellowed diplomas in their dusty frames.

Probably not one in a thousand of those who passed along Kenmare Street and observed the window card "Oenologist," had any idea of what it meant.

But that had never occurred to the stooping, white-haired man who maintained a certain elegance even though the tops of his woolen drawers showed through the opened top of his trousers. His diploma from the Royal College of Agriculture at Alba, Province of Cuneo, named him laureate in oenology. He spoke no English. The earlier diploma, from the agrarian school ta Cerignola, Province of Foggia, was dated 1855, and he must have been at least fifteen then.

Throughout the neighborhood basement restaurateurs and families who made a yearly barrel of wine for home consumption knew him as "that old guy who puts some powder in a barrel of wine that's gone punk and it comes out all right."

The powder, the Professor explained to me, was tartar that forms in wine barrels. "It is not a drug, like you get in a pharmacy. It is a wine product, so when you add it to wine with excess of acidosity, it restores the balance. Pharmacology is not oenology," he grandly concluded, with a pull at his white moustache.

Thirty years earlier he had come to this country to work for the California Vineyards Company. He had had a large library on the chemistry of wines. He had contributed articles to oenological publications.

Now it was finished. What he earned from the neighbors scarcely sufficed for an occasional black, gnarled Italian cigar. He lived with his son-in-law, who had started in life as a poet but had given it up to tour with an Indian herb tea medicine show.

The Stuff of Dreams

I made the acquaintance of M. Maurice shortly before the return bout between Max Schmeling and Jack Sharkey. M. Maurice was a dreamer. He used to dream the results of prizefights and elections in advance, and mail his predictions to newspapers. About this fight he had mailed us no prediction, so I called on him in his furnished room on West End Avenue to ask him what was the matter.

He said that he had dreamed the fight once and Sharkey had won. Then he had dreamed Schmeling. The third time he dreamed it, he regretted to say, it looked a little like a barney—as if there were some collusion. That was why he had not yet mailed a definitive prediction. Afterward Sharkey did win, by a very questionable decision. Joe Jacobs, Schmeling's manager, yelled "We was robbed." If Joe was right, so was M. Maurice's third dream.

M. Maurice was a French Jew, small and sleek, with large soft eyes. He was a quick dreamer. "I dream fifteen or twenty times a night," he told me. "If I dream more I forget sometimes." He had picked Hoover in 1928 and Tunney to beat Heeney. While most of his dream choices had been favorites like these two, he had picked Tunney to beat Dempsey in 1926, which had been a pretty exclusive dream. Dreaming was just an avocation with M. Maurice. He was the seventh son of a seventh son's seventh son, he said, so he couldn't help it. He said all of his ancestors were rabbis.

He had gone on the stage as a card manipulator at the age of twelve, and admitted he was still the world's greatest. But the card manipulation business was very slow, so M. Maurice had plenty of time for dreaming.

"Dream interpretation is twenty-five per cent foreknowledge, seventy-five per cent practical experience," he says. "The more dreams you have had the more infallible you become. Tenez—an example.

"A person dreams rats are climbing all over him? What is it mean? No, not what you say, he is one big cheese. It mean some lowly-spirited individual is trying to supplant him, beware." His system is not Freudian. It is not even a system. It is a gift.

"I am 127 per cent correct," he announced. "That is because oftentimes, on one dream I make three prophecies."

He had a furnished room instead of larger quarters, because of the decline in vaudeville booking and the failure of the Bank of United States.

He dreamed about the bank failure the night before it happened, but his wife, whom he had told to draw his money, forgot.

He put a photograph of the Lindbergh baby under his pillow after the kidnapping and tried to dream its whereabouts, but failed to dream about it at all, he said regretfully.

"I dreamed last night that everybody in the bread line wore spats and a gardenia in his buttonhole," he said.

"I was in a kind of desert, but green trees were growing out of beer barrels. Prosperity will be back next year.

* * *

Even ordinary labor sometimes becomes tragic merchandise. I once saw a boy of three playing with his father in front of the Waldrich Bleachery at Delawanna, N. J., outside Passaic, during a strike. The child, who wore a red sweater and blue leggings, threw a discarded water-logged tennis ball with his right hand, and between throws gnawed at a piece of bread in his left hand.

At length he lost interest in the bread and threw it away. His father stooped over and put the bread in his own trousers pocket, so he would have it when the kid got hungry again.

Bowery Boom

One of the saddest phenomena I ever observed was a boom on the Bowery. A boom on the Bowery would pass for a dull thud almost anywhere else. But habitués can notice it. It was the snow removal work coming right on top of the holidays that had brought in the money that winter. Christmas Eve and Christmas are the panhandlers' white stone dates.

"All these stories in the paper and ads about 'don't give to mendicants' hurt the racket this fall," said a hash house owner. "But it was a good Christmas, with the liquor and everything. I heard of one fellow who got $25 on Christmas Eve alone, working up around Columbus Circle. He doubled it by hiring himself a waiter's suit—he used to be a waiter before he hit the booze—and getting a job at a country club for New Year's Eve. But then he got to drinking again and by the time he woke up he had nothing."

The snow removal meant only a few dollars to each shoveler, but a dollar a day means a sybaritic existence to the man acclimated to the Bowery.

For 20 cents he may have a bed, for 25 cents a room, at any of two dozen hotels. The Montauk, at 197, advertises "rooms with windows," the acme of luxury, for 30 and 35 cents. He may sleep until noon. The old flophouse system of routing out the guests at 8 no longer obtains. Five cents pays for a shave at the barber college. For 20 cents the Boweryite may have "shave, massage, shampoo, singe and hair tonic," just like a 46th Street bookmaker. Ten cents will buy "pig snouts, vegetables, potatoes and coffee, bread or rolls," at the Pioneer Restaurant, 263, and 15 cents will buy an even more elaborate spread at Minder's Restaurant.

For 25 cents the man-about-the-Bowery may take in two movies, a burlesque show, five acts of vaudeville and a play, pleasurably killing a good eight hours.

The burlesque house is the People's Theatre, between Rivington and Houston Streets, where Weber and Fields played as boys. The first matinee begins at 9 in the morning and until 5 in the afternoon you can get in for 10 cents.

On Saturday nights, according to the master of ceremonies, the theatre runs a "snap-the-garter contest" and you can become acquainted with the members of the cast at Joe's Grill after the show. The picture on my last visit was a Western, with lines like, "So it was you who shot through that rope and saved my life."

It requires will power to get over to the other theatre, for it is on Clinton Street, half a dozen blocks east, but you can park a long time for fifteen cents when you get there.

A bill I saw there included an English society talking

picture which sounded as if all the actors had their mouths
full of hot knishes, and then two lads in top hats and dinner jackets who danced on roller skates, finishing with an
imitation of a train. A crooner featured this chorus:—

"Maybe yes, maybe no,
Efter all, you should know."

Then there was a sketch about a Jewish girl who marries
an Italian and they can't agree in a name for the baby.

The piece de resistance offered the great Jennie Goldstein in a Yiddish drama in which the pathos was easy to
follow because she died in pretty terrible agony after a
comic divertissement featuring a baby named Johnny Fitz-
patrick Grossman.

This makes, let us see: twenty-five for a room, five for
a shave, twenty-five for meals and twenty-five for the
theatre, leaving a dime for a pack of stale cutrate Camels
and another dime for liquor. The shock houses have cleaned
up their windows, put out restaurant signs and obtained
liquor licenses, but smoke is still obtainable. A trusted patron, who stands near the bar, carries a single bottle in his
hip pocket in many of the places. The thirsty client pays the
proprietor, the man with the bottle pours the drink. Ten
cents' worth of smoke will out-hit a pint of blended whiskey.

The only item unprovided for is female society, but
the Bowery is a republic of misogynists. You have to eat
regularly for at least a week before you begin worrying
about women.

La Bourse

Open air markets are a picturesque feature of many
regions in the sticks, and I am proud to say that New

York has an out-door market too. It is called the Tin Pan, but the cops chase it around from one corner to another on the lower East Side, so it will be hard to direct visitors to the World's Fair to this cheerful glimpse of colorful city life. The exact locale of the Tin Pan varies, but it is always in session in the same general neighborhood. The first time I caught up with it the Tin Pan was between Hester and Suffolk Streets, just outside the palings of Seward Park. A man named Patrick McGinn, a member of the floor committee of the Tin Pan, told me that time that short selling was the bane of it.

"Here I have ten magazines," said McGinn with feeling. "Good, substantial love stories and fact stories of crime, and like that—none of them older than 1930. A high school kid steps up and asks me how much I want for them.

" 'Fifteen cents.' I says, expecting to sell them for a dime. And along comes some blatherskite of an Eyetalian, yelling 'Fourteen magazines for five-a cents.' And I lose the sale. It ain't right."

Henry Ritzmeyer, McGinn's partner, returned from a tour of the Exchange with a padlock and a soiled shirt, discouraged.

"Five cents," he fairly spat. "Five cents for a shirt with collar attached yet. Not a bid for the lock.

"Moisha wanted to trade me a toothbrush for the lock, but who will buy a second-hand toothbrush?

"Get away from that. You think it's a toy?" he barked at a tipsy colored man who had spun a roulette wheel standing amid the firm's stock.

"We could get $1.50 for that wheel, easy," he mourned, "if we only had the ivory ball. Now we will be lucky to get a dollar."

"Look, good shoes," a tall man was roaring at a pockmarked Hindu. "Good soles. Good uppers. Good, strong laces. Fifty cents." His tone rose with each phrase.

The Hindu flexed the leather. "Forty cents," he said with determination.

"Oh, God bless you!" screamed the tall man. "Take them for twenty. I'll give you an overcoat in the bargain." This was pure sarcasm and he moved away.

From Essex Street to Suffolk the sidewalk was jammed with men pushing from one end of the block to the other. As each walked he carried in his hand a fountain pen, a pair of mules, a flutter of dirty handkerchiefs, a ragged sweater. A few had watches. Any object exposed was for sale or barter.

A knife-scarred Cuban carried a box of bargain cigars— one cent each. A fellow in a brown suit sold hunks of sausage and stale bakers' cakes. The two liveried young sharpers who wear N. Y. E. on their caps and drive about the city in their own delivery wagon with goods ostensibly stolen from the New York Express Company, "imported perfumes," and "real English tweeds" loitered about to replenish their stock. They sell their "stolen merchandise" to people they meet on the street who look unduly avaricious. The gulls believe they are getting bargains.

"Look," said a hawk-nosed Galician to an undersized Italian boy, "blue basketweave. A Hollywood cut. Two dollars. Cheap."

The boy compared the trousers with his own. "I want a twenty-two inch cuff," he said. "They ain't wide enough."

Hundreds of men of all races and ages attend the market every day. Where they get their stocks no one inquires.

Garbage barrels and morgue attendants are leading sources of supply.

Pat McGinn is short and florid and heavy set, with a broad, flat face. Henry, his partner, looks scholarly with his horn-rimmed spectacles and graying hair.

"Fellows shouldn't go around yelling prices," said McGinn. "People want to bargain with you, and you might as well start 'em off high. Then they get you down and go away feeling good."

"You feel good, too," said Ritzmeyer. "Because you know anyway they're stuck."

The next time I saw the Tin Pan it had acquired a roof. The traders had been driven from Seward Park.

They now went about their abject affairs on Delancey Street, under the west end of the Williamsburgh Bridge.

"The market meets now rain or shine," said McGinn. "It's a great advantage. But it's a bear market, all sellers. Would you believe it, I cannot sell these two good, clean vests for a nickel?"

"Yarmark, yarmark," shouted a Jew with long curly hair and a stubbly chin. This is Russian for a magnificent fair. "A whole hardware store, look," he yelled mockingly, pointing to a stock of rusty screws and one good monkey wrench.

A Japanese presided over a table burdened with five pairs of spectacles, a committeeman's badge of the Tenth Assembly District Republican Club and the sound box of a phonograph. The table was also for sale, but as it had only three legs, bidders lacked.

"The smell from that live poultry market isn't so good," said Mr. McGinn, nodding toward the shed where crated thousands awaited their fate at the hands of a tawny-bearded shochet. "At least, once I wouldn't have said it was so good, but now it makes me hungry."

A squint-eyed man tried on a pair of spectacles.

"No good," he said.

"Try these," advised the Japanese. "Maybe stronger."

"A suit, a beauty," urged a youth in a polo shirt.

"How much?"

"Two-and-a-half."

"Ain't got that much."

"Have you got two dollars?"

"It ain't my size."

"What's your size? Forty-two? It's a forty-two." No sale.

"The suit I got on," said Mr. McGinn, who wore a stiff collar, black tie, coat, vest and trousers, plus a homburg hat, "stood me ten cents. I got two for a half and sold one for forty cents. It was a clean-up.

"I can't make much today because I have no stock to speak of. I always keep my rosary beads in reserve. They're lucky. A couple of times I've sold them for a dime and then made a big comeback. I've had as much as $2 twice this winter. I always buy the beads back."

Lest We Forget to Remember

People who look back with nostalgia to the kindly days before the New Deal have probably forgotten the Hoover Cities; maybe they never noticed them. A Hoover city was a collection of burrows in the earth, with slanting roofs of corrugated tin and front walls made of timber salvaged from wrecking jobs. It was inhabited by men out of work who had not yet been pauperized by WPA, and they all had a fine time. They would send delegates to the wholesale food markets to collect partly spoiled fruit, and to the fish trucks to solicit fish that was not quite bad. Then they would cut the worst parts of the food away and cook the rest. There were Hoover Cities in a number of marginal neighborhoods back where I came from. All you needed to start one was a large vacant lot. Occasionally an accident occurred in a Hoover City, but there was never anything to arouse the indignation of the newspapers, as there evidently is in WPA.

I don't know why people called them all Hoover Cities —in all fairness they might have named a couple for other prominent Republicans like Sam Insull and Richard Whitney—but Hoover Cities they were. One of the accidents happened in a Hoover City behind the Todd Shipyards in Brooklyn. It was inhabited largely by stranded Scandinavian seamen. Four of the unpauperized were killed drinking wood alcohol, which was inexpensive in those days of low production costs. One was blinded. One of the dead was named Rider Johnson, and the fellow who had shared his burrow told me how he died.

"Johnson said, 'Bill, my eye is bothering me.' And I said, 'I go for the street cop.' And he said, 'No, I got no pine.' Then later he said, 'I got pine in the stomach.' I went for the cop. He couldn't see the cop. He could yust see me. He died before the bus came. He was a good man, mate's papers and all. He came from Moos, in Norway."

The corrugated iron shack had a fine sea view of the idle ships at their piers on Gowanus Bay.

"Years they drank alcohol here and nothing happened," the roommate continued. "Only when they drank this cheap stuff. It killed them. Fifty cents a gallon is too cheap.

Eighty cents a gallon it won't kill you. Still," he apologized, "when men are laying here for months, no ships, no work, good men with papers, some of them, it was no wonder they must do something. They drink what they can get."

To most of the seamen it seemed no great disaster. It was hard to locate the shacks where the different men had died.

"We all got to get it," philosophized a tough, stubby ship's carpenter. "Look how we live. That coffee, you could see bottom in t'ree fadum of it." He waved to a pot of viscous liquid that bubbled over a brick cooking place. "Maybe it wasn't alcohol at all. Maybe it was raw fish they copped from the trucks—spoiled, maybe."

"Andy Mellon got money," a tall lean fellow said, poking the fire under the "coffee."

"It's all graft," said the carpenter. "Now they got all the money out of the little fellows, wait until they squeeze dry a few small millionaires, then them big fellows will have it all."

In a cabin near the Halleck Street entrance to Hoover City Gus Johnson had died. He was a tugboat captain. He had a brother in Bay Ridge. He had a promise of another job soon.

"I don't believe that story a fellow came along and sold them wood alcohol telling them what it was," said his former bunkie, a vast Irishman. "They said in the papers this bird told them to boil it with milk, it would take the poison out. But I think they got it up on Cole Street, or Third Avenue, where they sell smoke."

Walter Johnson, another of the dead, was a deckhand

on a tug. Torval Anderson was a mechanic from the ship-yards, laid off, of course.

On the door of the shack where the drinking party had been held was a chalk inscription, "No admittance except to members."

There were no more members.

City Block

The most populous city block in the United States, and probably the world, is bounded by Seventh and Lenox Avenues and 142nd and 143rd Streets. With the exception of a couple of white women who have married colored men, and of three Chinese laundrymen who sleep behind their shops, all the 3,824 residents in the block are Negroes. It covers 150,000 square feet, and this means that the average density of population is 1,100 to the acre. If all the people of the United States were moved equally close together, they would fit in about half the area of the City of New York, leaving a couple of boroughs vacant for parking space.

The second most populous block is Knickerbocker Village, the housing development on the lower East Side, but it covers almost one-and-a-half times the area of the block in Harlem. Its 3,750 humans live above 217,000 square feet of land. The buildings have an average height of eleven stories, compared to six in the Harlem block. Third in the list of populous blocks is London Terrace in Chelsea, with 3,500 inhabitants on acreage very little larger than the Harlem one. But here the buildings are from seventeen to twenty stories tall. For number of human beings to the cubic foot, the block in Harlem is without a serious rival.

On first view, this block is hard to distinguish from those around it. All Harlem crawls with people. But by the hazards of architecture and commerce, this particular block is able to house more men, women, children, and dogs than any of its neighbors. Every inch of surface is covered by solid, boxlike houses of flats, with scarcely an areaway to break the mass. There isn't a garage, a public building, or any other non-residential structure on the block. There is only one saloon, a small one at the corner of Lenox Avenue and 143rd Street. It doesn't take up much room. There are stores on the Lenox Avenue side, but only one or two tailor shops and laundries on the side streets. On Seventh Avenue, a big, old apartment house, the Rose-Rita, runs half the length of the block. All the houses were built before the Negroes went to Harlem, but they seem to have been designed with a certain prescience, as if the architects knew that this would be the most congested district in the city.

Rents are high in relation to the means of the residents. Paradoxically, the high rents intensify the crowding. Few tenants can afford the whole rent of $60 for five rooms, or $80 for eight, the rates for apartments on either of the avenues. So each tenant takes in from two to four couples, or up to ten individuals, as lodgers. Single women often sleep three in a room. Rooms bring from $4 to $7 a week, according to size, and a fair proportion of the block's inhabitants live on the margin between the rent they pay and the money they collect from the lodgers.

The apartment houses on three sides of the block are especially well adapted to the lodging business. The flats, built for middle-class white families, have what Harlem today calls "private rooms." A long hall runs from the vestibule in each apartment to the kitchen in the rear. Rooms open off the hall, so that it is unnecessary to go through one to reach another. Each lodger gets his or her keys— one for the apartment and one for the room. If the lodgers are women, or man and wife, the landlady seldom goes into a room after renting it. If she has male lodgers, she usually makes up the beds. All the lodgers share one bathroom, as amicably as possible, and women generally have the privilege of preparing food in the kitchen.

The 143rd Street side is the poorest and toughest side of the block. It is also the only side where children are in constant evidence. Here again architecture has determined the character of the population. These flats were built by a man who evidently felt that the neighborhood was slipping. All the apartments to a floor, six floors to a house, and the average apartment shelters at least six persons. The lodger in such an apartment sacrifices even the semblance of privacy, but he gets a room for $2.50 or $3 a week. Couples with three or four children usually rent the apartments. If the family is on relief, it must take a lodger in order to meet the monthly rent of $35. The maximum Emergency Relief rent allowance for a family is $25.50. On this side of the block there are 132 relief cases, more than on the three other sides put together. Since they are mostly family cases, they involve perhaps 500 persons.

There are almost no relief cases on the two avenue sides of the block. Rents are too high. But on the 142nd Street side there are 90 cases. Many of these are single women, for the least desirable room of most apartments on that side of the block may be had for $3.50 a week, the maximum relief allowance for a single person's lodging. Approximately 80 per cent of the block's people support themselves, an unusually high proportion for Harlem.

To live in such close proximity to other human beings is wearing on the nerves. The people on the three "good" sides of the block resent their situation. They remain good-natured toward other Negroes, since obviously one's fellow-lodgers are not to blame for the crowding, and it's hard enough for four or five couples to make one bathroom do, without quarrelling about it. But they feel that the white world is taking advantage of them.

"For the rents we pay here, a man could get a *good* apartment off Riverside Drive or West End Avenue," they will tell you. "But we have no place to go. And the landlords know it. They never fix anything, and as soon as they read in the papers that prosperity was back, they raised the rents. Naturally, that means that a woman's just got to take more lodgers—rent out the living room, even. And if they one day late with the rent, out they go. Plenty more want the room. And if she one day late with the rent, out *she* go."

Old people, like children, are absent from the three sides of the block where there are private rooms. The lodgers are young men and women trying desperately to support themselves, keep up an appearance, and have a good time. In Harlem there are few blocks that attract this class. They shun the blocks of ruinous tenements east of Lenox Avenue, and the blocks of foul dumbbell flats under the "L" on Eighth Avenue, where people lose all self-respect. Prosperous Sugar Hill, west of Eighth Avenue, is beyond the private roomers' means. So they stay on in the central blocks, and seethe.

With much effort, they remain clean. Doctors at the

Harlem Health Center say that pediculosis, ringworm, and infectious skin diseases are almost unknown on the block. The rate of death from tuberculosis is twice that of white Manhattan, and an epidemic disease, like influenza, would inevitably run through the block like a fire through a paper-box factory. But there has been no major epidemic in New York since the block became crowded.

People maintain the forms of politeness, although with considerable difficulty. A girl has to receive her gentlemen friends in her bedroom, and because of its exiguity, they usually have to sit on her bed. It is impressive to see three gentlemen in bowler hats and Chesterfield overcoats simultaneously seated on one side of a young lady's bed while she, reclining on the other side, regrets that there are no hooks on which to hang the coats. It makes you wonder why she doesn't burst out crying.

There is only one house on the block where people live who are of a superior economic status. That is 137 West 142nd Street. It is owned coöperatively by twenty tenants, who include a lawyer, one or two school principals, several Harlem Hospital nurses, and a number of Pullman porters. The coöperative bought the building in 1923, before the opening to colored people of the region around St. Nicholas and Edgecomb Avenues that is now known as Sugar Hill. The members assumed a mortgage of $70,000, which they have reduced to $20,000. They now pay an average carrying charge of $6 a room, or $30 for a five-room apartment—about half what their neighbors pay. The coöperative house is beautifully kept.

John W. Walker, a real-estate man from South Carolina, who is the president of the coöperative, says, "We don't permit no harangue in the house. We keep it good."

Only three families out of the original twenty have had to sell their apartments, even with all the hard times. But some of the other members regret that the wave of fashion advancing up Sugar Hill has left them stranded—twenty social whales flopping among the minnows.

Most of the women who live on the block, unless they support themselves by renting rooms, go out by the day as house-workers. There may be a few sporting girls, but if so they don't work their own block. As for the males, they are elevator men, night-club waiters, garage mechanics, porters in stores, and hustlers. A steady income of $20 a week constitutes wealth. In Harlem, the word "hustler" denotes a man who lives modestly by his wits, perhaps as a policy-game collector, a doorman for a crap game, a pool shark, or a handbook man. The northwest corner of Seventh Avenue and 143rd, just across the street from the most populous block, is known through all Harlem as the numbers market, the bourse of the policy players.

Miss Ira, the beige proprietor of Miss Ira's Personal Shoppe in the Rose-Rita, gives the block its touch of chic. Miss Ira is a *couturière*, and conducts her Shoppe in the two front rooms of her first-floor apartment. She is a talkative young woman with long, narrow eyes and a thin nose, who wears exotic clothes and has her own automobile, pretty nearly paid for. Miss Ira drives a thriving trade with the ladies of the Kit Kat and Cotton Club ensembles, as well as with a great many general houseworkers. She decided to become a modiste nearly nine years ago, when she was a maid for a smart theatrical chiropodist on Fifty-seventh Street. Spring and fall openings at the Personal Shoppe are events of an intimate verve unknown to Vionnet. The mannequins, all ivory-tinted volunteers, parade in what Miss Ira calls "the things a girl would ordinarily wear during the course of a day," beginning with a negligee, continuing with a riding habit, and so through ten changes. She often wonders whether it would be nicer to call herself Madame Ira, but fears it might make her seem old.

Miss Ira is the only one on the block who drinks Scotch and soda in public; the wine of the country is a liquid sometimes called King Kong, sometimes Joe Louis. The better grade of King Kong, or Joe Louis, is moonshine prepared in kitchen stills from hominy grits and sugar. Initiates prefer it milk-warm, as it comes from the copper worm. There is a lower form made from grain alcohol adulterated with rye flavoring, but this is considered a lady's drink. When a hustler goes on a bender, his intimates say that he's "King-Konging it," or simply "Konging it." The stuff retails for twenty-five cents a pint. There is also a species of after-dinner liqueur known as shakeup, made by straining denatured alcohol through a felt hat. A taste for this has to be acquired, it is said. People on the block believe that bartenders refill their whiskey bottles with King Kong. It is therefore considered an affectation to drink in a saloon.

People on the 143rd Street side of the block do not have much social life. They have no money, or they wouldn't be there. That's the side where the children are, and a colored laborer with enough children to fill a five-room flat is always broke, even if he isn't on relief. Adults who live on this side of the block play policy, for infinitesimal sums, but for them it is neither a diversion nor a profession. It is a forlorn hope.

The United States Government, like Mussolini and Hitler, subsidizes the production of children. A pregnant woman client receives from the Emergency Relief Bureau a food allowance of $5.25 semi-monthly, instead of $3.85 granted to a woman who is not pregnant. The bounty of $1.40, however, evidently does not suffice to tempt the women of the block. The birth rate in Negro Harlem is one of the lowest in the city—about 90 births to every 1,000 women, compared to a general average of 130 for Manhattan, and of 150 for a neighborhood like Bushwick. On this particular block, the rate is far below the Harlem average. Few of the children on the block are infants. They are an active, noisy bunch. During the summer, the street is closed at both ends and used as a play street. During the fall, the children play as if it were still closed.

The adults, although not gay, are gregarious. All through the good weather they stand out on the sidewalks and cluster around the doorways, surveying their neighbors with quiet gloom. The first frost in the air sends everybody indoors, behind closed windows.

"The block is progressing from worse to worse," I was told by Mrs. Pearl Hankinson, a vast, scolding, chuckling mulatto woman who lives at 124 West 143rd. "Every week it is deteriating more and more." She has been watching it for twenty-three years now, about the only old resident left. Mrs. Hankinson's husband is a railroad man, which is the customary Harlem way of referring to a Pullman porter, and he sometimes makes $35 a week. So she doesn't really have to stay on the block. She thinks maybe she's just used to it. Her apartment is as clean and as full of mahogany furniture and embroidered sofa cushions as flats were in the cozy German Harlem that used to be. She scolds, feeds, and consoles the children of the block, and considers herself a civic worker. When she sees uncollected garbage on the street, she calls up the Commissioner of Sanitation. "Don't give me no underlin's or subordinates," she says. "Give me the Commissioner. This is Pearl Hankinson speaking." Sugar Hill friends cannot understand her preoccupation with a block so definitely *déclassé*.

"When I moved in here," Mrs. Hankinson says, "it was just like Park Avenue. White doctors across the street, with their signs right in the window. There was only six houses, counting all four sides of the clock, that took colored people. And over across Lenox Avenue there was nothing but woods with a fence around them, where people would carry their dogs at night. It was a telephone downstairs in the hall, and lights in front of the house, and a clicker on the front door that when you pressed a button up here it clicked, and your friends could come in. And we paid twenty-seven dollars. Then, during the good time, it got up to fifty dollars. And now I pay thirty-eight dollars. And it's all deteriated so it's just falling apart. It seem that every time I look out the window it's more people on the block. And more children. And more West Indians. Moving *in*. Moving *out*. Seem like they knocked down all the stairs just moving. But as soon as one is out, another is in."

For the number of apartments remains always less than the number of potential tenants in Negro Harlem. The district expands slowly, with the more prosperous Negroes always on the perimeter, fleeing the crowding in the centre. A landlord on the fringe of Harlem will turn over a building to colored tenants only when he sees certain profit in the move. As the comparatively affluent Negroes move outward, those behind occupy the apartments which the well-to-do have abandoned, and from that time on, the apartments are generally allowed to deteriorate. For Negroes who are poor even among Negroes, there is no escape from Harlem.

There is a growing colored settlement in south Jamaica about ten blocks from the 168th Street station of the Independent Subway, but this is helpful only to substantial people. There are no apartments. A Negro family coming there has to rent and furnish an entire house, and the supply of houses is limited. The settlement is expanding in the same haphazard manner as Harlem, with colored tenants moving into the old houses as whites move out.

Negro civic leaders talk of a planned low-cost development for Negroes, somewhere along the line of the new subway as it pushes east across Queens, but they say that no private builder will begin such a project. The builders blame the banks, which, they say, will not finance housing for Negroes. The block was once part of a farm owned by James De Lancey, that great Tory landowner who held half New York directly before the Revolution. Afterward it came into the family of one Archibald Watt, and stayed there for nearly a century. It was not until after the Spanish-American War that the speculators and the builders came and began covering the block with its solid layer of stone tenements. Germans, Jews, and a few Italians lived in them first. Negroes got their foothold in Harlem in 1906, when a landlord on West 135th Street accepted thirty-five families of colored tenants. From this focal spot they radiated over Harlem. They reached the block on 143rd Street in 1911. Its occupation was not completed until 1925, when the Rose-Rita, the most pretentious building on the block, surrendered.

The people on the north side of the block are an unenterprising lot. There are a number of hard characters, but they are too low in spirits to walk to a more prosperous neighborhood, where they might find somebody worth robbing. Instead they follow rent collectors, and even relief investigators, into the dark hallways and hold them up. Rent collectors seldom have large sums with them, as they get their money in small installments. Relief investigators are usually as broke as the stickup men. When the landlords put lights in the hallways, the hard characters steal the bulbs.

It would be difficult to find children so completely conditioned to city life anywhere else in the world. They go to schools within a block or two, attend neighborhood movie houses after school when they can assemble the price of admission—which is surprisingly often—and then come back and play on the block until long past midnight. They never feel inclined to walk outside Harlem, or even into a different part of Harlem. Last summer a number of boys on the block planned a camping trip. They spent a month assembling their outfit, which included several cartons of cigarettes; went out into the wilds of Harrison, New York, and came back after one night.

"It thundered and they was frogs in the water that we was supposed to drink," one of them said. "Ain't frogs poisonous?" This boy's parents came to New York from a farming district in North Carolina.

End of a Shop Union

Few newspaper men were unaware of the death struggles of the National Variety Artists' Club. They lasted for three years, and were punctuated by frequent indignation meetings that made fine feature stories. Every city editor knows that actors in trouble are sure fire. "It reminds me

of 'Pagliacci,' " one of my old bosses used to say senti-
mentally.

The N.V.A. was housed in a Doric building on West
Forty-sixth Street that resembled a branch bank. When
vaudeville was the largest American amusement industry,
toward 1915, the club had 11,000 members. Dues were
virtually nominal, for the club was supported from a fund
administered by the chief vaudeville managers. This fund
was replenished annually by benefit performances in a
couple of thousand vaudeville theatres. The clubhouse was
a fine exhibit for the industry, like the Walker-Gordon
stables of contented cows at Plainfield, N. J., or the model
chocolate factories at Hershey, Pa. When vaudeville
slumped, the managers, most of whom had gone over into
motion pictures, tried to get rid of their N.V.A. burden.
After a legal fight that began in the summer of 1931
and ended in that of 1934, they succeeded in evicting
the vaudeville actors, most of whom were by then unemployed. The clubhouse had never been a gratuity from the
management of the industry to the employees. It had been
a bribe to head off effective unionization. I remember talking to some of the old vaudevillians about it on the club's
penultimate day.

"This will be always the finish of every shop union,"
orated Jack McGowan, a monologist out of work, as he
stood with his straw hat under his arm and regarded the
red plush and marble interior of the Club lounge. The
plush was faded, the marble tarnished, the carpet worn
from its pristine thickness and the checker players on the
mezzanine moved their pieces along the board without
energy, even when they "jumped."

"I saw it come to hell in, and I just stopped by to see it go to hell out."

It did not look like the finish of the N.V.A., at least not much more like the finish than it had looked the previous week, and that week it had looked not much more like the finish than the week before. Plush does not fade, nor marble tarnish, suddenly, nor had vaudeville come to any abrupt, spectacular end. Slowly it had worn down, like the carpet.

The men who had dropped in to play checkers annually during the short layoffs between trips over the big circuits began coming around once a month, once a week. Of late you could count on their presence at the same tables every day.

The "single women" and sister acts and jugglers' assistants who had stopped around for mail once in awhile made more frequent calls at the desk. Instead of walking briskly out with their letters they commenced to sit around the big shady room. The membership of the N.V.A. dropped from 11,000 when vaudeville was good to 2,000, yet the clubhouse always seemed full. That was because there was no turnover. When you marched up the marble steps from the street, having been decorously announced by the page, who was a former dramatic artist, you saw the same faces.

They were there on the penultimate day.

"The dark hour is at hand," cried Al (E flat) Edwards, favorably known in minstrel circles as one of the Four Emperors of Music.

"This clubhouse was built by the White Rats," continued Mr. McGowan, disregarding Mr. Edwards. "We were all White Rats, the four of us here," and he waved to Mr.

Edwards, John Gilroy (song writer, acrobatic dancer and first comedian) and Ted Murphy (Irish comedy).

"The White Rats was a performers' union, created to fight for better working conditions. The Vaudeville Trust beat us. We lost our clubhouse. Then E. F. Albee, head man of the Keith circuit, gave us back the clubhouse as a sop. All we had to do to enjoy the privileges was to join the company union. He started the N.V.A. fund, supported by subscription drives in the Keith houses. It looked good to us saps. Then, when they had us eating out of their hands, the theatre men cut the heart out of vaudeville. Instead of playing eight acts twice a day they began playing four acts five times a day, with pictures.

"Also they let the theatre managers cut the acts. Suppose you had an act that ran fourteen minutes. A minute more or a minute less and the whole timing was off. Well, one week you worked on a bill with a long feature. The house manager, a janitor, would make you cut seven minutes. The next week you would be on with a shorter feature. The Siberian calf-stealer would tell you to put in some more business.

"They always gave the picture the best of it, because the theatre owners were producing the pictures. Then when they had knocked the spirit out of vaudeville they dropped it altogether from most of the houses. That saved musicians' salaries and stagehands' salaries. They had the theatre in a can."

"Now that they don't need us," said Mr. Gilroy, a studious-looking gentleman with hair parted in the middle and shell-rimmed spectacles, "they take away the bone."

"Next to actors, newspapermen are the next biggest fools," said Mr. McGowan. "Now that you fellows have an organization, why don't you rent the joint when they kick us out? Then we could come up and visit you. We will feel funny sitting on curbstones."

Frau Weinmann and the Third Reich

Fritz Weinmann, when I first met him, was of the opinion that the Hitler regime might be a good thing for Germany in the long run. While the government doubtless appeared to outsiders to be bitterly anti-Semitic, he said, its animus was directed only against the *Ost-Juden*, postwar Jewish immigrants from Galicia and Warsaw. Fritz, who had been living in New York for ten years, was of a Jewish family that had settled in Frankfurt-am-Main in 1489; he had an engraved *Stammbaum*, or family tree, to prove it. He remembered how, when his father had owned a leather-goods business in Frankfurt, an aggressive *Galizier*, with sideburns, had set up a firm in competition and cut all the prices; so Fritz could not find it in his heart to be angry with his old neighbors. They were just hostile to the *Galiziers* and in their indignation they were saying hard things about the Jews in general, which of course they didn't mean. He said he had had letters from his sister at home telling him how things were, and while she wrote that it was not nice for her children in school, she was sure Germans really liked German Jews as much as ever. That was in March, 1933.

What pleased Fritz about the new regime at that time was the way it had taken hold of the campaign to purify the German language. All words of foreign derivation were being officially exiled: railway tickets would no longer be known as *Billette* but as *Fahrkarten*, telephones no longer as *Telephons* but as *Fernsprecher*. Sporting terms were to be *"Deutscher Wort im Deutscher Sport."* Thus, Fritz said, the wrestling hold internationally known as a hammerlock would thereafter be called, in Germany, *"Ellenbogengelenkschlüssel."* These matters were the chief concern of the Deutscher Sprachverein, the German Language Society, which had now become a semi-official department of the German government. Fritz was the president; "that is to say," he once told me, catching himself in the use of a "foreign-derivated word," "the *Vorsitzer"* of Zweig Neu-York, the New York chapter of the Verein. The good effect of the government's vigorous attitude toward words with Greek roots would, he thought, eventually outweigh the temporary inconvenience of the Nazi regime to the German Jews. They were martyrs to an improvement of idiom.

Fritz Weinmann was a short, slender man, forty-four years old. The top of his head was even with the knot in my tie. He talked rapidly and endlessly, with much gesticulation. He had gentle eyes and heavy black eyebrows which almost joined—a characteristic, he said, which was common to all his mother's father's family, the Schwarzschilds. Fritz, ignoring three of his grandparents, considered himself a Schwarzschild. "In one house, the House of the Red Shield, Rothschild," he like to say. "Next door, the House of the Black Shield, Schwarzschild. It's one of the oldest Jewish families in Frankfurt-am-Main." Fritz was, on a very small scale, in the electrical window-display business, making such things as transparent pictures of coffee cups or cigars with lights flashing behind them. He also occasionally wrote poetry, which was published in the German-American newspapers. However, he devoted most of his time to the Deutscher Sprachverein, Zweig Neu-

York, because there was a great deal of correspondence connected with it.

I first came to visit Fritz because of a letter he had written to my newspaper about the Sprachverein. My city editor was a man who thought that any story with a lot of long, agglutinative German words in it was bound to be funny, and I was the accredited funny-story writer of the staff. Fritz sensed the irreverence in my tone when I asked him to spell out "*Ellenbogengelenkschlüssel.*"

"To you it sounds maybe peculiar a little," he said, "but to a hippopotamus is beautiful the words of a lady hippopotamus. So, to a German, sounds beautiful German."

I was astonished that the members of the Deutscher Sprachverein, Zweig Neu-York, retained a Jew as their *Vorsitzer.* It must place a strain on the relations with the parent society in Berlin, I suggested. But Fritz said that there was nothing political about the Sprachverein in America. It was just a philological and mildly social club. The members saw no reason he shouldn't continue as *Vorsitzer.* The Sprachverein here had lapsed when the United States entered the World War. Fritz had helped to revive it, and in 1932 he had been elected *Vorsitzer.* There were about seventy members, for the most part Gentiles, and they met every Thursday evening at the Blue Ribbon Restaurant on West Forty-fourth Street for *Plauder-Abende* ("chat evenings") conducted in German that was free of all "foreign-derivated" words. They received the monthly bulletin of the parent society, and also special booklets on German words in fashion-designing, musical criticism, sport, *und so weiter.* In all these fields, French and Italian and English words had established themselves in German usage. The Sprachverein rooted them out.

Fritz lived with his mother on the top floor of an old tenement on Greenwich Street, near Charlton. This is a depopulated district, under the "L," where lofts and warehouse now greatly outnumber dwellings. The few tenements that remain, built of red brick in Civil War days, are not popular even with the poor. Fritz therefore had been able to get two apartments, giving him six small rooms and the exclusive use of a toilet, at an extremely low rental. Two other apartments on the floor were vacant, and he had a key to them, too. He also had roof privileges, with a view, between the walls of two high warehouses, of a few yards of the North River. It was practically in Greenwich Village, he explained. He sometimes went to poetry readings in cellars, in his shirtsleeves, or walked the half-mile to Sheridan Square to sit in a favorite cafeteria there. The features of the apartment that pleased Fritz most, though, were the electrical devices which he had rigged up to amuse himself. He could push a button in the parlor of one apartment and make a red light go on in the kitchen of the other, or a green light in the bedroom; or start the electric heater going in the surplus kitchen, which he had fitted out with a bathtub. As for the radio set, which was in one of the parlors, he could select stations on it by turning a dial in any room of the six, and he could talk into a microphone in the toilet and project his voice all around the two apartments. He could switch the radio off and the phonograph on by pushing red and green buttons on his desk.

After the story I wrote about him—it consisted mostly of the longest words I could find in the Sprachverein booklets—Fritz used to call me on the *Fernsprecher* about twice a week and talk until I would be forced to hang up on him. At last, on a dull news day in August, I went back to see him, hoping he might have some new jawbreakers that could be worked into light summer reading. This time Fritz was elated about a new German decree, sponsored by the Deutscher Sprachverein, doing away with variant spellings of Christian names. "If you have a boy in Germany now and you want to name him Auguste or Augustin, or Agosto, or something, you can't do it," he said. "You got to name him Augustus." He seemed to find this admirable. "Here, if you got a boy and you want to name him George Wishington Jones—*Wishington*, mind you, instead Washington—you can do it," he said. "Nobody can stop you. What confusion!"

By that time things were much worse for the Jews in Germany, and I asked Fritz if he still thought that Hitler was not really anti-Semitic. He said it was taking longer than he had expected to clear up the misunderstanding, but he was sure everything would be all right soon. It was just that Hitler didn't understand how different the German Jews were from the *Ost-Juden*. After all, Hitler was an Austrian.

"My grandfather, Salomon Schwarzschild, wrote a book of patriotic poems about the War of 1871 and donated all the royalties to the war veterans of Frankfurt," Fritz said. "Myself, I have written poems in the *Staats-Zeitung*. When German sounded foreign in our ears, how could we have written poetry? How can anybody say we are a foreign race?"

He conceded, though, that he was having his troubles barring the Aryan question from the *Plauder-Abende* of the Sprachverein. Some of the members were importers. They feared the German end of their business would suffer if it became known in Berlin that they belonged to a *Zweig* with a non-Aryan *Vorsitzer*. "You understand, Herr Weinmann," they told Fritz, and he told me, "it isn't anything personal, but don't you think maybe it's more appropriate we pick somebody else?" But Fritz said that he wouldn't resign. Then the parent organization, which had always, even before the Nazis, provided a small monthly subsidy for stationery and stamps, had ordered Zweig Neu-York to abolish the weekly meetings and hold only one a month, in order to quarter the expense of sending out notices. Some of the members said that economy was not the only motive behind this order. With an Aryan *Vorsitzer*, the weekly meetings might have been encouraged.

It was on my second visit to Fritz's home that I met his mother. She had been calling on a neighbor the first time I went there. Frau Weinmann was sixty-eight years old, Fritz told me after introducing us. She was studying English at night school. Her spelling lessons, which she showed me, were marvels of Continental calligraphy, if not of English spelling. Neither the four flights of steps to reach the apartment nor the dismal neighborhood troubled her, she said. Life in America was like a continuous picnic with her little boy. Frau Weinmann's most awesome attribute, in Fritz's eyes, was that she had been a Schwarzschild, an *echte*. She was a merry woman, with a large, soft nose, a sensitive mouth, and the close eyebrows Fritz had taught me to expect. She wore spectacles with silver rims, a black silk dress, and large black beads. A character actress would have chosen exactly the same costume for the part of a *gemütlich* old German woman.

Like her son, Frau Weinmann enjoyed talking. Her English was not good, my German was worse. She wondered how I could have been so ill taught. She had come over to join her son in 1931, for some financial reason that she did not make quite clear. She wondered that our branch post offices were so shabby, our side streets so inadequately lighted, and everything so dirty everywhere. We drank many cups of coffee and ate a great deal of cake. I liked her very much. The little spread reminded me of a child's tea party. Fritz ate the sweet cakes greedily. "In my mother, the Schwarzschild penchant—excuse me, *Fühlung*—for art is expressed in cooking," he said, after he had wiped the crumbs from his mouth. "Such coffee cake you don't get anywhere in New York, I assure you."

Frau Weinmann was less optimistic than Fritz about affairs in Frankfurt. Her daughter wrote her sad letters; she could read between the lines. She wished she could bring her daughter and grandchildren here—the daughter was a divorcée—but there was not enough money. What money her daughter had in Germany, the Nazis would not let her bring out with her. Frau Weinmann looked mournful for a moment, and Fritz shouted, to change her mood, "The members call Mother the Mother of the Sprachverein! Such cakes she bakes for them!" Frau Weinmann smiled again, rather uncertainly.

For a long while I didn't hear from the Weinmanns, or think much about them, either. Then, one morning early last February, I was looking through a *Herald Tribune* and saw a small headline:

MOTHER DESPAIRS OF VISIT
FROM DAUGHTER, KILLS SELF
HOPED GIRL LIVING IN GERMANY COULD
EMIGRATE HERE

Something familiar in the situation made me pause, "How like Frau Weinmann," I thought. Then I read the story, and it was Frau Weinmann: ". . . committed suicide by gas in the kitchen of the apartment at 550 Greenwich Street which she shared with her son Frederick, a writer. She was seventy-one years old. The Weinmann family, her son explained, is one of the oldest Jewish families in Germany." Fritz must have said "Schwarzschild," I reflected. Careless reporting. Then there was a paragraph about the daughter—practically what Frau Weinmann had told me before. Things must have got worse in Frankfurt, I thought. Frau Weinmann must have had some more sad letters.

Several days later Fritz called me up. "I suppose you read the newspapers," he said. "The tratchety? You read about my mother?"

I said that I hadn't, ashamed that I hadn't got around to calling him first.

"Dead!" Fritz said. "Dead! Suicide!" He sniffled, like a kid trying to say something through tears. "It was in all the papers. She couldn't stand it any longer. From now on it's between me and Hitler. I show no mercy. I want to talk to you about the campaign I make."

He said he had moved from Greenwich Street, and gave me his telephone number. I promised to call him in a couple of days. He said the campaign needed publicity. When I called him, the girl at the switchboard—it seemed to be a hotel—said he had moved again, and when I called his new number, I was told that he had gone to Atlantic City. I let the search drop. It wasn't until last month that I accidentally met him again, on Sheridan Square, and he insisted that I go home with him.

Fritz was now established in a one-room-and-kitchenette in one of the big apartment houses on Christopher Street. He had installed his trick radio set, a forty-volume annotated edition of Goethe, and a portrait of his mother in a red blouse, painted from a photograph. The campaign he was waging against Hitler seemed to me at first to consist of sending typewritten copies of his own poems to expatriates like Thomas Mann and Professor Einstein. He showed me their letters of acknowledgement, which were all very gracious. "They are fighters, too," he said proudly.

Frau Weinmann had killed herself to make it possible for her daughter to come here, Fritz told me. One of Frau Weinmann's brothers, a wealthy hide merchant in San Francisco, had died several years before, leaving a trust fund equally divided between Fritz and Fritz's sister, with the provision that Frau Weinmann was to have the interest on the fund as long as she lived. She had been living on this income in the United States. But since the divorced daughter in Frankfurt had not prospered, Frau Weinmann had been sending back as much as she could spare of her income every month. That was why she had insisted that she and Fritz live in the cheap tenement on Greenwich Street. After the Nazis attained power in Germany, Frau Weinmann had wanted the daughter and her two children to come here. But the Nazis, having learned in some way that the daughter was heiress to an estate in America, refused to let her go until the estate had been transferred to her in Germany.

Then the German State could collect the inheritance tax, plus twenty per cent of the remainder as a fee for permission to emigrate. It meant, Fritz said, that the German government would receive at least three-quarters of the

San Francisco uncle's bequest. Even that wouldn't have been so bad, Frau Weinmann had thought. But while she lived, neither she nor her daughter had any control over the principal of the trust fund. Only her death could free that. "She had a very logical mind, my mother," Fritz said. "The strange part is, though, that now my sister doesn't want to leave Frankfurt anyway. She says she knows she would be unhappy in any foreign country, and she is unhappy there already, so what is the use to move?"

Fritz's appearance had changed a good deal. He had got tremendously fat below the waist, and his face looked sunken and gray. Since Frau Weinmann's death, Fritz had come into his share of the trust fund and had made a trip to Europe. Being an avowed enemy of Hitler, he hadn't dared to enter Germany, of course, but he had learned, from a cousin in Holland, of his sister's decision not to leave. The cousin sometimes travelled to Germany on business, and had a chance to talk to the sister.

I asked Fritz about the Deutcher Sprachverein, Zweig Neu-York. He said that a few months after our last conversation, the parent society had stopped the monthly subsidy. Zweig Neu-York had carried on for a brief period as an independent body, but a good many members had quit. Those who came to the meetings insisted on talking politics. So the Zweig had disbanded. "Maybe it wasn't the right time for a philological society," Fritz explained.

"Anyway," he said excitedly, "I have no time for such things now. I am an anti-Nazi-front fighter. I fight. We got to make propaganda it shouldn't happen here. Last week I was in the men's room of a restaurant on Seventy-second Street and I saw swastikas drawn in pencil on the walls.

I ran upstairs and told the proprietor. He sent a man right down to wash the walls."

The discovery of the swastikas, however, had been extra-routine. Fritz's principal method of combat, he explained to me, was more subtle. As I have said, Fritz writes German verse. He is moderately proud of one composition called *"Höll, Hitler,"* which means "To hell with Hitler!" But political satire is not his forte. He writes lyric poems of four classifications, which he listed for me. The first is *"Lieder, die Leuchten,"* or "Songs That Shine." They are pure lyrics. The second is *"Wir und die Tiere,"* or "We and the Beasts," rhymed satires in the style of LaFontaine. The third is *"Wir und die Welt,"* a philosophical series; and the fourth is *"Der Ritt auf dem Pegasus,"* long, heroic poems.

"These poems I send to the Chicago *Abendpost* or the *New Yorker Staats-Zeitung,*" he said. "Why? Because they are the only American papers that get into Germany, in the public libraries. So when people there read my beautiful poem, they say, 'Who writes it?' and they look at the signature. 'What?' they say. 'Weinmann? A Jew? But Hitler says a Jew can't write something good. This is good, so Hitler must be wrong. He's a liar.'"

I told Fritz that this seemed like a circuitous method of attack on a dictator, but he said that I didn't understand the situation. "The German people, they aren't really against us," he said, "if they only knew the truth. To illustrate what I mean, I give you an example. I was coming back on the boat from Amsterdam to London, and it so happened that the other man in my cabin was a German newspaperman. He thought at first I was English, but after a while I began talking German to him and I told him who I was, and that my family had lived five hundred years in Frankfurt-am-Main. 'Now tell me,' I said to him, 'we are only two here in the cabin, *unter vier Augen,* and nobody can hear us—really, do you think I am of a foreign race? Do you hate me?' He said, 'No, really, I don't.'

"So," Fritz said happily, "you see, in their hearts the Germans got nothing against us."

Thou Good and Faithful

About as fine a murder as we have had back home was that of Edward Albert Ridley, a loathsomely rich old man, in a basement under a building on Allen Street on May 11, 1933. Ridley was the last survivor of the firm of Edward Ridley and Sons, which in the nineties had been one of the great department stores of New York. The Ridleys had liquidated their business in 1902; they owned a great amount of property on the lower East Side. The neighborhood was no longer good for retail trade, but old unkempt buildings could be turned into tenements and flats could be rented to the Eastern European immigrants for whatever a landlord chose to demand. Edward Albert Ridley moved his office down into the basement, which was so dark and fetid that it was impossible to rent even to immigrants. He kept office hours there for thirty years, shabby, whitebearded, mean-tempered, one of the richest men in town. In New England he would have been considered a quaint local character.

He had a secretary named Herman Moensch, whom he had had with him from the old store days. In 1931 Moensch was found in the basement, shot to death. Nobody ever found out who had killed him. Old Ridley got a new secretary, a slim, neat young man named Lee Weinstein. Ridley's eyes were very bad; he wouldn't pay for new spectacles. So he could hardly see the papers offered to him for signature. Weinstein, young and active, looked after the details of most of Ridley's deals. Then in 1933 police found Weinstein and Ridley dead in the burrow. Weinstein had been shot with the same revolver that had killed the former secretary, Moensch. Ridley had been beaten to death with a club. There was a will in Ridley's desk. By its terms Weinstein was to have received $200,000, which was pretty fair recompense for two years in the old Harpagon's service. The sum of $2,500 was left to a man named John Meisinger, an inmate of a home conducted by the Association for Improving the Condition of the Poor, near Red Hook in Dutchess County. Meisinger had worked for Edward Ridley and Sons for thirty-six years, and when the will was published he was almost eighty years old. He had been the general buyer, what would now be called the merchandise man, in the store. It astonished most people that Ridley had remembered him at all.

A few days after the murder the detectives made an important discovery. Edward Albert Ridley had not made the will, although he had signed it. Arthur Hoffman and George Goodman, a pair of accountants, admitted that they had assisted Weinstein in the preparation of a false will. The near-sighted old man had signed it under the impression it was a tenement lease. Hoffman and Goodman went to jail for fraud, but the three murders have never been solved. On the day after the story of the false will appeared, I went up to Red Hook to see John Meisinger. It had seemed strange for Ridley to remember him, but it seemed positively fantastic for the embezzlers to have done so. Ward Manor, the A. I. C. P. home, is a fine baronial place, very refreshing for poor people to die in. Meisinger, who was staying there with his wife, was a precise, chirping, pot-bellied little man. He said he had been suspicious of the will from the beginning.

"Why should he have left $200,000 to Weinstein, his secretary, and only $2,500 to me?" he asked. "Weinstein must have used undue influence. He must have mixed Mr. Ridley up. Mr. Ridley probably meant to leave $2,500 to him and $200,000 to me." He found it impossible to believe that the insinuating and sinister Weinstein had written him in for his $2,500, failing which he would have received nothing at all.

The detectives on the case thought that Weinstein had done this to give the will an air of verisimilitude.

Meisinger said, "There must be another will concealed somewhere with a larger bequest for me. Mr. Ridley always gave me to understand he would take care of me." No other will was ever found.

"When my wife and I applied to enter the home, three years ago," Meisinger insisted, "Herman Moensch, his old secretary, promised that Mr. Ridley would send us each $200 a year for spending money and clothes. You know you are supposed to buy your clothes here, if you can.

"But after Moensch was killed—I remember Herman when he was a cash boy, I was buyer of furniture, crockery, blankets and miscellaneous already—I went to see Mr. Ridley in his office, down where we used to keep the delivery wagons when the store was going.

" 'No, I will not sign anything,' he told me. 'I cannot

make myself responsible for anybody. Go up to the home,'
he said. 'You will be taken care of.'

"Then as I was walking up that long runway to the
street, I met Weinstein. He was a slim man, quite neat and
decent-looking. He asked me what I wanted and I told
him. He went down into the basement and I went on, and
he came back and caught me again before I reached the
street. He must have spoken to Mr. Ridley very quick.
'It's all right,' he said, 'we will send you a check every
now and then.' So after that they did, didn't they, Mrs.
Hunt?"

Parchment-faced little Mr. Meisinger, with his bright
automatic, store-clerk smile, appealed to the superintend-
ent of the hall.

Mrs. Hunt nodded:—

"The checks were always signed by Weinstein," she said.

"But I always used to write to Mr. Ridley, thanking
him," said Mr. Meisinger.

"Perhaps Weinstein opened his mail," suggested the
matron.

"Why should a fellow like Weinstein send me money?"
argued the former general buyer. "If he cared for money
enough to steal it—Did you read in the paper how he took
10 per cent of all the money he paid out for Mr. Ridley on
contracts? Besides the $210,000 he made Mr. Ridley pay
to fake companies.

"I worked for the Ridleys thirty-six years. I started for
$1.50 a week in 1866 when I was 12 years old. It was a
little store at 309½ Grand Street. Albert and his brother
worked in the store and slept in the attic. I used to deliver
packages, hitching on the back of wagons."

The old employes used to call Edward Albert Ridley

'Albert' to distinguish him from the head of the firm, Meisinger explained.

"We had no delivery wagon then, and of course no one would think of giving a boy carfare. I was with them so long that when they wound up the business, people said to me, 'You might have been a very good man with Ridley's but you have been too long in one place.' I was getting $65 a week then.

"In the late sixties I used to take notes for Mr. Albert to a woman on Forsyth Street. That was a good neighborhood then. She lived in a brick house, three-story-and-basement. She was a plain-looking woman, nothing flashy about her. No. I don't know if she was married.

"I never heard of her afterward, and as the years went on Mr. Albert got to be a confirmed bachelor. When I was general buyer and the store covered the whole block, we used to have a joke on new girls in the store. We would send them up to Mr. Albert's office to take him papers, and we would say to them. 'Here's your chance. Mr. Ridley is a rich old bach.' But they would come down saying, 'Say, what's the matter with that guy?' they would say. 'He acted as if he was afraid I would touch him.'

"His office was up in a cupolo, then, windows on all sides, bright and airy, just the opposite of that cellar he moved into when the store closed. I asked him last September why he moved down there underground, and he said, 'Nobody bothers me here.' He wasn't afraid of any-thing, and a wiry man for his age. I bet he found the fellow who shot Weinstein and he grabbed hold and wouldn't let go until the fellow killed him.

"Arthur Ridley was more of a sport. He liked horses, and he lived good, and he bought that house up on 64th

Street near Central Park when there was nothing up there but rocks and pools with wild goldfish in 'em.

"When he married Miss Nelson from the store they didn't feel they was rich enough to set up house; so they lived in a furnished room at first. Maybe Mr. Albert didn't marry the woman on Forsyth St. because he didn't think he had enough money. But afterward he could have afforded any woman.

"I brought the store lots of good luck. I bought a spotted white-and-black wooden horse once and put it up in the harness and lap robe department. It was a sensation, children begged their parents to take them to see Ridley's horse. I started most of them departments in fact. When I went to work they had nothing in the store but millinery, ribbons, velvets, and hosiery—women wore mostly cotton stockings.

"The biggest stroke of luck I brought them was in March, 1888. A fellow failed and they auctioned off a carload of snow shovels. It was so late in the season nobody wanted them and I bought 'em for six cents each. Just my luck, a week later there come the blizzard, and we sold 'em at a handsome profit. Thirty-nine cents, I think.

"It is impossible that Mr. Ridley would do nothing for me."

I never saw poor Meisinger again, but I have heard that the relatives who eventually got the Ridley money voluntarily gave the old man his $2,500.

GETTING BY

The chief industry in my part of the country is getting by. You can get by in several million ways. I know a professional faster and a professional eater, and both were getting by all right when I last saw them. The faster weighs 260 pounds when he isn't working. The eater weighs only 180 pounds. The faster, as you might expect, has to eat a lot when he is laying off so he will be in condition to fast when he gets an engagement. But the eater trains by eating. He says appetite comes that way.

The faster is named Ben Green. He is not a mere passive non-eater. He fasts for fifty days at a clip, lifting a 100-pound weight on the first day and adding two pounds to the lift on each succeeding day, so that on the last morning of his fast he hoists two hundred pounds. He does this to advertise swimming pools and department stores, on the same principle as a flagpole sitter. During the course of each of his fasts Green studies geometry, algebra, chemistry and accounting, and sometimes he sings.

Tony Di Laurentis is the professional eater. I met him when he was doing a stint for Billy the Oysterman's restaurant a few years ago. It was September 1, and Tony was eating a couple of hundred oysters to signalize the opening of the season. After eating the oysters, he was going to meet all-comers in an eating contest.

"Have another dozen, Tony," Billy the Oysterman urged. Billy the Oysterman has a voice like a foghorn and a bluff, hearty, grasping manner.

"Maybe some challenge comes," argued Mr. Di Laurentis. "I don't want to get full before the contests. I don't need to eat these. I just eat them for show how good sport I am."

There is something more ingratiating about a professional eater than a professional faster. Most people are prejudiced in favor of eating. But Green is a more intellectual fellow than Di Laurentis. Mrs. Green is a chiropractor.

It was the economic depression that led Green, like so many others, to discover his talent for fasting. Not directly. It did not actually cut him off from lunch money. But when the laundry he had established in Belle Harbor, one of our most charming suburbs, failed in 1929, he had time to consider his figure. It was shocking, he says.

"At the age of 38 I weighed 278 pounds," he told me once. "I was in a fair way to become a laughing stock.

"I tried dieting and then I tried exercise. Neither seemed to help, so I decided to try both together. One day when my wife called me to dinner in our home at 74 Beach 132nd Street. I put on my hat. 'Instead of eating further viands,' I told her, 'I am going for a nice nourishing twelve-mile walk.'

"I went, and I went to bed afterward without having eaten. The next day I got up feeling fine, and instead of breakfast I took a five-mile walk. For lunch I had a juicy eight-mile hike, and for dinner I ran a luscious marathon on the Rockaway Boardwalk.

"During the fast my wife and I went down to Philadelphia, and on the thirty-seventh day I said I had to return to New York on business. She said I was too weak. My wife weighs 130 pounds, and I picked her up in my arms and tossed her up and down in the air like a rubber ball.

"I went back to New York, and might have continued my fast indefinitely had I not been tempted with a herring. I never could resist a broiled herring with onions. So I ended my first fast after thirty-eight days. I had lost forty-one pounds, but felt improved physically by the reduction of my obesity, and mentally by the absorption of large quantities of algebra, geometry, chemistry and accountancy." The extemporaneous fast was the beginning of a career.

Consuming for Prosperity

Di Laurentis, who like many another worthy fellow is an immigrant from out-of-town, discovered his talent while he was working as a barber in Hatboro, Pennsylvania, where he speedily became known as Old Quicklime.

"I train hard for this contess," he told me at Billy's. "For lunch I take just a steak and a couple of eggs and three or four glasses of whiskey and some fried potatoes. And I walk around the block twice. Yesterday is the first time I eat oysters. I like them fine. No seeds in them. I guess you read about the Lion's Club picnic in Hatboro. I eat 130 apples in 1 hour 34 minutes. You could say I am the most popola fellow in town. This is my first big money shot. I am not nervous. I don't sweat, huh?"

Mr. Di Laurentis was square shouldered and blocky, but not overly fat. He stood five feet eight inches, weighed 180 pounds, and was 37 years old. His black hair was pomaded, and he wore a wristwatch on a gold link bracelet. His jaw was broad at the base and he bent dimes with his teeth.

"Don't tell anybody I do this," he said, as he demonstrated on Billy the Oysterman's favorite ten-cent piece, a family heirloom. It seems somebody had once told Mr. Di Laurentis it was against the law.

"I start in this way to make pleasure to my friends," he stated when asked for an account of his career. "Nine of us went down to Atlantic City once for a picnic. We got plenty dinner, chicken and spaghetti and fruit, and a gallon of wine in the car.

"While they swim, I go back to the car, eat up the nine dinners and drink the wine. They come back, they say, 'You hog!' I say no, to prove I eat nothing, we all go to the restaurant and I eat as much as anybody. Which I did."

"I don't restrain myself unless I got a good competition," said the man who was known in Hatboro, Pa., as The Maw. "I risk my life for my championship. The doctor he say not one man in thousand could eat them 130 apples and live. I don't eat against any bum that ain't eat for three days, maybe. He gotto got a reputation, and been eating regular, like me. You blame me?

"I can make a lot of money if I get the breaks. After I make popola the oyster business, maybe the pork butcher hire me for eat how many pigs I can. Maybe the apple pie business, the spaghetti business, the mozzarella in carozza business, they all need advertising. I got a reputation."

"The man's a wonder!" shouted the oysterman.

"You bet my life," conceded Mr. Di Laurentis.

It is harder to get by as a professional drinker, but I have heard of a fellow who did very well that way. Patrolman Bill Finn of the Poplar Street station, who pounded a beat outside the Brooklyn Navy Yard for thirty years, told me about this fellow. He was a Marine stationed at the Yard. "Whenever any ships was in and men with money to spend," Patrolman Finn said, "this Marine would walk into them sailors' rendyviews and bet anybody there that he could drink a half barrel of beer and eat eight pounds of raw potatoes. He wouldn't drink the beer without eating the potatoes—he thought they brought him luck. He done so well with the betting that he bought himself out of the service and set up his own saloon over on Prospect Street. There was some very talented men in the Navy in them days."

Jongleur

You would not think that a guy could get by as a jongleur nowadays, but I once met one. He was on a mattress under a ticket window at the Yankee Stadium, two nights before the World Series opened. He was one of those first-in-line addicts who show up at big murder trials, bridge and tunnel openings, the six-day bike race and things like that. This was just by way of obtaining *reclame*. The fellow really supported himself by jongling. His name was Stanley Corcoran.

"I turned in early tonight to get me a good night's sleep, so I'd be fresh for the wait tomorrow night," he said, to explain his presence in the hay at 11:30. "I don't suppose I'll get any at all then, waiting in line. Have a seat over there," he invited, with a sweep of the hand toward an overstuffed chair some admirer had planked down next to the ticket booth.

Corcoran paused as the overhead subway roared by.

"Just as I'm getting used to that thing," he said, "the series is actually going to start and pretty soon I won't be able to sleep here no more. I'm doing fine here, too. I brought my blankets from Seattle and a fellow give me this mattress for reciting some poems."

Over by Gate B, in the railed runway leading to another ticket window, William Cunningham, of Kansas City, snored under canvas. Mr. Cunningham who was the jongleur's rival for the honor of leading world series filbert, had spread a tarpaulin over the rails, forming a tent. Cunningham was the first to encamp outside the Stadium gates, awaiting the sale of the unreserved seats on Wednesday morning, but Corcoran said that he had been in town earlier.

Cunningham refused to stop snoring to argue the point, which the jongleur took by default.

"The American public has been slandered," said Corcoran, aroused by an opportunity for business. "There is them that says Americans thinks of nothing but practical things. But it is not so. No matter how hard times is the American people will pay for poetry. I had a job as a railroad section foreman out in the State of Washington. It was a good practical job, but I couldn't make a living at it, because they laid me off.

"I worked my way across the country reciting smokehouse poetry, such as 'The Hoboes' Convention' and 'The Lehigh Valley' for dimes and quarters, and I haven't missed a meal. Of course, you got to have a good memory."

"Say me a dime's worth," I requested. Corcoran evidently expected it.

"Toledo Slim" announced the jongleur, and began:—

"We were seated in a pool hall one cold December day
"Telling jokes and funny stories just to pass the time away,

"When the door was slowly opened and a form walked
slowly in;
"The boys all stopped their kidding when they seen
Toledo Slim."

"How long is it?" I asked.

"About five hundred lines," the merchant of the muses
said. "If you ain't satisfied I'll throw in 'The Shooting of
Dan McGrew.'"

"I think it would be all right if you skipped some," I
suggested, when Slim got to:—

"We were fleet as greyhounds, and were nearly down
the street,
"When a bullet hit me in the leg, and I knew that I was
beat."

"No," said the honest Mr. Corcoran, "I ain't got no
change of the dime." So he went on to:—

"I swore that I would have his life, for the trick that he
had done,
"And I searched the country everywhere, knowing well
my turn would come. . . ."

It was impossible to stop him now. Gehrig could have
stepped to the plate without drawing him from his elocu-
tion. Half an hour later it had reached:—

"One foggy day on Market Street I met him sure as fate,
"He tried to get the drop on me but was a moment late.
"I sent a bullet crashing into my false pal's brain,
"And then I made my getaway, and glommed an
Eastern train."

A milkman rattled by.

"And as he finished talking, from his hip he drew a
gun—
"In a moment came a sharp report. His grafting days
were done."

"Gimme the dime," said the last of the jongleurs. His
head dropped back upon the mattress.

Hi-fo-be-yo

There are some purists in the New York language who
would say that meter reading was not getting by at all.
They would classify it as working for a living. In a larger
sense, however, getting by includes working. The latter
is merely a tough way of getting by.

The least assuming world champion I ever met was a
young man named Rubin Fisher of 214 Broome Street who
had at that date read 146,444 gas meters without a mistake. He had been invited by officers of the Consolidated
Edison Company to give a seminar course for other meter
readers. I always covered those big stories.

"The first point in meter readings," the champion said,
"is to find the meter. This is very easy. If there is a cellar
with three walls clear and the fourth wall stacked to the
ceiling with junk, the meter is on the fourth wall."

Mr. Fisher's usual district comprised Mott Street, Elizabeth Street, Attorney Street, East Houston Street, Spring,
Stanton, his native Broome, Orchard, Suffolk and over
toward the East River. These streets form a kind of ethno-
logical crazy quilt.

In the performance of his duties Fisher had become

quite a linguist. His Chinese vocabulary included the word
for meter reader—a test which would have stumped Con-
fucius. It is, according to the champion, "Hi-fo-be-yo." In
Italian it is "meeta' read," and in Jewish it is "gess men."

The idea that with the coming of the automatic re-
frigerator the meter reader replaced the iceman in the role
of romance met indignant rebuttal by Mr. Fisher.

"In the first place, I am a married man," he said, "and,
in the second place, if you are reading 450 meters a day you
don't have time.

The meters on South Street and West Street are the
hardest to read, he said, because of the tides that flood the
cellars. Every meter reader carries hip boots when working
those books (a book contains from 250 to 400 accounts to be
worked in sequence). Once in a cellar in South Street he
nearly drowned.

"There was a deep hole in the floor of the cellar," he
said. "I couldn't see it because I was up to my waist in
water already."

Wherever a householder keeps a dog the first meter
reader makes a note for the protection of his successors.

"But you don't always know where the dog is," com-
plained the professor. "You might think he is tied up and
he is loose. But dogs are nothing next to one time I went
down cellar in one of those animal dealers. I flashed my
light and there I saw about a dozen six-foot alligators.

"I got out of there pretty fast."

Neighborhoods vary from a meter reader's standpoint.
In Chinatown nobody is ever home at night. On Cherry
Street and Elizabeth Street, where there are many laborers,
nobody is home during the day.

"In a neighborhood like Washington Heights, now," Fisher said, "where there are lots of young married couples, both working and meeting in the evening to eat chop suey and go to the movies, the only time you can catch them in is in the morning.

"A reader sees a lot of things," said Mr. Fisher, sententiously, "but it is none of his business.

"Meter reading is a very interesting business. Ninetynine per cent of the people are O.K. Now and then you get some man who has been working nights, and he raises hell when you wake him up."

The champion was then in the prime of his meter-reading career—twenty-six years old, with eight years of service behind him. He hoped to establish an all-time record of 1,000,000 meters, if a bulldog didn't get him.

He is not a playboy.

"When I get home," he said, "I just like to sit quiet."

The Flying Mail

The innate fineness of the New Yorker is epitomized in Professor Fisher's statement, "A reader sees a lot of things, but it is none of his business." This is perhaps the reason why so few New Yorkers become newspapermen.

A dignified municipal employee whom I remember only as Operative 2,020, Department of Sanitation, once expressed the same world outlook. He said: "If somebody trow someting in a street I turn my eye out. It's no my business. I sweep it up. *That's* my business." A lot of fellows get by as municipal employees who push cans on wheels. A new Commissioner some years ago invited them to submit suggestions for improving the street cleaning service.

"It's too bad," said Operative 2,020, "I guess I never get promote. I tink everyting is a ho kay."

A foreman in the Department could think of one improvement, but not of how to effect it. "I wish I could think of a way to stop the flying mail," he said. "That is what we call it when a window opens right after you have given a block a good polish, and, bing, down comes a bag of slops.

"Why only this morning Dominick had canned this block beautiful. Those older fellows are the best brushmen. They're more methodical. It takes years to get the stroke. And just as he starts to cross Broome Street, a bag of raw chicken guts hits him in the head.

"That was just an accident. People do not aim at us. They save the stuff to throw at policemen. Only sometimes they get tired waiting for a policeman, so they let it go. Last summer I had my coat off and was walking along Suffolk Street in my cap and blue uniform shirt. Suffolk Street is a fish market street with cobblestones. Well, somebody must of took me for a cop."

I could sympathize with the foreman, but I hope the flying mail is never grounded. It is a symbol of the proud spirit of the burghers back where I came from. A well developed flying mail might have saved Germany, the first time the National Socialists paraded. I never see a strutter like Grover Whalen or Bob Moses without thinking of the flying mail and feeling reassured.

Leap No More

Charlie Bell sat on a trunk by one of the entries to the circus ring, watching the elephants.

"Ain't nobody leaped over 'em for twenty-four years

now," he said pityingly. "I don't see how they handle
'em. Nothing keeps an elephant in place like being leaped
over. Makes 'em feel they ain't so big."

The last principal leaper with the Ringling Bros. Greatest Show on Earth cast a sad glance down upon his slap-
stick. Since 1908 the man who jumped over the elephants
had been one of an army of clowns. In that year the circus
abandoned the leaps.

"It's a good show this year," he admitted diplomatically,
"but it's gone soft. Just because a few fellows landed on
their foreheads and broke their necks they gave up the
leaps. But why? Because those fellows was either layout
leapers that was trying doubles or double somersault leapers that was trying a triple.

"That was the way with leapers, an ambitious lot.
Always trying to better themselves. They was always adding another elephant to the line or trying to do an extra
somersault in the air and, naturally, there was trouble. But
how the crowd used to love it!"

Mr. Bell became meditative, assisted by the soft music
to which Tamara does her trapeze act.

"Leaping was an American sport," he said. "It should be
in the Olympic Games. Europeans are all right for balanc-
ing acts or trapeze, but, shucks, they used to leap off a little
springboard on the ground. We used to have a fifty-foot
sloping run, hit the board, with both feet and out thirty
feet, twenty feet in the air, do a double somesault and land
on the tick standing up.

"I could lay a handkerchief on the tick—that was the
landing mat, stuffed with straw—and hit it every time. Of
course, there was greater leapers before me. There was
Frank A. Gardiner, my teacher, who won the gold belt in

the old Madison Square Garden. He leaped forty-two feet over eleven elephants.

"Then there was George Klein, the clown leaper, who wore a big belly. Leaping was infectious. Kids practiced in backyards. Even the musicians in the circus got so they wanted to leap, it looked so easy. I remember a clarinet player once bothered me until I let him go off the board. He went straight up in the air, come down and knocked out his front teeth and he lost his job with the band because he couldn't blow right."

The principal qualification for leaping, according to the last of the leapers, was "good revolution." Strong leg muscles counted, but so did the acrobatic knack of turning in the air. Under canvas the leaper had to consider the slope of the ground.

"You would leap different on a sidehill from what you would on a upslope," said Mr. Bell.

Charlie was the only double somersault man with the show in the 1908 twilight of the art. He was like the lone heath hen of Martha's Vineyard, and the circus management determined to preserve him as the last specimen of a vanished race. Sedulously they kept him away from anything that could be leaped off, and now he is said to be quite sane.

Animal Husbandry: I

There is probably no region in the United States where live stock flourishes in so many different forms as New York City. I have known commercial dealers in yeasts, leeches, rabbits, monkeys and escorts. Our husbandry runs the whole gamut of evolution. A yeast is a plant, but it is not very different from a low-grade animal, and yeast keepers get to thinking of yeasts as people. The man I met riding herd on yeasts was named Hjalmar Winther, an officer of a brewers' academy.

"He is from Berlin," Mr. Winther told me, gently shaking a phial of sugar water which contained a yeast culture, "a type M,—no, a type K." The water turned milky.

"Pure culture," said Mr. Winther. "All the billions of yeast cells of this strain trace to a single ancestral cell. Aristocracy."

If the officials of the Brewers' Academy ever should mix the phials, strange consequences might follow. Within a year Schaefer's beer might taste like Ruppert's, Molson's Ale like Muenchener Augustinerbrau.

Most of the great brewers are constantly engaged in the breeding of pure culture yeasts, colonies of microscopic cells which reproduce with dizzying speed on a diet of unfermented beer.

"As the vats cool impurities creep in," Mr. Winther said. "The wild yeasts from the air, they get in with the thoroughbred yeast.

"If this continued, the taste of the brewery's product would change. So the brewers must renew the strain from the pure cultures they leave with laboratories. A few yeasts in a ten per cent sugar solution like this may be kept at low temperature for five or six years.

"Hansen of Copenhagen hangs on the wall there," continued Mr. Winther. "He developed the pure culture system in 1880. Until then there was, you might say, no studbook. You brewed beer according to the yeasts that happened to be in your district. The Carlsberg Brewery in Copenhagen has the oldest strain of pure culture yeast in the world."

Yeast has affected world history, according to some authorities.

It just happened that the air of England was filled with top-fermenting ale yeasts, while Germany developed lager beer bottom-fermenters. So Britons became ale drinkers. In order to acquire mutton chops to accompany the ale they colonized Australia. In quest of potato chips they conquered Ireland.

The Germans became lager beer drinkers. Needing only pretzels to complete their happiness, they settled Reading, Pa. Recently something has apparently gone wrong with their yeasts.

Animal Husbandry: II

For thirty-five years I. Berkitz has lived on the blood of his fellow-citizens. Mr. Berkitz is a mild, bald man, with a generous stomach and a German accent. He deals in leeches.

"The best leeches come from Germany and Sweden," Mr. Berkitz says. "See what a nice leech," and from a jar apparently containing rubber bands in water he draws one and puts it on his left wrist.

"See how quick it takes," he says fondly, as he pulls the hind end of the leech, which stretches like a piece of chewing gum. "The domestic leech sticks, but it does not absorb. It is no good. It has not nice red and green stripes on the back. Wait."

He pours a liquid on the leech, which promptly lets go.

"Salt water," Mr. Berkitz explains. "The leech is an epicure. If he is not hungry, you put a little sugar water on the skin to coax him. To make him let go you put salt water.

"He is also a social barometer. If prohibition had been a success then there would have been less drunks, less black eyes, less demand for leeches. But no, the leech business was good."

Mr. Berkitz knows how many leeches he sells for work on shiners, because small sizes are used for this work.

"The big leeches are better for rheumatism," he says. "But the American doctors won't use leeches enough for it. They would rather cut or give long, expensive treatments."

You use a leech only once, it seems, because the blood it takes may be infected. That means a constant demand for new leeches. They are especially popular in Germanic sections of the country, like Illinois and Eastern Pennsylvania.

"During the war we could not get German leeches," Berkitz once told me. "I imported some Greek leeches and they were very good, too, but somehow I could not feel at home with them."

Other Germans like to lounge about Berkitz' leech shop and talk to him.

The leeches live in ponds, it seems, and this once reminded Fritz Ritzmeyer, a visitor, of the quaint Old World custom of collecting them by driving an old horse into the water until the worm-like creatures collect on it. Ritzmeyer liked to tell stories.

"But better yet is a nice fat lady," said he. "It 'minds me on Otto Hundschlager, the richest man in my town, Glugglau a. Donnerwetter. The principal export from Glugglau is leeches, blut-egel, we call them. Glugglau leeches are famous wherever the sun sets on a black eye.

"This Hundschlager married a wonderful pretty girl,

it weighed not a hundred pounds. She was so slender like a fairy, with golden hair and blue eyes like heaven und so weiter. But in a couple of years she gets fat like anything, and he is a sad man.

"At last one day he took her for a picnic, with the idea he would thrown her in the water and letting her drown. So he took her to a nice little pond in the woods, and when she had unwrapped nice the pinkelwurst, and also the schlackwurst, plockwurst, teewurst, bratwurst, leberwurst, blutwurst and mettwurst, he pushed her in the water. Instead drowning she could swim and she got out.

"In one minute, would you believe it, she had on her for 10 marks and 45 pfennigs blut-egels. When he saw this, Hundschlager was so happy he could cry. After this he bought her a one-piece bathing suit, and going in swimming every day, she made gradually his fortune."

Animal Husbandry: III

Norman Bernstein, my rabbit breeder, raises mice and guinea pigs, too. He would like to get an AAA crop limitation on all of them, but the rabbits, mice and guinea pigs will not stand for it.

"Over-production broke the price of white mice and guinea pigs," he said to me, explaining why he would not bid on a city contract for 9,000 white mice. "Rabbits, too, although I won't say that we won't throw them a bid on the 1,600 rabbits and 2,000 guinea pigs they want for the hospitals.

"What was the cause of over-production? Over-capitalization, just like among bulls and bears.

"You see a lot of fake small-stock schemes sprang up in the beginning of the depression—small livestock, I mean.

The rabbit racket, we called it. Companies with impressive names—the Pink Eye Imperial Universal Rabbitries, or such names—started out selling individuals say ten rabbits or ten mice for breeding.

"They picked mostly on people who were out of work but who had some savings. They would sell these people ten rabbits with a hutch and one month's food for $500 or $300 or whatever they could get. Then the company would give a contract to buy back all the future rabbits at a fancy price.

"Well, at first they would buy back a few rabbits. The rabbits they bought back at 32 cents a pound, say, they would plant on new suckers at $500 for ten. It was like the Ponzi business. Then they would begin to shut down, buying the rabbits back at market prices, 14 cents a pound, say, but not cash. They would dump those rabbits in the market by the thousands, breaking the price to four cents a pound and grab the cash.

"So all over the country there are too many white mice, too many guinea pigs, too many white rats, too many rabbits.

"The millionaires who used to endow research foundations every time their wives had birthdays have quit, so there is less demand for laboratory animals. That is why I expect mice may go for a nickel on these sealed bids for the city."

The Breeder Co., Bernstein's firm, occupies a barnlike, white-washed building which resounds with the continual "eek, eek," of cavies (the correct name for guinea pigs) and mice. Even with the checked production, there are about 10,000 mice, 1,000 rats and 1,000 cavies and rabbits in stock.

There is a large white Angora cat, which feeds on mice. Not the 15-cent-straight mice, but the house mice who appear at night.

"They carry mouse typhoid," Mr. Bernstein explains. "They might start an epidemic.

"We don't need the city's business," he said. "We got quality customers like the Rockefeller Institute and hospitals all over the East.

"Kill Mrs. Horowitz today, Jerry," he directed a helper. "How is Mrs. O'Shaughnessy?

"You see," he explained, "doctors come here to make tests on rabbits.

"They inject the rabbit with urine taken from a patient and in a certain number of hours they know from the condition of the rabbits' ovaries whether the patient is pregnant or not.

"Naturally, we can't afford to get those rabbits mixed or it would come out that one woman was going to have a baby when, as a matter of fact, she had some kind of other trouble altogether. So we put each rabbit in a separate box labelled Mrs. Grossman or Mrs. Schmidt, according to the patient's name. Then we refer to the rabbit by that name as long as it lives, which is not so long, of course."

Animal Husbandry: IV

Henry Trefflich advertises in Billboard, the show business weekly, as The Monkey King.

Medicine show doctors, managers of amusement parks and up-and-coming administrators of filling stations and roadside hot dog stands, lease monkeys from him. The organ grinder trade unfortunately has fallen off to virtually nothing.

Mr. Trefflich will rent out any kind of a monkey, but he propagandizes for the Indian rhesus.

"The rhesus is the most human monkey, the friend of man and his closest imitator," he declares. "But if you prefer a ringtail, or a baboon, or a pigtail monkey, maybe that is a matter of taste and we will rent you one to suit." Terms on a macacus rhesus for restaurant lobby or show window use are $10 a day, fee in advance, plus a deposit of $20.

"When you want a monkey for all summer, that is a transaction," said Mr. Trefflich. "You pay us $15 for the average monkey, and at the end of the season you turn him in and we refund 40 per cent.

"Any monkeys born while you have the parents, we buy them each and every one at the same rate. You could have the use of the monkey all season and make money. But if you lose the monkey, that's the end."

Mr. Trefflich specializes also in pythons for snake oil shows. Lucknow, India, is the wholesale center for pythons and rhesus both. Trefflich imports large shipments.

"A chimpanzee I wouldn't rent," he says. "If you want a chimp, I import him from Africa in three weeks, but only if you want to buy him. Orang-utangs and gorillas is out. The Dutch government in the East Indies has an embargo on export orangs, and the Belgians in the Congo won't ship any gorillas. Gibbons we can get, but there is no demand."

George Wohlstadt, another dealer, will rent a chimpanzee any time, however.

"Of course you have to deposit the full price," he said. "On a chimp like Mae West, there," and he gestured toward a two-year-old female who leers at visitors, "I would want five hundred deposit. And fifty for the evening."

Wohlstadt is a ringtail booster. "The cleverest and gentlest of monkeys," he says. "There is something Oriental about a rhesus, but a ringtail—you feel at home with him right away. He is like one of the family. He is an American, just like you and me."

Trained monkeys naturally come higher than the unskilled.

Trefflich, a pale, blond young man who inherited the business from his father, gets as high as $50 for a rhesus that will use a knife and fork and ride a bicycle. But he prefers to sell them unbroken.

"The minute you have to keep a monkey a month or so and feed him, the profit is gone," he said. "Besides, there is always a chance you lose him."

He is a great friend of the pigtail monkey and the giant rhesus from the Naga Hills.

"The pigtail is a one-man monkey," he said. "So is the giant. They are ideal bodyguards. I had a couple of pigtails in my place up at the Bronx as watchdogs. But the African green, a very beautiful monkey, you can't trust ever."

People often ask Mr. Trefflich why, when a theater can buy a monkey outright for $20 it costs $10 to rent one for a day.

"Because, if the monkey bites a couple of children, or pulls off an old lady's eyeglass, we are responsible," he said. "We own the monkeys."

We also have a fellow named Ted Peckham who conducts an Escort Service, renting out male escorts for an evening. This, in my opinion, is merely an extension of Mr. Trefflich's business.

Animal Husbandry: V

Even the Mexican jumping bean experiences machine competition.

A vendor on Nassau Street displays a tray of weighted red and blue capsules which when he shifts his tray leap end over end like well-kicked footballs. The tray bears the inscription, "Mexican Jumping Beans," and the price is three for five cents, underselling the imported article, which retails two for five.

But David Mayer, importer and popularizer of the jumping bean and its compatriot, the tarantula, says that the genuine article, the Brincadore Mexicano or Sebastiana pringlei, need fear no celluloid capsule with a buckshot inside.

"To a nature lover a piece of celluloid has no soul," Mr. Mayer declared. "Inside the genuine Mexican bean, of which in some years I have sold 35,000,000 to nature lovers all over the United States, there is a nice, interesting worm. I have had an individual bean which lived five-and-a-half years without feeding—that is to say, the worm lived.

"I have had a bean which leaped six and seven-sixteenths inches. I had another bean which could do seven inches in practice, but it could never do it in an official meet. It lacked competitive spirit.

"The artificial jumping bean, on the other hand, is inanimate and inert unless you give it a push. It cannot get off the ground under its own power. It is a fraud, devoid of scientific interest."

Mr. Mayer, who is broad and benevolent of appearance, wiped his spectacles, which had become misted by emotion. With his brother, Michael, he has been in the pet shop for forty-two years. They specialize in embalmed cats for scientific institutions, and David used to go on the road with a troupe of trained tarantulas (he once had one sixteen inches in diameter) to exhibit in drugstore windows. Occasionally a tarantula would fly away. He says they fly like mantises. Mr. Mayer would be too busy to go looking for it.

"In cool weather like this the Mexican bean hibernates," said Mr. Mayer. "That is to say, to get good results you should carry the beans in your vest pocket for a couple of hours. When you feel a gentle tickling you know the beans are warming up.

"In Mexico," added Michael, "they grow on trees, and people eat them like snails—a delicacy."

"We invented the hand-painted turtles, too," said David with pride. "We took small Florida turtles and stencilled mottoes on the back, like 'God Bless Our Happy Home.' They were a sensation at the Century of Progress.

"I have even sold those Moroccan snails, which some Italians eat, as Oriental novelties, for 10 cents apiece, and done very well with them."

He paused to brush a few fleas over a stuffed dog to give the final touch of authenticity.

"But these buckshot jumping beans, now, that is a fake," he said.

Animal Husbandry: VI

Miguel Roginsky is a reliable man.

If he sells you a black jaguar the color will not run, and

when he shows you a "mother of ants" snake he points out that it hasn't two real heads—just a head and a knob in its tail.

When in New York he lives on East 61st Street, and if you can speak a bit of French or Russian or German or Portuguese or almost anything but English he will tell you of his bad luck with electric eels.

"I had sixteen in tins of water on the ship," he said, "and I informed the officers that they were highly charged.

"But such is the scepticism of sailors that when I was not present some of those officers touched some of the eels. It is a peculiarity of the electric eel, monsieur, that when you touch it you cannot let go. The hand closes convulsively, shutting off the eel's breathing and inflicting internal injuries.

"The ship's electrician detached the officers from the eels.

"Unhappily, the officers survived but the eels didn't. So I lost several fine specimens. Then when I arrived in this country I learned that the venaticus, the so-rare fox-dog that I brought here for the Bronx Zoo, had died. *Il etait si gentil,* that dog—he sang like a bird. How I regret his departure!"

M. Roginsky sipped meditatively at his frosted chocolate.

The electric eel, it is a very interesting beast," he said. "For the hunt one wears rubber gloves."

M. Roginsky's home is in Para-Belem, Brazil. He is a Russian who fought in France during the World War. After the war he decided he could get along better with jaguars than with other Russians, so he became a naturalized Brazilian, collecting the animals and fish of the upper

Amazon. Twice a year he visits New York, bringing his acquisitions to an animal dealer.

On electric eels there is no authority of higher voltage.

"The eels live in holes in the bank of the river," he explains. "They come out of the holes to breathe, and by the number of bubbles which show on the surface one knows how large is the eel. By the bubbles one marks the location of the hole, and when the bubbles cease one knows that the eel is in its home again.

"One then enters the water, making sure first that there are no araya on the bottom. Araya are flat fish with barbed bony spikes on their tails. They stick their prey and leave the poisoned dart in the wound. One enters the water, then, and plugs up the entry to the hold.

"Then, from the land side, natives dig down until they find the eel in his lair. They pick him up with rubber gloves and place him in a tin case filled with water.

"The electric eel shocks its prey to death," he said. "It is very instructive to watch, very amusing. It is quite conscious of its power. There is a fruit down there called asai, like a black wild cherry.

"The branches hang down over the river, and the roots jut into the water. The Indians say that the electric eel will swim up next to the roots and turn on the juice until the tree trembles, and the asai rain down on the water. Of course, that is only what the Indians say."

The eels sell for $50 a foot.

The Professor, the Captain, the Prince

To sit on a flagpole, to hang upside down by one's heels, to squawk loudly "Hello, Sucker!" at utter strangers, or to play baseball with Satan on a platform, may seem today actions intrinsically curious. But during the blessed time of late Coolidge and early Hoover prosperity people earned good livings in all of these ways, and none of them was locked up. They more than got by.

It was at the very apogee of that era, in May, 1929, that Professor Alexander Meyer, the Rockerless Chair Rocking Champion of the World, rocketed, or perhaps it would be more fitting to say rocked into fame and a temporary place in the high income class. His feats were chronicled in the daily press; thousands of persons saw him with their own eyes. It is astonishing therefore that some of these same persons when you speak of him today, choose to treat Professor Meyer as a myth. They might as well refuse to believe there existed such persons as Mr. Coolidge, Texas Guinan, or Milton H. Crandall, the dance marathon promoter.

Professor Meyer lives, breathes and eats coffee cake today as in 1929. He performs all these functions in a four-room, fifth-floor walk-up apartment in the Bronx. Last year he sent out cards lettered in his exquisite hand, which is indistinguishable from engraving, announcing the birth to Capt. Emily Meyer, his wife, of "Baby Helen Meyer, first child in seventeen years marriage." This year Baby Helen won first prize in a baby contest at the neighborhood health centre.

Friends calling on the Meyers to congratulate them are greeted by the barking of Prince (short for Prince Kouropatkine) the Professor's dog. Then the Professor himself comes to the door, a well-proportioned athlete just under six feet tall and weighing 180 pounds. He has a rugged, aquiline countenance dominated by expressive eyebrows, and his black hair, pointed with grey like a silver fox scarf, is parted exactly in the middle.

The baby is either asleep or requesting nourishment in her crib in the middle of the living room. Capt. Meyer, if it is after working hours at the corset factory where she is employed, joins in astonished group contemplation of the little phenomenon. Then the Captain, a blonde, deep bosomed, dimpled woman who has reduced to 210 pounds from a 1929 high of 260, goes into the kitchen to prepare coffee.

"I wanted to name the baby Marta," the Professor confides when she has gone out of the room. "She was born on Washington's Birthday. Of course was not born on Washington's Birthday Marta Washington, yet it was kind of nice idea. But the mother liked better Helen. I think she will make goot octeress, becowss she mades very goot cockice. This she gets from me. I make cockice like Ben Turpin."

Before Milton H. Crandall launched his second Madison Square Garden Olympic Dance Marathon in May, 1929, the title of Rockerless Chair Rocking Champion had little significance for the American public. The first Garden marathon, conducted by Mr. Crandall in the summer of 1928, had netted its promoters $120,000. It had included among its officials Bossy Gillis, the noisy Mayor of Newburyport, Mass., Peaches Browning and Mae West, then appearing in "Diamond Lil." It had profited by a skillfully fomented dispute with the Health Department, hinging on the supposed inhumanity of the competition, and had ended in a tie among nine couples after twenty consecutive days of dancing. It was incumbent upon Mr. Crandall to top this effort by providing a more eccentric entertainment for a public which had developed an unparalleled tolerance for goofiness.

As side attractions he had engaged Alvin (Shipwreck) Kelly, a gentleman who sat atop a sixty-foot mast, Art Huffman, another gentleman who circled the Garden twenty-four hours a day, handcuffed to the steering wheel of an automobile, and a selection of winners from Mr. Crandall's own recently-completed talking marathon at the 71st Regiment Armory. The main event consisted of sixty men and women somnolently shuffling over the Garden floor, the women waking fitfully to claw their partners' faces and scream. This was known as "going squirrelly," and gave everybody a lot of laughs.

While Mr. Crandall was still uncertain of the success of his new venture, he received a letter signed "Alexander Meyer, physiotherapist, Mt. Sinai Hospital," which introduced a new giant to the American scene. The letter read approximately as follows:

"Mr. Grandel:—I have been classified as the strongest endurance athlete in the world, having defeated thousands of athletes without a scratch and injuries yet by rocking in a ordinary chair without rockers for from 100 to 500 hours without any stopping. My wife also is a good rocker. You can engage both of our services for $2,000 for your Marathon, which will then be surely a success."

The enterprising but sceptical Mr. Crandall wrote to Dr. Meyer, offering him and his wife $12.50 an hour each, provided that they rocked without any pause during the sixty minutes. They were to sit in ordinary straight legged chairs, swaying forward from the waist to an angle of 45 degrees.

It was thus that Professor Meyer came to introduce

rockerless chair rocking to the American public. The promoter would have done better to close with the Meyers for the flat price of $2,000. They rocked for 108 hours and collected $2,700 for their work. Mrs. Meyer lost 26 pounds.

The Meyers made their debut before a large audience of unemployed comedians, night club chorus girls killing time between shows, winners of beauty contests hoping to be photographed, drunks and shipping clerks out for a good time. It was like a six-day bike race crowd minus the Italians. Their chairs were placed upon a platform overlooking the dance floor, and they met a series of opponents provided by Mr. Crandall, who had discovered instantaneously that a Mr. and Mrs. Johnson of Brooklyn were mixed doubles rockerless chair rocking champions of Latvia, and therefore fitting adversaries for the Meyers. They rocked the Johnsons down easily.

Then the promoter brought against Professor Meyer a galaxy of athletes from the Y. M. C. A. One, appropriately named Bender, Professor Meyer regards as the best natural rocker he ever met. It was the age of gangsters. Bookmakers infested the Garden, taking bets on the endurance of marathon couples, and the rocking also became a medium of speculation.

A sinister personage approached Professor Meyer and offered him $100 to let himself be outrocked by a Y. M. C. A. boy named Palmer. The Professor declined. After a while the fellow came back and offered $500. It was evident he was heavily committed on the rival rocker. He raised the bid hour by hour to $2,000.

"Not if you offered me $2,000 morer," hissed the Professor. "Go away. You are a rockerteer."

"Then," says the Professor, who has a highly dramatic memory, "I seen the judges was against me. When they thought I wasn't looking they slipped a rubber cushion under the end of my opponent, so he would bounce more easier. But in the end he had to give up."

The performance of the Meyers had a hypnotic effect upon the drowsy audience. Once they looked at the rocking the belated Broadwayites could not take their eyes away. Gently at first, then violently, they began to sway in unison with the rockers. Even Mr. Kelly on his mast teeter-tottered dangerously, until Mr. Crandall had to beg the Meyers to rock half time, to avert an accident.

"We stopped because the dancers was getting jealous," the Professor says. "They said unless somebody looked at them they would quit."

Crandall next promoted a marathon at Boston, but there his creditors closed in on him. The Meyers rocked for nothing, despite the Spartan courage of the Captain who rocked for hours upon an exposed nail in the seat of her chair. Due to her construction, she did not become aware of the nail until she had rocked for several minutes, and then she could not stop without breaking her contract. So she gritted her teeth and carried on, winning the undying admiration of her husband when, after the expedition, he viewed her wounds.

The bankruptcy of Crandall did not shut off Professor Meyer's vista of a golden future for rockerless chair rocking. He rocked for 58 consecutive hours on a kitchen chair perched on top of a church steeple at Monticello, Ill., for the benefit of a local fraternal organization. Then for 74 hours he rocked standing up to attract attention to the opening of a swimming pool at 351 West Forty-second St.

This was in competition with Bill Goll, a professional marathon swimmer, who splashed up and down the tank, periodically receiving nourishment through a rubber hose, while Meyer rocked. Goll quit first. For the newsreels Professor Meyer placed a chair on the roof of the Hearst building on South Street, with two legs in space, and rocked on it as long as they pleased. This, he explained, is done by keeping the weight well back while rocking. It is one of his best tricks.

The swimming pool opened early in October, 1929. Everybody remembers what happened later that month. There was no more demand for rockerless chair rocking. The Meyers had invested their money in common stocks. But Professor Meyer never went back to therapy. He has developed a machine called a rockoswayscope. By its means he hopes to extend the benefit of rockerless chair rocking to all. While he works on it he takes care of the baby. Capt. Emily supports the household.

"The rocking chair deteriates the spine," he says. "The chair gets the benefits of the exercise, not the body. My ambition is to knock out the rocking chair."

The rockoswayscope, which he gladly demonstrates, is a red-lacquered, straight-legged chair with a banjo clock rising from its back. There are springs, covered by a leather cushion, on the back of the chair, and every time Professor Meyer, sitting in the chair, rocks his body, touching the cushion, rubber bands attached to the springs jerk the minute-hand of the clock forward one-sixteenth of a space. On the back of the rocking clock is a common clock, and if one rocks correctly, the two should keep pace. One should rock 3,600 times in an hour, and the Professor always does.

He rocks three hours a day to insure a straight spine,

calm nerves and a good appetite. Under normal circumstances, he says, this is sufficient. But when he is making up an invention or a poem, he goes on a regular rocking bender. He then sways with such force that you can hear his bones creak, while a yogi expression forms a film over his face. He says the rocking induces inspiration. The Professor has computed that during his life he has rocked 47,-000,000 times.

"If you had two chairs like this in parlor you would have owlways fun," he says. "Comes it company, you say, 'I show you a little sport. I bet you dollar I could rock morer times as you.' So passes off quickly the visits." His dream is to place rockoswayscopes of chromium steel on all subway platforms, with slots for nickels and attachments to register correct weight and blood pressure.

Although the rockoswayscope is foremost in his mind, it is by no means the champion's only invention. He is the originator of the one-piece four-piece suit, for which he was awarded a prize of $50 by the Daily Mirror, and on which he expects soon to receive a final patent. The garment consists of a dickie, a strip of vest, a jacket and trousers with open side-lattices for ventilation. It is all made together, like a union suit. He cannot see the sense of concentric layers of coat, vest and shirt when only small portions of the latter garments show.

The same unwillingness to take anything as a matter of course marks his approach to music. He does not write new tunes for old media. He invents new instruments, opening entire fields to future generations of composers. In this realm his most notable discovery is the mando-saxophone, an aluminum mandolin with a horn growing out of the seat of its pants. One may strum and blow simultaneously:

for instance "Ach, Du Lieber Augustine" on the mandolin part and "The Star-Spangled Banner" in the saxophone department, producing an unusual effect clearly audible at four miles. He has also created a celluloid violin and a double mandolin which sounds like a wood-wind because a raised deck over the strings deflects the sound vibrations into a hole. He paints frames around his water colors, a trick he shares with Eilshemius. In everything he is the Man of the Renaissance, self-sufficient.

Naturally, rockerless rocking chair champions do not spring full-muscled from the brains of marathon promoters. Experts say it requires at least five years to develop a champion boxer and ten for a champion wrestler. Professor Meyer, who is now fifty-two, has been rocking without rockers since he was ten years old.

He was born in St. Petersburg of Lettish Lutheran parents, tri-lingual Baltics who spoke Russian, German and Lettish interchangeably. His father was master of a sailing ship. He took his son with him on a voyage to the Black Sea, and in Sebastopol young Alex saw certain old Mohammedan sweetmeat sellers squatting in the market place and swaying from their haunches.

"For why you do this?" he asked them.

"This way we grow strength," they replied. "Also, we forget our troubles. We make our bellies small, so we do not feel so hungry. And we stop ourselves to fall entirely asleep, in which case a policeman might steel our *halvah*."

The boy returned to his ship delighted. He began swaying immediately. A couple of summers later he was sent to peasants, in accord with a middle-class Russian theory that city boys should be hardened in the country.

"They puts me out with fifty pieces cows and ships, to

be haird boy," the Professor reminisces resentfully, "and gave me to eat only block braid and boader. And I don't like boader. So to overcome the hungry I began rocking myself."

Other herd boys, observing his conduct, were inveigled into contests. By practice young Meyer had already developed phenomenal loin and stomach muscles, so he always won. This flattered him, so he went about to country fairs introducing his new game. At the end of each summer he returned to the city with regret.

His father was killed in an accident aboard ship, and Alex became a nomad, journeying to the great fairs of Mittau and Nizhny-Novgorod, at which latter place he defeated 80 competitors in a rocking match that lasted 300 hours.

" 'What kind new contest is this?' was asking the mouzhiks," he chuckles. " 'Here is young boy defeating in endurance strongest Roshian wrastlers.' "

But there was not much money in athletics under the Romanoffs, so in 1899 he decided to emigrate to the United States. He lived in a Russian boarding house in Elizabeth, N. J., and worked in the Singer Sewing Machine Company plant at Elizabeth. He earned a little money on the side by playing the violin at Russian entertainments. It did not take him long to discover there was no field for competitive rocking in a country where James J. Jeffries was heavyweight champion and the Baltimore Orioles were playing baseball. Moreover the land was infested with the pernicious rocking chairs.

Rockerless chair rocking was regarded as not merely exotic, but possibly pathological, and since he had no wish to visit a hospital for mental diseases, he ceased to rock in public. But in private he kept it up for his own benefit. This proved to be a break for Holy Russia, when in 1905 he saved the entire Imperial Army from freezing to death on the Liang-chao Peninsula.

"I was owlways a wild young fellow," he says in recounting this exploit, "so when was the war with Japan I went back as volunteer. I was non-commissioned offizier which we call cadet. But the Prince Kouropatkine, the general, was with the monk Rossputztzin hand in hand to make us lose the war. So instett he should lead us in attacking the Japanese, he kept us waiting in cowld and freezing wit'out anytings to eat so we was pretty near debt.

"So then when I saw how it was I said to the men in my squat: 'Come, little pigeons, I will show you an exercise.' So I folded my arms on my chest, put out one foot, and began to rock, so, back and forth."

The result, according to him, was astonishing. His squad emulated him. Soon the motion hypnotized the entire platoon, then the company, the battalion, the regiment, the division, General Headquarters. Click-clack; click-clack; sixty bends a minute. All the way south to Port Arthur and back to Mukden the soldiers swayed, and the baffled Japanese snipers might as well have been shooting at nigger dodgers. So the frostbitten paladins escaped cold and bullets. Like most true history, the incident is unrecorded, but the Professor recalls it vividly.

Of his dog, Prince Kauropatkine which is nine years old and like the Meyers a native of Russia, the Professor delights to report remarkable traits. He says Prince is the only thoroughbred Blue Snooper in America. That is the way he understood the name of the breed when he first heard it. Although he has been told that he should say blue schnauzer, he sticks by his version.

"He is blue and is owlways snooping around," he says.

Prince in shape and coat resembles a cairn terrier, but latterly he has developed a high crest of wiry gray hair over his skull. His most remarkable quality, according to the Meyers, is his tact. Thus, if an indelicate guest should palm a silver spoon or fork—this has happened to the Meyers, they are sorry to say—Prince would not embarrass the crude person by barking. He would wait until the guest took his leave, and then follow him out into the street. Mutely, unobtrusively, he would follow the fellow, until the culprit turned around. If the reminder produced no effect, Prince would follow him some more. Once he was away from home six weeks, but the Meyers got the purloined spoon by mail.

Alex returned to the United States from the war and became a citizen. He attended a special course at Johns Hopkins and learned hydro-therapy and electro-therapy, by which he maintained himself comfortably for years, rocking and inventing in camera. Shortly before the World War he made another trip to Russia, this time as a rich American. It was then he met his present wife. After the Armistice he sent her money to come to America, but he did not know she would arrive a commissioned officer. Emily had, in fact, become a captain in the Kerensky Battalion of Death. She says it never did any fighting, just guarded railroad stations. She is one of the best-natured and most powerful women in New York. The difference between her own grade in the Russian army and her husband's has never made the slightest difference in their relations.

She is an excellent housekeeper, knowing for example that it costs exactly $7.66 a week to feed her menage, including Prince Kouropatkine, and that the upkeep of the baby amounts to precisely $1.25 of this total. She earns a fair salary in the corset factory, and supports the family during the Professor's efforts to launch the rockoswayscope commercially.

The Captain admires the Professor's superior erudition. Her naivete amuses him. They are a model of compatibility. Thus they were discussing the other evening one of the Captain's former employers, a cake-vending company that went into bankruptcy.

"I could see it coming," said the Professor. "They were lavish."

"So?" exclaimed the Captain in benign wonderment. "I thought they was Irish."

Albertus Magnus and Mr. Wehman

One can even get by in New York by publishing educational books, which proves that people still read back here where I came from.

Frank Wehman, says that the "Sixth and Seventh Books of Moses," "Albertus Magnus, the Approved, Verified Sympathetic and Natural Egyptian Secrets," and "Pow-Wows, or Long Lost Friend," still are best sellers across the counter in his shop and publishing house at 153 Park Row.

"Of course, they have never sold over a short stretch like our 'Bartenders' Guide,' did during the three months after repeal," Wehman says. "That number remained pretty dead for years, and then with repeal it jumped into the best-seller class. Our books of toasts also made a great comeback.

"But the interest in black magic is constant. It does not vary from year to year. Why, only last week a woman was in here to ask me for a book containing specific instructions on how to sell her soul to the devil. Said she had nothing else to hock.

"Then there was the convict in Louisiana who wrote that he was to be hanged in two weeks, and wanted us to ship him, postpaid, special delivery, a book with a charm he could use to prevent the rope breaking his neck. And the wife in Texas, who wrote that she and her husband got along fine, but his family always made trouble, and would we please send her a charm to get rid of them."

Wehman is not an adept in black magic, any more than he is an expert on how to be a detective, or clog dancing in ten lessons, but the firm has sold the paper-bound books ever since 1876, along with manuals on mending broken china, French self-taught and "Bones, His Gags and Speeches." Most of the books are reprinted again and again from the plates of volumes compiled by his uncle, Henry Wehman, the founder.

"The 'Book of Love-Letters for Ladies and Gentlemen,' and the 'Book of Flirtations' have a steady sale," said the publisher. "But it is mostly a mail-order business now. The telephone has killed the love-letter business in the city. But we get a great many orders from the British West Indies and from the Gold Coast and Nigeria, where they appreciate flowery writing.

Mr. Wehman offered a sample, headed "From a Gentleman to a Lady, Declaring his Love":

"My dear Miss Rogers:—Ever since the day I was introduced to you my mind has been so filled with the one idea of yourself, and my whole soul so absorbed by the passion of love, that my thoughts have been completely distracted from daily pursuits."

"It goes on like that," he said, "and here is the answer:

"Dear Sir:—I was not a little surprised at the tenor of your letter of yesterday, and while I am deeply sensible of the ardor and earnestness of your passion, I think the acquaintance you have with me is so slight that it is possible a closer intimacy might produce an alteration or modification of your sentiment."

The "Book of Flirtations" contains directions for postage-stamp, handkerchief, hat, glove, fan, eye, parasol, cigar, pencil, whip, window, dining-table and lovers' telegraph flirtations, as well as the language of jewels, the language of flowers, and a selection of Ingenious Letters with Double Constructions.

The language of flowers is sometimes precious, as "I hope you may be happy and offer you pecuniary aid," which is expressed by a bouquet of flowering almond, volka-menia and calceolaria. "I weep for your indifference and am melancholy on account of your coldness," may be conveyed by a simple bouquet of purple verbena, mustard seed, dead leaves and agnus castus.

But even the book repertoire is not sufficient for the Wehman mail order customers.

"I got a letter from a farmhand in Arkansas," said the bookseller, "who said he had read all the kinds of flirtations in the book, but what did it mean when the hired girl stood on the back porch and waved a tablecloth at him?"

"Aunt Sally's Policy Players' Dream Book," justifies two printings a year of 5,000 copies each, even although it is in direct conflict with another best seller. "Policy Pete's Mutuel Number Dream Book." If you dream of your wife, according to "Aunt Sally," you should play number 29. Policy Pete says 128. Mr. Wehman says he gets favorable reports from users of both books.

The most familiar volumes published by the House of Wehman, however, are the seventy-two joke books sold by five-and-ten-cent stores.

There are Irish, Jewish, Scotch, Hobo, Married Life, Darkey and Laughable Jokes, among others in this famous series, and none of them has been revised since they first were compiled thirty, forty or fifty years ago.

"Jokes get better with age," said Mr. Wehman, "and also, there are no new jokes, so what is the use? The demand for joke books has risen tremendously in the last few years. We sell them to the authors of radio programs."

International Banker

Crime was never my specialty when I was a reporter. Editors didn't think there was any Hildy Johnson in my blood. Once I went to the Tombs to interview a confidence man named Stewart Donnelly, but he turned out to be an international banker, so I turned him over to the financial editor. Donnelly had been a pretty fair lightweight out of Indianapolis, and it made me sad to find him in a racket like banking. He was brazen about it, however. "I am an international banker," he said. He did not appear to think it discreditable. He was a square-shouldered, compact little man who had given the warden as his permanent address "the Ritz, Place Vendome, Paris."

"I am a financier," he told me as he looked out through the wire mesh of the visiting room. "That is why they connect me with $150,000 worth of swindles that I don't know anything about. I have made thirty-five round trips on first-class passenger ships.

"What kind of a bank did I run, a faro bank?" The "financier" indulged in a well-bred laugh. "I should say not. Too risky. No, I just banked money. I made a great deal when the franc broke in 1926 buying francs at two cents and holding for the rise. Then they send two detectives to bring me back to the United States in connection with a $16,000 swindle five years old.

"Now I hear they want me in Montreal because a Los Angeles lieutenant of detectives lost $22,000 in a race tipping swindle two weeks after I had travelled in the same plane with him as far as Chicago, when he was coming home from Ireland.

"Just because I was in the same plane! When I knew he was a detective, of course that predisposed me in his favor, but I see I should never have spoken to him. He just didn't belong.

"It's like Al Capone, a fine fellow, a gentleman, a stand-out. He only went out of his way to help people, and what happened? As soon as anything went wrong he got the beef. That is to say," the banker corrected himself hastily, "suspicion was pointed in his direction. You can't make that too strong about Capone. I want him to know how I feel about him.

"As to that rumor that I had some of the Lindbergh money, it horrified me. Why, everybody knows I am too smart to touch that kind of money. Why, if I were outside and somebody accused me of such a thing I would recall some of my old boxing prowess to resent it.

"It all started because somebody said that Charlie Mc-

Cord had some of that money, and I know Charlie Mc-Cord. He is an international confidence man. I have to know all sorts of people.

"But Charlie would never touch anything like that, either. Why, at Scotland Yard in London they refused to question him! They said:— "We know Charlie; he's a bit of all right, an international confidence man." He wouldn't do anything so crude.

"It's too ridiculous. Please say that I am very disgusted. And remember to boost Capone. You say that there are no marks on me for an old fighter? Well, I always knew how to keep out of trouble."

The international banker stroked his moustache with some slight complacency. His voice is high and seemed a little tense.

"I had 267 fights and lost only seven. Yes, a lot of them were no-decision. I knocked out Rudy Unholtz, the South African Boer, in one round, Ad Wolgast in three, in 1916.

"How is it, if I am a banker, I just finished fifteen months in prison in France? Why, the French police got to fighting over my profits. You see, whenever an international confidence man, that is, a confidential banker, makes a profit in France he has to cut the police in. Well, I made $100,000 and they cut it so many ways there was nothing left for me. So to shut me up they stuck me in jail. And what a jail. They take your money but they give you the worst of it just the same.

"It is positively mediaeval. It reminded me of Charlemagne. You remember Charlemagne? Well, it is like the old gladiatorial days.

"Anyway, they took the money, and $1,500 worth of

personal jewelry, and charged me with being a known confidence man. Get that. *They* took *my* money and I am a confidence man. And who has Stavisky's money? The same guys that got my money.

"Well, I expect to furnish bail soon and get out of here. They haven't got a thing on me, but there is a prejudice against bankers and they once arrested me with Nicky Arnstein."

P. S.—Jack Curley, the sports promoter, when asked to verify Donnelly's ring story, said:—"Sure he was a fighter. He fought Bat Nelson down in a beer garden in Havana a couple of nights before the Johnson-Willard fight. His end of the purse was $800 and he gave it to the promoter for safe-keeping. The promoter skipped."

On the Whiz

It is barely possible that the World's Fair next spring will see a revival of an ancient regional art: picking pockets. The pickpocket is a product of urban civilization. His development presupposes a culture in which people—1. Wear pants. 2. Have money in their pants. These conditions have obtained in New York for centuries, but nowhere else in the United States except for brief spasms. Naturally the New York pickpocket got to be the best in the world. However, an organism exposed to a disease develops anti-bodies. The New York pickpocket squad got so smart that it just about starved the pickpocket. Old pickpocket detectives sometimes are sad about this, because they find life a bore.

Picking pockets is a high type of crime. Pickpockets never carry revolvers except when they are going to fight with other pickpockets over a violated trade agreement. The old New York pickpocket worked a twelve-hour week, which put him well in advance of contemporary labor practice. He worked one hour every morning when people were going to their offices in the street cars, and one hour in the evening when they were coming back.

The pickpocket generally lived in a Turkish bath, where no professional opportunity could tempt him during his hours of leisure. In the bath he played pinochle or stuss with other pickpockets, from nine in the morning until five in the afternoon. At five he boarded an uptown street car; at six he debarked and returned downtown in a hansom cab, to dine off a peck of steamed oysters and six poached eggs on lobsterfat toast at Jack's. At nine he was back in the Turkish bath, dealing stuss. He kept regular hours; it was essential for his success that he should appear bright-eyed and clean-shaven in the morning. A man with rings under his eyes would have appeared conspicuous in a carload of officeworkers starting their day.

Police Captain William J. Raftis, retired, once said that there would never be a revival of the art in New York. But he had not at that time seen drawings of the 1939 World's Fair trylon and perisphere, which should induce millions of visitors to look upward at an acute angle, making them soft touches even for novices.

"It took years to make a good tool," Captain Raftis said. "There may be some old-timers who will go on the whiz again, but there's no new blood in the profession. Just lush rollers and moll buzzers and patch pocket workers. There hasn't been a good watch lifter in New York in twenty years."

A tool, Captain Raftis explained, is the operative who actually removes money from a victim's pocket. A tool may be called a wire; the terms are interchangeable. The stall stands behind the tool and covers his operations from public view. A moll buzzer is a woman who opens other women's handbags in department stores. A patch pocket worker takes the change purse from a woman's outside pocket in a crowd. A lush roller rolls lushes.

A fob pocket worker is a decrepit cannon or dip (both generic terms for pickpockets) who takes change from men's overcoat pockets. Shaky from booze or dope, his fine touch lost, the fob pocket man makes Captain Raftis blue.

"It is a lesson in the vanity of criminal pursuits to see a fine man reduced to grabbing dimes from commuters," he said.

"The best pants pocket workers came from New York. They still do, but there are few of them." Captain Raftis sighed, like a buffalo hunter recalling the days when countless herds covered the prairie. "We used to have 1,500 complaints a year."

The Captain was quite sure of the reason for this early decline.

"It was the pickpocket squad," he said modestly. "We have sixty-five of the best pickpocket detectives in the country riding criss-cross on the subway, working wherever there is a crowd. Also, New York City has the only law in the country that is specifically aimed against pickpockets.

"It is section 722, subdivision 6, and it makes it disorderly conduct to approach a person and place the hand in proximity to his pockets or act in concert with such an attempt. The officer's testimony, based on observation, is enough."

ONE JUMP TO FOUR MILES

We have better riders in New York than any place else in the United States. The best riders cannot afford to live in the country; there are no horse races there.

Although Eddie Arcaro, the jockey, is only twenty-two, he has a mature, Metropolitan understanding of his public, which is largely made up of investors. When he canters back to the winner's circle at Belmont or Saratoga or wherever he is riding, he peers sadly down his long, pointed nose and touches the peak of his cap with his whip in perfunctory acknowledgment of the applause. He knows that the hatless man in the polo shirt who hangs over the rail screaming "Attaboy Eddie!" has had two dollars on his mount to win; he knows that if he loses the next race, the same fellow may be yelling, "Yah, Arcaro—you bum!" Neither the handclap nor the hiss moves him very much.

What really interests Eddie is his income. As the leading rider on New York tracks last year, he collected about forty thousand dollars. With a win in the Kentucky Derby to start him off and good prospective mounts in the fall two-year-old classics, he ought to do even better this year. Since a jockey's career is usually short, Eddie works hard at his trade, knowing he'll get heavy eventually. He puts his money in annuities.

"You know how old jockeys wind up—with eppes," he once said. "You know, they got nothing." *Eppes* is a Yiddish word, meaning something of indefinite value, which Eddie learned from Jockey Sammy Renick. His talk, like that of all jockeys, is a strange mixture of New Yorkese, Westernisms (about half the riders hail from the horse-range country), Southern idioms picked up from Negro swipes, and trade terms pertaining to race riding. All these elements are fused into one standard jargon in the jockey rooms, where the boys spend the greater part of their afternoons.

Eddie is five feet three inches tall and can ride at a hundred and twelve pounds. This means he is able to strip to a hundred and seven, for riding weight includes a racing saddle, pad, the jockey's garments and boots, and any extra equipment, like a martingale or blinkers, worn by the horse. Bridle and whip are not counted in the weight. Eddie got his first stable job when he was fourteen, and his view of the world, although sharp, is limited. He has never assumed a knowledge of champagne vintages or a hunt-club accent. Mrs. Payne Whitney is his contract employer, but he has never met her. He thinks well of Mrs. Charles Shipman Payson, Mrs. Whitney's daughter, whom he sees occasionally around stables. "She's a high-class woman," Eddie says. "She never has nothing to say."

During the season he receives scores of letters from people who want inside tips on the races. They generally say that they need the money for an operation, or to lift a mortgage, or to buy themselves a pardon from a penitentiary. Eddie never answers them. He is not a successful bettor himself. When occasionally he backs one of his own mounts, he says it "just seems to jinx everything." "Anybody is a sucker to bet their own money," he says. Usually, if the horse he is riding looks like a fairly sure thing, the trainer or owner will put a bet on it for Eddie, which costs Eddie nothing. He likes that kind of bet all right.

Arcaro is a sociable sort, but he has little time for pleasure. With the increase in the importance of winter racing, there is a strong inducement for him to work all year round. Arcaro usually knocks off in November every year to mitigate the strain of continual weight-making. In a few luxurious weeks his weight goes up thirteen pounds, which he works off gradually during December and January. In winter he rides in Florida and California, and in spring in Maryland and Kentucky.

Six mornings a week, during the Belmont season, Arcaro rises at five-thirty in his apartment at Jamaica, gets into riding togs, has a cup of coffee, and then drives a long maroon automobile out to the barn of the Greentree Stable, at the end of a hedge-lined, studiously English lane in the stable colony at Belmont Park. The Greentree Stable is Mrs. Whitney's *nom de course*. The stable pays him a retainer of a thousand dollars a month for first call on his services. When Greentree has no horse in a race, he is free to ride for other owners.

At the barn, Arcaro joins the exercise boys and rides one of the Greentree horses out to the track for its morning gallop. He gallops three horses around the mile-and-a-half oval every morning. Sometimes he shakes one out for a time trial. He performs this morning chore in order to hold his riding form. After the gallops he may chat a while with Bill Brennan, the Greentree trainer, or Nick Huff, who is at the same time the stable agent and Arcaro's jockey agent. As stable agent, Huff acts as a combined purchasing officer, paymaster, and auditor. As Arcaro's agent, he arranges for the jockey's outside mounts. Eddie starts for home at about eight-thirty and has breakfast there with Mrs. Arcaro. He has been married a year. At breakfast he follows no special diet, but is careful not to eat as much as he wants of any-thing. Then he takes a nap until noon. He must report at the jockey room at the track at one o'clock, even when his first engagement comes late in the afternoon. After he has ridden his last race for the day, he is free to go.

At the track Arcaro changes from street clothes into the colors of the first owner he is to represent, then sits around or plays catch with other boys in back of the jockey house until it is time to go out to the saddling shed. A valet in a khaki uniform helps Eddie dress. For this service the valet receives two dollars from Eddie each time Eddie rides. If Eddie wins, he must pay the valet three dollars instead of two. On a typical program, Arcaro may ride six races.

A certain Wednesday early this summer was a fair sam-ple of his day. Arriving at the Belmont jockey room, in a white one-story building next to the saddling shed, he changed into the "salmon pink jacket, emerald green hoops, salmon pink sleeves and cap" of Mrs. Ethel Jacobs, owner of the two-year-old General Howes, which he was to ride in the first race. Hirsch Jacobs, Mrs. Jacobs' husband, sad-dles more winners than any other trainer on the American turf. Jockeys like to ride his horses because, Eddie says, "they always have a chance." A jockey receives only ten dollars for a ride unless the animal wins. If it wins, he gets twenty-five dollars plus ten per cent of the purse. The mil-lionaire establishments like Greentree, Foxcatcher Farms, and the Wheatley Stable retain contract riders in view of the great stake races toward which they aim their seasons. Jacobs has no contract rider, but few of his horses run in the big stake races, and he usually has his pick of the high-salaried riders in the cheap races.

General Howes was wild and hard to ride going to the starting gate for a straightaway dash of five-eighths of a mile. But he got off well, led all the way, and won by half a length, making a profit of ninety-five dollars fee and ten per cent of the seven hundred dollars first money. Eddie said, "I bounced the sucker out in front when the man throwed it, and then at the eighth pole I showered down." Jockeys call the starter "the man." When he pressed the buzzer to signal the start, they say he "throws the gate," or, more colloquially, "throws it." "When he throwed it, I had it," a boy will say to express satisfaction with a start. To "shower down" means to whip.

Eddie had a breathing spell during the steeplechase which followed the opening dash, meanwhile changing into the "pink jacket, black and white striped sleeves, white cap" of John Hay Whitney, the son of Eddie's contract employer. He rode a Whitney two-year-old in the third race and finished next to last. The horses in this race were of a distinctly higher grade than those he had beaten in the first. He then prepared for the feature of the day, the Hollis Selling Stakes, in which he was scheduled to ride the four-year-old chestnut filly North Riding for the Howe Stable. The race was worth $2,750 to the first horse, which would mean a round three hundred dollars for the winning jockey. The Howe Stable has second call on Arcaro's services, for which it pays him three hundred dollars a month. If there is a Howe entry in a race and no Greentree starter, Arcaro must ride the Howe horse. The stable is not large. Most of its horses are a little better than platers but not quite of stake calibre. North Riding is a heartbreaking mare for a jockey. She is very fast but what Eddie calls "a rank, rapid horse that you can't reserve." This means that she goes out to run her head off at the start and that if the jockey tries to conserve her speed for the finish, she stops altogether. There is a horseman's adage, which Eddie accepts, that no horse can run more than three-eighths of a mile at top speed. A horse that insists on running this magic three-eighths at the beginning tires and must be coaxed into finishing on its nerve. "When this mare stops, she sticks her feet in the ground," Arcaro says. "If you whip her she sulks. All you can do is hand-ride her and pray." On this day his prayer was answered. North Riding started fast, as usual, but didn't stop. The race was over before the other horses could catch her.

Eddie then went on to ride another horse of John Hay Whitney's, finishing last this time, and two more Jacobs platers, finishing second on one called Celestino and third on another named Mama's Choice. This brought his gross income for the day to four hundred and thirty-five dollars; three hundred for his win on North Riding, ninety-five for General Howes, and ten dollars for each of the four losing mounts. For a week-day, this had been an excellent program for Eddie. Out of his earnings he had to pay fourteen dollars to his valet and fifty-seven fifty to Huff, the agent. A jockey agent, like a valet gets two dollars for losing and three dollars for winning mounts, but he also gets ten per cent of the jockey's ten per cent of the purse. When Eddie won the Kentucky Derby on Lawrin this spring, he received five thousand dollars as his share of the purse and paid Huff five hundred.

After his ride on Mama's Choice in the last race, Eddie had his shower, got into street clothes, and drove his car into New York to meet Mrs. Arcaro for dinner at a place called Leone's. She seldom goes to the track when there is not an important race. The Arcaros like to eat at Leone's, the Hickory House, or Gallagher's—all Broadway places where the food is good and fairly expensive and the patrons include a sprinkling of sporting people. After dinner they usually go to a "show." Eddie always calls moving pictures shows. He gets to bed by eleven o'clock except on Saturday nights, when, with Mrs. Arcaro, he invariably goes to a night club. His wife, who used to be a photographer's model, is blonde, pretty, and five inches taller than her husband. They met while Eddie was riding at Hialeah a few winters back. "I guess I'm pretty miserable to get along with during the hot weather when I dassn't drink much water on account of my weight," Eddie says. Being thirsty irritates him, but his wife makes allowances.

Since horses generally carry between a hundred and a hundred and twenty-six pounds in races, it might seem to the layman that very small men, weighing around ninety pounds, would make the best jockeys. They would not have to weaken themselves by sweating or dieting. But, as trainers will point out, ten pounds of dead-weight shows a horse more than fifteen pounds of live weight. The difference between the weight of the jockey with his tack and total weight assigned by the handicapper is made up by loading the saddle pad with thin sheets of lead. The trainer's ideal is a jockey who, with saddle and tack, weighs exactly the figure allotted to his horse. A jockey can vary his weight for races on the same day by using different saddles. Eddie has three, of which the lightest weighs twenty-four ounces and the heaviest five pounds. A heavier saddle is considered preferable to lead. Eddie is close to the trainer's ideal and doesn't have to use lead as often as some other jockeys. But an extra three pounds on Eddie's frame would decrease his chances of employment by about twenty per cent. A gain of five or six pounds would be a vigorous push toward retirement. A "heavy" jockey—118 to 125 pounds—gets engagements so infrequently that he is apt to lose his form, after which he gets no engagements at all. Raymond ("Sonny") Workman, considered by most of his jockey-room colleagues to be Arcaro's only peer, is a deep-chested, bull-necked little man of twenty-nine with a roast-beef complexion, who is afraid of getting heavy. He goes on the road like a prize-fighter every morning, wearing rubber garments under his sweater and trousers. When the weather becomes really hot, he often plays eighteen holes of golf in the late morning, wearing the same rubber clothes. He can count calories like a movie actress.

Boys in the jockey room carry on interminable technical discussions during the waits between races, and there is an argument after each race. "If there is fifteen in a race," Eddie says, "you would think to hear them holler that fifteen should of win it. And when you do win, some other kid will come up and say, 'Gee, you was lucky. I should of galloped.'" Angry little men shout they were bumped or shut off by other jockeys, but a boy who hits another in the jockey room is liable to a hundred-dollar fine, so blows are seldom struck.

Eddie rides "ace-deuce," with the left stirrup a good three inches longer than the right. Most American jockeys ride ace-deuce, the theory being that since they ride with the rail to their left they throw more weight in that direction to keep the horse from running out. They learn the style on the half-mile tracks, where a jockey feels that he is on a continual turn from start to finish. Arcaro rides ace-deuce even in straightaway dashes. He says he is so used to it that

if he evened up he would get seasick. He rides with his
knees high and gets his grip on a horse with his lower
calves. Workman, whose legs are shorter than Eddie's,
grips the horse's withers with his knees. He rides ace-deuce,
but less ace-deuce, than Eddie, he says.

Arcaro was born and brought up in Newport, Kentucky,
a little town across the Ohio River from Cincinnati and only
a few miles from the Latonia race track. Like many Italian-
Americans reared where they have few compatriots, he
talks with the inflections of a local product. His name and
his mobile Latin features, with deep brown eyes and large
white teeth, hardly seem to fit the Ohio River twang in
his voice. His father, who runs a small crockery and restau-
rant-supply store in Newport, was born in Texas. Eddie
started out to be a jockey after one year in Newport High
School, when he decided he never would be big enough
to make the football team. A Latonia horseman named Mc-
Caffrey offered him a job as stableboy. Eddie agreed to
work for him for a year in return for food and clothes and
a chance to ride.

The boy was with the McCaffrey stable for several
months before he got on a horse. He carried water, pol-
ished tack, and amused himself in his spare time by twirling
a stick and riding exciting whip finishes on bales of hay.
This is the traditional stableboy method of learning to handle a whip. He is an ambidextrous whipper now, and can
change the whip from the right to the left hand in two
strides of his mount. After a while, McCaffrey allowed
Eddie to ride the lead pony, the stolid, cold-blooded brute
that is used to lead a string of thoroughbreds to and from
the race track. A boy riding a lead pony begins with his
stirrups long, like a novice in a riding academy. As he gains

confidence he shortens his leathers in imitation of the jockeys he sees about him, until finally he is balanced high on the horse's withers like a real race rider. Eddie has never read the elaborate arguments in favor of the forward seat which are written by cavalry officers and published in limited editions. American jockeys have used it for forty years. A new boy around a stable usually is promoted from the lead pony to the back of a quiet old thoroughbred for his first morning gallops. That was about as far as Eddie got with McCaffrey. At the end of the year the boy's employer advised him to go back to school. McCaffrey told Eddie he would never make a jockey.

Instead of taking his advice, Eddie signed a three-year contract with a gyp horseman named Booker, who was taking a small string to the Pacific Coast for the winter racing. "Gyp," as applied to horsemen, is a term without opprobrium. Gyp stables try to make a profit, contrasted with the de-luxe establishments that operate at a deficit. With Booker, Eddie landed out in Agua Caliente in the fall of 1931. His contract bound him to serve his employer faithfully in return for twenty dollars a month and found for the first six months, with a ten-dollar raise every six months thereafter. The contract was signed by Booker, Eddie's parents, and Eddie. An apprentice who breaks such a contract may not be employed by another horseman even as a stableboy.

It is the gyp horsemen, for the most part, who "make" riders. They run their horses often and they cannot afford to pay the regular fees for outside jockeys. If they can develop a good apprentice, they get their riding done for nothing. If he continues to improve, they turn a profit by selling his contract to a major stable, just as a minor-league baseball club sells a player to a big-league team. Booker had too few horses to give Eddie a complete education. The curriculum was limited. But Eddie won his first race in Booker's colors, on a four-year-old named Eagle Bird that had never won before. Horses begin racing at two, and a four-year-old maiden is usually phenomenally bad. Eddie says, in the pungent race-track phrase, "Him and me lost our maidens in the same race." Eddie won a few more races during that meeting, but Booker kept selling horses or losing them in claiming races until finally he had no need of a jockey. He transferred Eddie's contract to a kindly man named Clarence E. Davison, who still runs a highly successful gyp stable in the Middle West. Davison paid nothing for the contract. "It was give to him," the jockey modestly states. "I wasn't doing no good."

Davison is a former Missouri farmer who races his horses methodically. "Everybody in that stable had to earn his keep," Arcaro says. "Even the lead pony could run like hell. The feed was counted right down to the ounce and every horse had to be rode out in every race, because even fourth money meant twenty-five dollars on the feed bill." The Davison horses provided a fine range of experience.

In the morning Davison taught Eddie pace. A jockey unable to gauge his mount's rate of speed may run his horse into the ground early in a race. Or else, fooled by a slow pace, he may dawdle along and be beaten by an inferior horse. Davison would tell Eddie to work a horse a mile in 1:46 or six furlongs in 1:16. He would wave to the boy to slow down when he was riding too fast or to come on when the pace was too slow. In the end Eddie' caught onto it. When the boy made mistakes in races, like getting pocketed behind other horses on the rail or running a mount into heavy footing to save a couple of lengths and thereby sacrificing in speed more than he gained in distance, Davison never was angry. He took Eddie home with him after the races and drew diagrams of the jockey's mistakes.

At every track where these horses ran, Mr. and Mrs. Davison would engage a cottage. They made Eddie live with them. Davison never let the boy associate with hustlers or scufflers, the race-track small fry who ingratiate themselves with young jockeys and try to fix races. He never let Eddie shoot pool or smoke cigarettes. "S'all he ever did to me was preach to me," Eddie says now, his tone a mixture of gratitude and relief at his escape. Under the intensive tutelage the young rider improved, and at Sportsman's Park, near Chicago, he won fourteen races in one week in the fall of 1932. That set him up in his own estimation. Before losing his "bug," he rode seventy winners. A rider's "bug," is the asterisk at the left of a horse's handicap on a race program. It indicates that the rider won his first race within a year, or that the rider has not attained his fortieth win and that the horse therefore is allowed a deduction of five pounds from the weight assigned. The bug always remains with a rider until he has won forty races, and it is a bitter jockey-room reproach to say "You had your bug for five years."

In midsummer of 1934, Davison sold Arcaro's contract for $5,000 to Warren Wright, the Chicago baking-powder millionaire who owns the Calumet Stock Farm. The contract had five months to run. Davison had been paying Eddie his contract salary of sixty dollars a month; the Calumet owner started him at three hundred, plus mount money and a percentage of stakes. The Calumet horses moved

East to Narragansett Park near Providence, and Eddie engaged a suite at the Biltmore, the city's leading hotel. Mr. Wright presented him with a Chevrolet because he didn't like to see his contract rider waiting for buses. Later, in one of his first races at Belmont, Eddie won the Matron Stakes on a Calumet filly named Nellie Flag. His ten per cent of the purse was two thousand dollars, more than he had earned in his entire previous career. He was the contract rider for Calumet through 1935 and 1936, then switched to Greentree at a higher retainer.

While Calumet and Greentree are both millionaire stables, neither has had a real champion in recent years. Some horsemen, indeed, unkindly compare Greentree with the White Knight, who kept a mouse-trap on his saddle in case a mouse ever got up there. The stable, they say, has the jockey in case it gets a horse. Arcaro's reputation has been gained chiefly on outside mounts. He is not sure that he has ever ridden a first-class horse. His greatest triumph was this year's Kentucky Derby, but he is not certain that his Derby mount, Lawrin, who is now out of training because of an injury, is a champion. "Maybe the other three-year-olds just ain't so good," he says.

It is the skill with which Arcaro handles all sorts of mounts that makes him a favorite of the ordinary racegoer. Last year he won 96 races on New York tracks, finishing first with about twenty per cent of his mounts. Including his races in other parts of the country, he had 153 winners. Nine other jockeys led him in number of victories, but they were riders on the minor circuits. His 717 mounts won $205,874 in purses.

The most important figure in Eddie's business life, he thinks, is Nick Huff, who tries to get him on horses that can win. "You very seldom hear of a jockey getting in a slump riding good horses," Arcaro says sincerely.

Huff used to be a jockey himself, although not one of the top rank. He is a small-boned, keen-featured little man who wears snappy suits. He always speaks of Eddie in the first person plural, a custom jockey agents share with fight managers. "We won on Lawrin when nobody gave us a chance, didn't we?" he asks pugnaciously. "We could have won The Withers on Menow—Headley wanted us to ride —but on account of our contract we had to ride Redbreast. We are par excellence the best rider in the country, from one jump to four miles."

Eddie knows from his own experience, or has learned in talks with a trainer before a race, just how to handle whatever horse he is riding. One difficulty of race riding is that some horses are opinionated and stubborn. There are the rapid, rank horses that will run only when they're out front, and there are hardened devils that refuse to run until they reach the stretch. Either type will quit if forced out of its natural way of going. There are old horses that have been knocked about on the rail in their youth and won't go near it, and there are rapid luggers that will make for the rail no matter what the jockey does, and often disqualify themselves because they block other horses. Eddie remembers a rapid lugger named Hot Shot; he drew six ten-day suspensions in one year riding that horse. Then there are horses that will run up on the other horses' heels. Such a one was Gunfire, which stepped on the horse in front of it at Washington Park in 1933 and went down. Eddie, who was on Gunfire, came out of the jam with two fractured ribs, one of which punctured his lung. That is the only serious spill he's ever had.

When Eddie has a mount amenable to reason, he likes to break fast from the gate, then take back to third or fourth position, and come through when the leaders tire. You get two horses out there fighting for the lead for a quarter of a mile, you see, and they will kill theirself off every time. Then you can come on and win. But sometimes when you are set for the rush, the horse isn't. You shower down and he sulks. He loses his action and goes limber on you like, and you know he's stuck his feet in the ground.

THE WORLD OF ART

People back where I came from are receptive to artistic influences from outside, and among the visiting priestesses of the arts I remember was a dancer named Princess White Wing. Shortly before her arrival the City License Department had prescribed opaque clothing over the critical portions of all dancers' anatomies.

"What is the use of opaque clothing?" demanded the Princess. "You can see right through it."

The Princess, who was a graduate of a college in Sherman, Tex., had abandoned the brick-and-stucco tepees of the Cherokee nation to carve out a career as a feather dancer. She employed as many as two feathers at a single performance, and she had been all set to open at a new night club when along came this theatrical reform business.

She had done a strip act in Chicago burlesque for a while during the previous summer under her "American" name of Billie Joyce, but thought Sally Rand went too far.

"When a girl comes out startlely naked, that is too much," said the Princess. "Besides I bet she is thirty years old."

For herself she thought a feather here and another there quite enough costume. "Because there is really nothing more beautiful than a beautiful body," she said, "or what do you think?"

The story of how Princess White Wing came to the stage is very romantic. Her father, whose Indian name she did not precisely remember (she thought probably it was White

Wing) owned $1,000,000 worth of oil lands. The Pale Faces performed a famous Oklahoma dance known as The Run Around, and Chief White Wing died brokenhearted, without enough oil to lubricate a sardine.

Now the Princess was suing the Pale Faces for the lands of her ancestors, and in the meanwhile she was performing this dance with the feathers.

"Sally Rand makes me sick," she said. "She hasn't got no dance, you know."

"The Princess does a richwel dance," said Sam Burger, her Broadway representative. "You know, it is like a strip number a little, but it is part of her religion."

Double Life

Steamships occasionally deposit on the fringe of our west side exquisite gentlemen named Hyacinthe, of Paris, or Schnuck of Vienna, or Salciccia, of Bologna, who willingly admit that they are coiffeurs-artistes, great artistes even, and that when they run their fingers through Madame's hair the hair is as the marble of Phidias and the fingers are as the chisel. The chisel fits right into the picture.

The coiffeurs-artistes try to avert public attention by such ruses as sleeping in glass beds wearing false teeth to match their mauve wigs, picking the fifteen best-dressed women in America and the fifteen who look best undressed.

Such singeries (monkey business in the neighborhood where he keeps shop) cause Paul Mommer to smile.

It happens that he is a hair-dresser and also an artist, but he keeps the two callings neatly separated—by a partition dividing Paul's Beauty Shoppe into a front three-quarters, where ladies sit with medieval looking contraptions on their heads or recline with mudpacks on their faces, and a rear room where at night he paints by the light of a blue bulb and a yellow to simulate daylight.

In front of the partition, during the day and early evening, he is "Mr. Paul" (beauticians, like bartenders, have no last names), a slender, fair-haired man in his 30's, with blue eyes, a longish nose and a ready smile featuring one gold tooth. The office girls from the Guardian Life on the corner and even from as far as the Edison Co. on Irving Place consider his haircuts "real works of art."

They are ignorant of his trans-partitional activities, because, as the painter explains, "It might not be good for the business. And then to be known just as a hairdresser who paints—critics would not take me seriously as a painter. I began painting when I was a boy of 7 years. Hairdressing I began only a few years ago. I am a painter who dresses hair for a living. The two things do not interfere with each other, except sometimes I have to hide my fingernails from the customers. No matter how I scrub I can't get the paint out sometimes."

When Mommer was a boy of 13 he painted a picture of a cottage near Metz, in Lorraine—a cottage where he lived. He still has the painting, a gay presentation of a house with a bright red roof and whitewashed walls, perched on a green rise with a canary yellow bridge in front of it and skies like washing blue with cotton clouds.

A couple of years ago he painted the same cottage in retrospect. The dead white walls evoke the word-association "sepulchre."

The gray sky and the gray light suffusing the picture have turned the roof to blackish brown. The black clouds racing across convey a feeling of menace over the house, like one of Poe's haunted mansions, and the sensitive onlooker can hear the ugly rumble of the swollen brook under the bridge.

"That seems to me the permanent aspect of life. I have experienced it," the painter says with his pleasant smile. "Rain, snow, sun are passing things. I don't paint things as they look for the time being. I paint the truth about them as I see it, and when I paint I don't feel any truth in other colors than dark ones. It is a mood I am related to.

"I don't want to paint a picture of a scene as it is for the time being—in a certain shadow. I want to paint without beautifying."

The white smocks of his employes hang on the same walls with paintings of a stark white church overwhelmed with foreboding, of imaginary men and women with dark brown and green faces, of pitifully commonplace backyards and taxpayers in Astoria, where Mommer lives.

He was born in Luxembourg. An uncle, a sculpture, encouraged him to draw. When he was 16 he was drafted into a Bavarian regiment. He spent a year in France, two years in a British prison camp. In the prison camp the men used to take turns cutting one another's hair. He came to the United States after the war and became an X-ray technician at Mount Sinai Hospital.

"I tired of seeing always sick people around me," he said, "and I had, one day, temperament. I quit. And by that time I had a wife and children. I remembered the haircutting. I saw a barber shop with a sign 'Barber Wanted,' so I got into the haircutting business. I make always a living by it."

The somber mood of his painting does not obsess him in ordinary life.

"It is easy to be pleasant with people," he said. "Only

once in my life I argued with a customer. She was one of those women that tell you once they went to Emil on Fifth Avenue and for $5 he cut their hair a certain way so that is the best way, but they cannot remember the way exactly, because they have had several haircuts since.

"So no way I could start to cut it was like the way Emil cut it. So there were other customers waiting. So at last she said:—'Oh, these Fourth Avenue hairdressers! Emil, he is a real artist.'

"So I thought then of Rembrandt and El Greco and Daumier, and I said to her:—'Madame, I am sorry. I am not an artist. I am a hairdresser. If you want an artist go back to Emil.' It was very foolish, because I lost a dollar."

Roll Like a Cannery

The diversity of regional arts back here is breath-taking. We even have a Swiss Yodel Club. Most of the yodelers live in New York, but the clubhouse is in Irvington, New Jersey, because when anybody yodels in our well-ordered city the bulls throw him in the pokey as drunk and disorderly. This is not necessarily so. The Yodel Club is moderately prosperous, but it lacks competition because it includes all the good yodelers in the district. Gus Ochsner, the president of the club, told me that there were not enough unattached yodelers to fill a tournament, without including Bavarian and Tyrolean yodelers. There is nothing sadder than a Bavarian or Tyrolean yodel, he said.

"It is a low yodel with an open face. The Swiss yodel is the highest yodel because it is the highest country.

"You take a Swiss yodeler in good voice, he rolls like a cannery bird."

Paul Naef, secretary of the club, and Rudy Hohwald,

the junior yodeler, solemnly nodded confirmation of Ochsner's dictum.

American yodelers? Hohwald, foreman in charge of the
delicate color processes of a dollar magazine, smiled.

"You are born with the yodel in your throat," he said.
"It comes out natural or not, not? Singers everywhere
are born, but yodelers only in Switzerland. And then sometimes the yodel won't come out."

A yodel quartet has five members, only one of whom
yodels.

"We all sing," the secretary said, "and the yodeler comes
on top of it." When, as sometimes occurs, the yodeler finds
himself temporarily yodelless, the quartet sounds just like
any quartet. So the club has a double quartet, with two
yodelers, and then everything is pretty safe.

Hans Pruemm, the musical director, explained that
there exists a great deal of music for yodel quartets. Switzerland has a yodel composer named Oskar Franz Schmalz,
who outranks Irving Berlin above the timberline.

Some of the lyrics are very catchy:—

> U-li, o-li-o, u-i-u-li,
> Jo duli diu duia-ho, dui duia, ho duli du.

A discussion arose anent the results of the national Jod-
lerfest in Interlaken, as chronicled by the Swiss newspapers
received at the clubhouse.

"The champion einzeljodler without singing is again
Peter Bachmann, of Hongg," chortled Walter Altorfer,
first bass and bartender. "I always said the most refined
yodelers are by Zurich. You don't have to chase on a mountain a cow to be an artist.

Herr Bachmann, he elucidated, is not a mountaineer but a floorwalker in a department store.

The champion jodlerin (it is spelled with a "j" in the original but the "j" is pronounced like a "y") is Frau J. Balmer-Baudenbacher, of Interlaken, who by her unaided voice, summons Herr Balmer-Baudenbacher from skat games fifteen miles away.

Mr. Ochsner, before he attended the late conflict as an American soldier and was pretty well shot to pieces, yodeled forty-two weeks at the Hippodrome. As he has made no stage appearances since the war he is no longer classed as a professional, but, instead, is considered a simon-pure amateur.

The organization feels the need of an Alphornblaser, or performer on the Alpine horn—a wooden instrument twelve feet long, which lies along the ground like a length of pipe while the artist blows into a moderate-sized orifice at one end. Five years ago Pruemm thought he heard one down near Perth Amboy, but it turned out to be only the steamer Roma, which had run aground and was blowing her foghorn.

A Window on the World

Every so often we folks back here have an opportunity to talk to some visiting artiste or literary figure, like one of the Abbe children, about Europe, and this helps to broaden our point of view. Distinguished visitors are like a window on the outside world. New Yorkers are very narrow, as folks from the country like to remind us, and we need contact with visiting minds for stimulation. I well remember a talk I had with Clara Bow, who was at that time one of the best minds of Hollywood, the artistic capital of the world. Miss Bow had just returned from Europe, which she was glad to interpret for me.

"The French have their idea about the war debts," Miss Bow began, "and we have ours. So really there is no use talking about it. Oh, they were very, very angry. The government fell while we were in Paris. No, it didn't make any noise when it fell. It didn't actually fall down, you know. It lost the election.

"But everybody was very nice to me. We stayed at the Hotel George Sank Fifth, and admirers came to see me every day. They talked French to me fluently, but of course I don't understand French; but I knew they wanted my autograph.

"The Tower of London was very fascinating," she said.

"The guide knows the history of everything by heart. Of course it makes you sleepy now and then, but you wake up when he shows you the chair where the Kings of England have been crowned for quite some time, and, my dear, the plush is entirely worn off.

"Then they tell you a story about the changing of the guards. Of course that is quite an old custom, and it seems they had a new guard there and when they change the guards one guard delivers the keys, and the other guard says, 'Who goes there?' and the guard says, 'The King's Keys,' and the other guard says, 'What king?' and the first guard says 'King George,' and the other guard says 'Amen.'

"So the new guard, instead of saying amen, said 'Sez you.' I thought it was a scream. But of course it sounds better in an English accent."

Miss Bow, with her husband, Rex Bell, and her manager, Sam Rorke, had visited London, Berlin, Paris and St. Moritz during her trip.

St. Moritz was her favorite spot in Europe. "The French and Germans are practically civilized," she said, "so it is not much fun travelling there. I want to go to Egypt some time to see the Pyramids and the natives. They say the architecture is marvelous."

"It is quite educational to travel," Miss Bow said, "if you meet the right people. Rex and I met a lot of Counts and Dukes. I forgot their names, but they all said they'd write, so I suppose they'll sign the letters."

Monkeyhouse Hero

Frank Salerno is a bail bondsman who is known in the vicinity of the Tombs Prison as Valentino. This is because at one period of his life he thought he looked like Valentino, and gave an agent a thousand dollars to get him into the moving pictures. The agent disappeared, and Frank has never since consented to bail out anybody connected with the theatrical profession, even on excellent security. Yet he himself has an artistic past. For several years he presided at the Metropolitan as chef de claque. The office has been abolished, and it is to this gaffe that Frank attributes the decline of grand opera in America.

"Without a claque no artist can have success in America," he insists. "The American public is no good to clap. It is ashamed to be the first one. Before it makes up its mind another aria has started. The artist she's discouraged, she's nervous, some applause comes when she's singing up then when she gets to the top they let her go. So really the claque is necessary.

"It's just like a story. You got two words, you can make a big lie around it, fine story. Still and all, you gotta have those two substantial words. Don't? So, you gotta have a claque to start the applause. Then the rest follow."

In the old days, when a dozen opera companies cruised the railroad seas, when even the smaller cities had civic opera ventures and when "Mr. Omblestein" was giving the Met red hot competition, there was a bull market on claqueurs.

"To lead a claque you gotta be musician," Frank explained. "Like one of these boys rides a horse race, you gotta know just when to make your move. For years, when they get a new opera, the leaders of the claque always attend the rehearsal to learn the score, know just when to clap. The rest follow.

"The artist, she's encourage, she sing better and better. Without, she's a flop. I made-a Galli-Curci," Mr. Salerno boasted. "I made-a Tita Ruffo, Muratore, Amato, De Lucca. I make them success, and success make them to sing better.

"I save the Metropolitan, but that was what you call publicity. I put Caruso in the monkey house, and break Mr. Omblestein's heart." The vast Neapolitan eyes of the great musician flashed with pride.

"In that time," he said, "Mr. Omblestein was have a better opera company than the Metropolitan. Was no so strong subscription as now, and the Metropolitan was licked. Only draw they got was Caruso, and he draw only in 'Pagliacci', 'Aida,' 'Rigoletto.' Outside those three operas, nothing. So one day Caruso was advertised to sing 'La Boheme' that night.

"Mr. Guard, the press agent, send for me. I hire a fat woman. I go to Caruso's hotel. I say, 'It's a nice day for walk.' I lead him to the monkey house in Central Park.

When he pass by the woman she yell. 'He pinch me.' The detective he's plant right there, he arrest Caruso. In five minutes every newspaper office got the story.

"In court is sensation. He pays $10 fine. It's more head-lines of a murder trial. 'Caruso in the Monkey House,' it's call. That night people pay $50, $100 for a seat. There was not so much scandal ever before. Caruso is nervous. He say, 'What shall I do?' I say, 'Go ahead, sing like you never sang before.' He do.

"After that all New York know he can sing something beside just 'Aida,' 'Pagliacci' and 'Rigoletto.' Mr. Omble-stein is lick."

Martial Notes

Back where I came from the people are profoundly and diversely musical. There are not many regions where you could find a virtuoso like Master Fifer James J. Gillespie of the Seventy-first Regiment, N.Y.N.G. He was born in West Thirty-ninth Street, learned to fife on Governor's Island in 1875 (a completely regional artist, you may note) and was perched on a fence at Camp Smith like a leathery little satyr the last time I saw him, playing "Garry Owen."

Te-oodle-de-doodle-de-doo-de-doo,
Te-oodle-de-doodle-de-doo-de-doo,

he played.

"Do you know whose favorite tune that was?" he inquired, taking his fife from his lips.

"Stravinsky's?"

"Naw, General Custer's," affirmed Master Fifer Gillespie. "Many a time at review he used to ask, 'Have the boys play "Garry Owen." ' Billy Morris, what was a drummer in the Seventh Cavalry, told me himself. Afterward Morris was a judge in the Bronx.

"Well, sir, I was stationed at Fort Vancouver in what was then Washington Territory and playing baseball the day we heard about Custer. A fellow named Sweeney was pitching, but underhand, and when he heard the news he said, 'Ah, you're only trying to distract me attention,' but when we saw the flag at half-mast we knew it was true."

Gillespie raised the fife again.

Te-oodle-de-aadle-de-doo-de-doo,
Te-oodle-te-oodle-te-oodle-te-oo.

"That's the hard part," he paused to say. Then—

Te-do-doo, te-doo, te-dee-doo, de-de-do.

"General Howard, was a fine man too," said the fifer when he stopped. "He had only one arm, but he got along fine except when them mule skinners began to swear. Then, being a kind of a Sunday school kind of a man, he would try to put his fingers in his ears, but, with only the one hand, there was always one ear open to a flank attack.

" 'There is something about association with mules,' he would say, 'that is very corrupting to the language.' But he didn't hinder them to swear because otherwise, they said, they couldn't handle the mules.

"Ah, it was in June, 1877, that we set out from Fort Vancouver for to keep the Nez Perces on the reservation.

"General Howard picks out 100 men, some from the cavalry and some he mounted from the 21st Infantry, and he detached them and instructed the captain."

It was a long story and I no longer recall the first ten thousand words of it.

"And out of the tree tumbled an Indian with a head as big as a buffalo," related Sergeant Gillespie an hour and a half later. "He was the one that had been doing all the sniping. He must of killed thirty-six men altogether. He had a rifle with telescope sights, and as soon as Cody seen it he said: 'That is what happened to them two English lords that disappeared hunting in the Bitter Root last winter.' Dr. Fitzgerald decapitated the Indian's head and sent it to the Smithsonian.

"General Howard had a pal named Chief Winnemuka, and his daughter Sally Winnemuka, got married. So the General says to me, 'Fifer, play them Injuns a nice wedding march.' So what did I play, only—

Te-oodle-te-oodle, te-do, te-do."

and as far as I know, he is still playing it.

Flap No More

In the days of my youth, the creation of flapjacks was an indigenous art. It had its relation to the drama, for the artists appeared in the flesh, and to the motion pictures of the period, for the artists were silent. Flapjack men worked behind the plate glass windows of restaurants. Each had his own following. Any boy could tell you who, in his opinion, put the wickedest twirl on a wheatcake, the man in Walsh's on Third Avenue or Dennett's on Park Row. If you asked a boy what he wanted to be when he grew up his first choice usually was driver of a white horse fire team and second was a flapjack man. A flapjack man mixed his own batter, a butter tub full at a time. Getting the right consistency was a gift, like mixing colors. By the time I reached adolescence, the firehorses and the flapjack men had disappeared. This probably accounts for the feeling of frustration which has nagged me all through life.

I did meet an ex-flapjack man once. It was in an employment agency. He was a gray-haired man named William Hall, and the only job he could count on was that of assistant cook at six-day bike races, which only occur twice a year in New York. Naturally that left him with a lot of time for reminiscence. Hall did not disappoint me. He was a dignified man with a profound analytical mind.

"It was the cheap places that struck flapjacks the first blow," said Mr. Hall. "They started making flapjacks as big as your hat, three for a dime, but they were only flour and water. They were like leather. They brought the flapjack into disrepute."

"The efficiency men finished the flapjack," he went on bitterly. "They put girls in the windows, as if you could put sex appeal in a flapjack. I don't say you can't teach a girl to turn a griddle cake, but she is too serious about it. Humor is as much an ingredient of a flapjack as flour.

"Also, unless it is flapped, it is not a flapjack. Turning it over isn't the same thing. It must make two somersaults in the air and then you catch it with the plate in your left hand."

Gustav Gartner, the employment agent, nodded. "Yes," he said, "sometimes I see a night man in a chain restaurant on Union Square try a few flips when the manager is not looking, but he is not very competent. Always it flips either once or three times.

"It is no more novelty in flapjacks; that is why the art

has died. Now the men who carve hot meat in sandwich grills are the public favorites. Girls will never become sandwich carvers because the heat from the grill would melt the makeup."

"Ten orders of flapjacks is all one man could keep going in the old days," Mr. Hall resumed. "By the time you got to the one at the left of the line to turn it the one at the other end was done. You couldn't take your eye off your work, and maybe that is how I missed a lot of romance, for I was a presentable young man, and the most beautiful girls in the city had their favorite flapjackers. They would stand in front of windows by the hour, but we were too busy to smile."

SHOW BUSINESS

The Shuberts, in an affable mood, once likened Chicago to a blind beggar with a tin cup, bound to be grateful for any contributions of amusement New York might drop in it. Most folks back where I came from take a kindlier view of what used to be known as the road. For years New York has shouldered the burden of amusing the rest of the country, which appears to be rather dull. The city has even established a *succursale* or bargain basement in California, where retired New Yorkers manufacture a diluted species of dramatics not good enough for New York consumption but fine for the regions without a flesh theatre of their own. No one better exemplifies the kindliness of the New York showman than Joe Hughes, who sells acts to county fairs for George A. Hamid, Inc.

Hamid loves agriculture. He loves it so much that he gets people to do astonishing things for the advancement of agriculture.

He will induce a beautiful California bathing girl to dive 110 feet into a four-foot tank of water to improve the grade of beef cattle at Ormestown, P. Q., or a quartet of reckless daredevils to toy with eternity far over the heads of the thronging populace of Gouverneur, N. Y., the idea in the latter case being to stimulate the production of imitation Camembert cheese.

But Hughes is the man who actually ventures outside the city bounds to bestow the firm's bounty on the peasantry.

Hughes, if brought to the attention of an artist like Gilbert White,* who painted the panels for the Department of Agriculture Building in Washington, might well be represented in a group with Ceres and Proserpine and Flora and other agricultural deities, without belittling the classically draped ladies. All through the cold months he circulates in the bucolic, rustic, sylvan and otherwise discontented regions away from the big city and sells performers to country fair secretaries for the festivities designed to encourage husbandry.

He has no need to consult the index of farm prices, the quotations on International Harvester or the speeches of Senator Smith, of South Carolina, to gauge the condition of American agriculture. When Hamburg, N. Y., asks for three more acts than last year, including a four-high teeterboard specialty that will put it over Dunkirk, he knows that the dairy farmers are doing all right. And when South Boston, Va., asks for a few more girls on the line in the tabloid revue which is staged in front of the grandstand Mr. Hughes knows that all is well with the tobacco boys.

"The acts in front of the grandstand are always free, to draw the crowd to the fair grounds," he told me a while back. "The fairs get their income from renting space to exhibitors. When they spend more money for acts it means they are counting on a good income. This year we haven't enough high-wire acts to go around. Of course, you never can tell what might happen. The milk riots hurt the milk fairs up-State last year. I wouldn't like to hold the contracts of some of those Middle Western fair associations this year with the drought. Fairs pay off every time, but in drought years they are a long time getting 'round to it."

* White is a pretty good showman too.—Ed. Note

From long association with fair secretaries, most of whom are farmers serving for the glory of agriculture, Mr. Hughes, who grew up east of Third Avenue, has contracted an honest, sun-tanned and loose-girthed appearance, so that as he wades along Seventh Avenue, under his broad-brimmed straw, heading for the B.M.T. and Jackson Heights, he is frequently accosted by young men who offer to show him the town.

This does not displease Mr. Hughes, who is an excellent judge of summer squash, Poland China pigs, embroidery, cookies, Houdan roosters and even record halibut, an annual feature of the fair at Lunenburg, Nova Scotia, where fishing and farming divide interest.

"I admire the farmers of the United States," he says. "Their resourcefulness is amazing. During prohibition each district fell back upon its natural resources, and from the spring berry fairs in Florida with their blackberry wine through the peach wine districts of Georgia, the tomato wine areas of New Jersey and right up to the alcohol and soda pop drinkers of Maine, they got along better than the big city slickers, who had to drink bootleg gin."

Political speeches (as well as trotting races and midway attractions) are a part of the agenda at most fairs, and many a State Senator or Governor starts his campaign with a ringing address to the multitude which has assembled to view the Four Queens of the Air, four dazzling examples of radiant young American womanhood performing miss-outs and hock catches on a rigging 110 feet high.

Mr. Hughes, however, refrains from taking political sides, except that he is for the farmer all the time. I would give plenty to see a farmer who is for a New Yorker any part of the time.

"Take the potato men, now," Hughes will say. "When they get a crop they don't get a price, and when they get a price they don't get a crop. Or the milk producers. How do they know how many pounds the distributor sells as liquid and how much goes into cheese?"

He is ready to take up the cudgels for any group of farmers anywhere, and he is up in his lines like a repertoire actor. He gets across the impression that only the titanic efforts of Hamid acrobats have kept agriculture going this long, and that there have been periods in the past when the whole business hung by two fingers or one heel, like the sensational Vesse Troupe, which has just finished an engagement to encourage the agriculture of Pascoag, R. I., by performing the most startling stunts 137 feet in the air.

There are about 3,000 fairs in the United States and Canada which use talent, he estimates, and outlays vary from $1,000 a week for the smallest district fairs to big State fairs like Syracuse, which sometimes spend up to $75,000 for acrobats, a revue, bands of music and auto races (which may be booked through the same office).

As for Hughes' boss, he is the only business executive in New York who is an accomplished acrobat. He can do handsprings backward and forward, somersaults in the air, flip-flops, and a number of other more complicated tumbles called brynies, Rudolphs, pinwheels, and tinsikas. These nimble gyrations serve him much as conventional conversational gestures serve other business executives. Instead of pointing a finger, slapping a thigh, or banging a fist, Hamid is apt to do three or four back flip-flops or a triple handspring. In his roomy offices on the fifteenth floor of the Bond Building, at Forty-sixth and Broadway, he has been known to get up from his desk, take off his coat, and

finish up an interview with an employee or a client by saying "Hai! Hai!" and going into a spirited pinwheel around
the border of the rug.

Handspring Hall

To keep the rest of the country happy, New York maintains an ever-normal granary of acrobats in hotels in cross-
streets off Eighth Avenue. These hotels have succeeded the
theatrical boarding houses of the nineties. My favorite is
one named Irvington Hall, on West Fifty-first Street, in
the halls of which I used to encounter a pair of magnificent
Mexican sisters. They were hand-balancers, and used to
take turns carrying each other, with the top sister's toes
pointed at the ceiling. When they were doing a head-to-
head Rosita, the younger sister, would wave in response to
my greeting. But when they were doing a hand-to-hand she
could only smile.

Irvington Hall was the home of the Braatz family, excellent friends of mine. Mickey, the daughter, was a genius.
She could turn seventy-five successive pinwheels without
pausing. I well remember the first time I visited her.

"The greatest inventions come by accident," said Harry
Braatz, her proud but modest father.

"Like the time I was rehearsing headstands with an
understander and the boss of the troupe said to another
fellow:—'Let him rest his feet on your head, instead of
coming down to the ground every time he gets tired.' I
bridged back with my head on the understander's head,
until my feet were on the head of the third fellow—and we
had made the first Human Bridge!' Mr. Braatz sighed
with pleasure.

"So when my daughter tried her first tinsika—she was

four years old—and she fell in so natural—right there I knew she would be a credit to the family. But never did I imagine—seventy-five! If I would measure my words carefully I would say it was superhuman."

Daughter Mickey, a straight and sturdy blonde of 17, with level eyes in a boyish, pugnacious face, accepted the adjective without delight or demurrer.

"I don't get out of breath," she said. "Not a bit. I could do pinwheels all night on a dime."

She used the layman's word for the trick—her father preferred the more erudite "tinsika."

"The trick was named after Tinsika, the Arab who invented it," he says, "and he should have credit."

But he was not angry with his daughter, who, by combining a tap dance with her seventy-five successive head-over-heels revolutions on one spot (that is what makes it a "spotted" tinsika)—had moved out of the acrobats' world and into music show business.

"There used to be a great future in acrobatics," he said, "but no more. If I had a son I would not teach him further than a backbend."

"I like flip flops," said Mickey. "But I like pinwheels better. Every year I can do more pinwheels, but I think seventy-five is enough. One might injure one's heart."

"Yes," said Mrs. Selma Braatz, the champion lady juggler of the world, Mickey's mother. "Remember Ernst, the handstander? He jumped from four tables down on his hands. He was on his hands more than his feet and finally he became religious crazy and ran around nude. Too much is too much."

Mrs. Braatz, although about to leave the house when I called, consented to doff her furs and balance a wheel on her forehead on the end of a long stem. She made the wheel revolve, with a red ball in its innner rim, and juggled four balls through and around the whirling circumference.

"There," she said, allowing the apparatus to crash to the floor. "Practice, practice, always you got to practice. That is what I always tell Mickey. When I was a little girl my father made me practice twelve, fourteen hours a day. Now sometimes when I sit down in a restaurant, absentminded I begin to juggle the knife, the fork, soon a plate—it's very embarrassing."

"Her brother used to juggle cannon-balls on the back of his neck," Mr. Braatz confided as his wife departed, with a commission from Mickey to bring back "any kind of cake but not apple cake."

Although Tinsika was a man, the pinwheel has become an exclusively feminine trick, Mr. Braatz says, because women are quicker and more supple. Three is about the limit for male tinsikas, and they are not spotted.

"I speak lines in the show," said Mickey. "I met Rudy Vallee at a party, but he has a terrible voice. I do not like the way his left eye droops."

It was a matter of dispute in the hotel, although naturally nobody told Mickey, whether she or Bozo, who lived two floors above the Braatzes, was the more prodigious prodigy.

Bozo is the greatest canine hand-balancer of all time, the only dog to circumambulate Madison Square Garden arena on forefeet exclusively, a feature of Ringling Brothers' and Barnum and Bailey's combined circus.

He is the property of Shorty Flenn, a clown who works in a rube outfit, with white chin whiskers.

Bozo weighs four pounds, and in relation to his bulk, one circumference of the ten-lap arena is equivalent to four miles for a human acrobat walking on his hands.

He is 9 years old, nearly 10, an age which would entitle him to rank as a DeWolf Hopper among canine performers, but he acts more like a juvenile.

If you pretend to ignore him he goes into his act spontaneously, sitting up, waltzing on his hind legs, imitating a crippled dog, and finally, for the sock, going into his hand-walk. If you still ignore him, he scratches at your knee and raises a squawk like a columnist whom nobody reads.

He is a native of Iowa, and like most bright Iowans, an emigre. Mr. Cameron, the manager of the State Fair, perhaps ashamed of such a small dog in a fiesta devoted to such large hogs, presented him to his present owner, who was appearing with a refined divertissement known as "Peck's Bad Boys and Girls," doing a rube character bit.

Bozo is black and tan, and his brain capacity is so phenomenal in proportion to his body weight, Shorty reports, that a professor from the University of Iowa asked him to appear before a university course in psychology during one of his triumphal tours.

"They had him away from me for nearly an hour," Shorty recalls, "and he nearly died for lack of some intelligent conversation. Intelligent? Do you know how I trained him to live in an apartment? I clapped my hands once, and he has never done anything wrong since."

Shorty has a cauliflower ear, a legacy from a boxing kangaroo which he once owned and which hit him after the bell rang. He says all kangaroos are punchers, but none of them can take beating around the head.

Chesty, the Boxing Clown, who shares Shorty's suite, agrees fully as to Bozo's "qualities magnifiques, extraordinaires." Chesty is a Belgian, whose gestures of a pantaloon (he has been a clown from childhood), ill accord with the melancholy grandeur of his thought.

Chesty is a clown by profession, and in Europe a clown wears beautiful clothes, like a matador. The fellow who gets slapped around by the clown is the Auguste. Here nobody knows the difference; it is give and take. The audience distinguishes not even a contortionist who is a front-bender from a contortionist who is a back-bender. But Bozo —he is better than the Fratellinis, Chesty says.

Bozo has never been sick. He never overeats. When left alone he spends hours rehearsing.

"I don't think a dog trainer could ever do as well," says Mr. Flenn. "I have just one animal at a time. There was the kangaroo, a good fellow even if he did sneak a punch on me. He died of pneumonia. And then I had the smallest mule in the world, but a llama fell on him with the Wallace show."

The Minstrel Boys

Before the taste of the rest of the United States had been educated up to acrobats, New York used to amuse the perioeci with minstrel shows. The antiquarian usually can find a quorum of minstrel alumni near the bar of the Hotel Cadillac.

"When I see an old codger around here I don't recognise," said Al E Flat Edwards as he leaned on that bar, "I whistle like this:—'Tu-whee, tu-whee.'

"If he comes over to me, he is a minstrel man."

The whistle was the signal for the minstrel men, in their

purple or scarlet ulsters, to form their two-block line of march and start the 11:45 parade.

"With fifty men you could easily have a parade that stretched two blocks," confided Mr. Edwards, Frank Cushman '93. "You would have two lines of single file, with the men spaced wide apart, on each side of the street, and in the centre the boys with the banners. The band would lead the way. No band ever sounded like a minstrel band. The boys doubling in brass were performers, and each wanted the centre of the stage. Real window-breakers.

"The drum major would throw his baton over the trolley wires and catch it again.

"The girls would line the curb and smile. The kids would run behind. The minstrels probably all had hangovers, and the morning air was a great thing for the fellows who were just kicking cobblestones.

"But the band," Mr. Edwards' unfurred top turned pale green at the memory. "Say, you just try blowing out strong like that after you have been up all night playing poker. Most people think a cornetist blows with his lungs, but really he works with his stomach muscles. Oh, an empty morning-after stomach. And the smell of lunch in the streets."

E-flat, who won his appellation because he habitually blew in that lofty key, mopped his reminiscently agonized brow.

"That's why I had to quit the minstrels," he said. "I became one of the Four Emperors of Music, a variety act which, if I may say so, lives as standard. But there never was anything like the minstrels."

"Never," breathed Tom Barrett, Haverley's Augmented Mastodon Minstrels, '79.

"Never," echoed Poodle Jones, Al G. Fields vintage undetermined.

"On the coldest mornings we had to turn out," said Tom. "It didn't make no difference. Sometimes it was so cold the horns'd freeze and we'd all have to step into a beer saloon to thaw them out."

"Not having been a member of the band," said E-flat, "you don't know that we were supposed to carry little bottles of alcohol to look out for that. But we always managed to lose them."

Whereas most of the variety actors, whose calling has fallen victim to the talking pictures and the depression only during the last decade, are ready to believe the worst, the minstrel men, whose game went on the rocks twenty years ago, are full of hope.

"We have a little organization here right now," Billy Heins confessed without the slightest reluctance, "that is looking for bookings and will give a better show than any of these kids. Why, Billy Maxwell, our interlocutor and tenor soloist, hits high C like eating candy." Billy, at one time with the Gus Hill Minstrels, is on an end with the youthful organization, the Empire State Minstrels.

"I do the dancing," said Tom. "I hoof as good as I did fifty-three years ago. And in those days there was dancers. You danced American clog, or Lancashire clog, or trick clog, or song-and-dance—that was soft shoe, or you were a jigger.

"Afterward they made up the buck-and-wing, and that was the beginning of the end. It was a bastard dance, with a little of this and a little of that all mixed, and now there is no dancing left, only acrobatics.

"I remember when my brother Dan and I were out in

Minneapolis, playing the Comique, in '79. Jack Haverley's show came to town and we went in as clog dancers. There was a bit where all the clog dancers appeared bronzed up like statues, and each man did all his stuff on a little pedestal. Howe and Doyle used to wind up with a back flip right on that tiny space.

"Charley Queen, from Kansas City, the principal clog dancer, used to tap so fast he had to take off his shoes after every performance and pass them around the audience to show there was no instruments inside. Some did just double rolls, but he never tapped that it wasn't a thrible.

"How about John E. Drew?" challenged a listener.

"Or Johnny Williams?"

"Or Billy Hale?"

"There were clog dancers in those days," concluded Tom, with inclusiveness and dignity.

"There never was anything like a minstrel tenor," said High Tom Ward, who should know. He won his nickname because, in Mr. Heins' words, he could 'hit a high C like eating ice cream.'

"They would break your heart," said Mr. Edwards solemnly.

"Do you remember Dick Jose singing 'Silver Threads'?" Tom whispered.

"Or Freddy Bowers and that tearjerker of his, 'Always'?" countered E-flat.

"And Stewart, the Male Patti and Master Julius?"

"They could hit high C like eating cake," asserted Mr. Heins.

"First, there was the first part," he began with what seemed a truism. "That was where all the boys were seated in a semicircle. In the beginning they was right down on the stage, but afterward we got them up in tiers. That was when the interlocutor gagged with the end men and members of the company sang and danced as requested. Haverley carried two interlocutors and four end men, working in two editions, but later shows got up to four and eight.

"Then came the olio. That was a sort of vaudeville performance between the big numbers. We had George Wilson, the monologist, who delivered a comic stump speech— Lew Dockstader was his only rival. Then there would be a comedy musical act—Swiss bell ringers or sleigh bell performers, or such. Every show had a quartet, and most every show had a female impersonator, but he had to keep his place. Another kind of specialty that was popular was gun-juggling.

"And of course Harry Kennedy, the ventriloquist and composer, was a great olio feature.

"With the big show you had a singing and dancing eight, usually, and then came the second part, what we usually called the big act. That was where some of the boys would put on wench dresses and they would play some fool sketch or travesty.

"The scene might be out on a levee, just as it would be on any day down South, with lots of Negroes playing the banjo and singing and shooting craps, and two steamboats racing and one of them blowing up—all a typical Southern everyday scene.*

"Well, Dan and I went out to the coast with Haverley, and it was a wonderful trip. We played all the Western towns like Butte and Helena, but the talk about the gunplay and such is mostly a joke.

* Even the most discriminating New Yorkers are sometimes duped by regional literature.

"The bartender would always tip you off which fellow with a gun might really shoot it off, and those fellows you gave a wide berth. But most of those bold, bad Westerners wore guns for personal adornment only.

"My brother and I left Haverley and went into variety, and later we ran a theatre down in Oklahoma City when they opened the Indian Territory. There was local option, so all the beer was labelled hop tea, and the fellows would also get stewed up on Peruvian Bitters and Hostetter's Bitters and come in and shoot out the lights.

"The next day they would come around and 'pologize, but we had lost a night's business and they had no money.

"We also ran into some stiff impromptu competition in the town of Natchez, where there was a double lynching day and date with us. Admission to the lynching was free.

"About thirty years ago I came East, and along in 1910 I went with Al G. Fields."

"I suppose you found a lot of changes in minstrelsy?"

Tom looked astonished.

"Why, no," he said. "What was there to change?"

A post-mortem on the noble art then began, with half the old boys arguing that this sameness had killed the business, and the others contending that, on the contrary, such innovations as elaborate scenery by destroying the true spirit had hastened the end.

It ended, like most theatrical discussions, with the burden squarely on "the interests," who, E-flat said, had denied the minstrel troupes good dates in order to capitalize more highly on their own musical comedy companies.

"Minstrel shows would go fine now," said Billy Heins, "but the talking picture people control all the theatres and they don't want anything else."

"The automobile struck minstrelsy a terrible blow," declared Poodle Jones. "How could you run a two-block parade with all this traffic?"

Cut yourself a piece of throat

It is unlikely that the names of Adelman and Millman will figure conspicuously in the annals of the American theatre. Yet they are the authors, producers and cast of, "Cut Yourself a Piece of Throat", a drama which is undoubtedly the run leader of the century (more than twenty years), and which must have earned gross receipts comparing favorably with "Tobacco Road's."

Adelman and Millman put on their show in the window of a vacant store. Since there are always vacant stores, this custom frees Adelman and Millman from the necessity of dickering with the Shuberts. Their production is audience-proof. I have caught them on the road, in the notoriously unenthusiastic city of Providence, as well as back where I came from. They always click.

Adelman and Millman are, with Charlie Chaplin, the sole surviving exponents of pure pantomime.

"The show is a wow," the senior partner admits. "Every time you see it it is as if you had never seen it before. But it is exhausting, so we can only put it on every other week. If we did it in two successive weeks we would go stale and lose our punch. We alternate it with the 39 cent fountain pen demonstration, and consequently we never give a dull or indifferent performance."

The act is set in a show window, and this is important, because, as Mr. Adelman says, "You see a man selling something on a street corner, and right away the mental reaction is 'faker'. You see him in a store window and you think 'business man'." Never does the Adelman-Millman Consolidated Show play a street engagement.

The setting, the finesse of the performers, the breathtaking qualities of the scenario and a ton of cheese a year combine to prolong the run of the performance.

The act starts when the partner in the window picks up a fair-sized kitchen knife, pounds the edge of the blade with a hammer and then presses the knife against his throat, draws it past his ears and pushes it against his wrists, showing how thoroughly it has been dulled. He then picks a Belgian whetstone from a stack by his side, sharpens the knife with a few strokes, and drops a page of a magazine or newspaper from shoulder height. As the paper falls he slices it into shreds with the newly sharpened knife.

Next he produces a bread knife with a serrated edge like a Malay kris. When he draws this across his throat, grimacing like a policy collector being put on the spot, the crowd outside his window comes as near applause as a street crowd ever does. He sharpens it and slices some more paper.

Then comes a scissors, with which he earnestly tries to cut his nose off. He fails, sharpens the instrument, moistens it with his tongue and shaves hair off his arm with one blade. Then comes a butcher's cleaver and then, if he is in fettle, the big punch. This is a monster cleaver with a blade three feet by two.

The pantomimist leans his weight upon it. He is unscathed. A few deft strokes of the stone, he whirls the monster chopper through the air and cuts page 156 of the Saturday Evening Post to confetti.

The partner who is not acting stays inside the store and sells whetstones, fifteen apiece and two for a quarter. Fifteen minutes in the window is enough—then they change roles.

The fountain pen act consists of drawing in the style of various cartoonists, then writing out in fancy script:—"You can do it, too," or something of that nature. It is lucrative, because, as the partners explain, nobody has the price of a dollar fountain pen any more.

But their hearts are in whetstones—long, ship-shaped articles that weigh at least half a pound. That is why they carry the cheese.

"You see," said Mr. Adelman, "the market for whetstones is not limitless. They don't wear out, and they are hard to mislay. Yet we must sell several thousand a week to pay our way. So what do we do?

"We distribute this cheese where young mice will get it. The mice eat it, flourish and multiply. They grow fat and dull witted, not having to hunt their food. Cats feed upon the mice and they, too, multiply.

"The cats go out on back fences and express their high spirits. Householders cannot sleep. They go to their windows, and what is so handy to throw as a cheap, hard, heavy whetstone? In this way millions of stones pass into oblivion every year."

Danse Antique

There is some quaint regional place back in the Rocky Mountains where sixty years ago they had a theatre, and now every summer the quaint regional people go out and hold a sentimental revival of the dear dead theatre and get a feeling of having deep roots in the dear dead American past. It is not like New York, they say, where there were plenty of theatres fifty years before their dear dead theatre was built, and where there still are plenty of theatres. It is very vulgar not to be dead, and this is what many writers hold against New York. As soon as they get a stake they move out into the mortuary atmosphere of Connecticut, which reminds them of their dear dreary homes but is handier to their agents' offices.

Because of the city's resolute aversion from the past, there probably will never be a revival of the great cakewalking days. I once met the greatest cakewalker that ever lived, and hardly anybody remembered him.

Young Harlem, then dotingly aware of Snakehips Tucker, the Mills Brothers, Cab Calloway and old Bill Robinson, failed to notice the broadshouldered dignified, middle-aged man of the complexion of a sherry flip, freckled with grated nutmeg, who walked up Lenox Avenue and turned west on 135th Street into the dusk.

Old-timers, lounging in front of the corner barbecue and bar, rubbed their eyes in amazement.

"Can this be you, Billy?" they mumbled.

"It is, indeed, I," replied Billy Farrell, the Paragon of Negro Aestheticians and holder of the Richard K. Fox Three-Decker World's Championship Medal for the Cakewalk. "Produce a cake and I will willingly demonstate my identity."

"Feel good to be back?"

"Back?" echoed the Paragon, who taught the cakewalk to the present Duke of Westminster. "I've never been here before."

Billy Farrell, who had been in Europe for thirty-three years, was pre-Harlem. When his beautiful first wife, Willie, and he embarked for a triumphal tour of the British music halls 53rd St. was the center of Negro life in

Manhattan. Bert Williams and George Walker were rising young comedians. A pair of white boys, Dave Montgomery and Fred Stone, could walk a few, too, but the Farrells held the medal.

Willie (she was a quadroon from Trinidad, an ivory tinted replica of Anna Held) came back for a visit and died. Billy stayed on the other side, married Edna Alexander, another colored actress whom he met in London, ran a dance hall in Cairo, led the band at Shepheards Hotel, acted the role of Battling Siki in a French play, "Le Champion," taught American dancing to Parisian stage artists. He had a son, an officer in an Egyptian regiment. His younger daughter was a special student at Cambridge. Edna died in Vienna.

"I was quite prepared for the skyline," he said in the lounge of the handsome new 135th Street Y. M. C. A., "but I can't get used to seeing so many colored people. And no more walking for the cake! I'd like to do it once again, maybe at a benefit."

"Why, just mention cakewalk to these young people and they say, 'Oh, yes, that old dance where you throw your head back and kick your legs in 'the air.' That isn't the straight cakewalk at all. That is the grotesque cakewalk, a plebeian variation. Willie and I walked with grace. It was like a ballet, interpreting a flirtation. Magnificent. Thousands of dollars were thrown on the floor the night we won the championship, March 2, 1895."

Farrell tapped his very British brogues with his malacca stick.

"Mr. and Mrs. Luke Blackburn, the favorites—they were society people from the West—they were too dignified to pick up any of that money. But Willie and I, you

bet we picked it up. We hadn't worked in two months before that. I had $10,000 worth of diamonds on me and two
bits in my pocket.

"Mayor Strong and Jim Corbett and Richard K. Fox
and Willie Vanderbilt were the judges. It was in the old
Madison Square Garden, and there were 108 couples competing. Nobody gave us a chance. We were just part of the
field. I had been in the show business all my life since I
was nine, singing tenor and imitating De Wolf Hopper
and end man in colored minstrel combinations, but I wasn't
known for a cakewalker. Neither was my wife.

"We were living in two rooms, just two little rooms,
over on 30th Street between Sixth and Seventh, in the heart
of the Tenderloin. Willie saw the poster in the windows
about this great cakewalk contest. She was a clever seam-
stress. She fixed herself up a dress that looked like a million. I went down to the Bowery and saw a pawnbroker
named Goldstein. I performed a lot for nothing for those
Jewish lodges on the east side. He loaned me $10,000
worth of diamonds, but he didn't let me out of his sight
while I wore 'em. Not once.

"There were a lot of theatrical people in the walk, as
well as those colored society cakewalkers. We saved our
best business for the second time around the hall. The first
time around those society walkers made us look pretty
small. But the second time around we did a lot of new stuff,
like me kneeling and tying my wife's shoelace without
missing a beat.

"We walked from 10 until 4 the next morning. One
by one the judges sent the other couples away, until at last
we walked one round alone. And the next day firms that

had donated prizes delivered three sets of furniture and four pianos to our two-room flat. I had about two dozen silk hats and Willie got miles of stockings. And after that we never looked back."

THE LAUGHING JEW

Seven or eight years ago, when I began to cover trick assignments on the East Side, I was agreeably astonished to find that Jews enjoyed themselves. My early reading had taught me to think of Jews as pale, sad people, persecuted for their insufferable virtues, like Isaac and Rebecca in "Ivanhoe" or Ludwig Lewisohn in "Upstream." This view was tacitly endorsed by my parents' friends, although they were neither pale nor sad. Still, they seldom got drunk, and their chief diversions, bridge and tennis, were conducted with the acerbity of Talmudic dispute. My secret inclination toward less orderly enjoyments sometimes made me feel lonely and atypical. It pleased me enormously to find that back where I came from there were hundreds of thousands of Jews who stuffed themselves with highly flavored food, got pie-eyed, sang dirty songs and occasionally punched each other on the nose. A saloonkeeper I know on Delancey Street once made me a proposition that would have delighted Villon. "We'll eat good," he said, "then we'll get shikker, go upstairs and see the girls, and then we'll go to a Turkish bath and have a good sweat." * Beroald de Verville could have thought of nothing to add.

* This association of ideas, the reader will at once perceive, is richly mediaeval. It is a survival of the period when *bordel* a brothel, and *etuve*, a public sweat bath, were virtually interchangeable terms. Back where I came from all the regional customs have origins, and practically everybody has ancestors.

For the first time I felt a desire to learn Hebrew and Yiddish. Then I hoped to write a history of the laughing Jew, which would establish Noah, the bad kings of Israel and Harpo Marx as the authentic leaders of Jewish thought and put the blast on people like Jeremiah and Stephen S. Wise.

An event I always liked to cover was the fall opening of Mayor Abe Haimowitz's Roumanian restaurant on Forsyth Street. Abe is a vast fat man the color of a tallow candle, and his jowl is as deep as an ordinary face. People who came to Haimowitz's to dance and drink were almost all heavy and happy, and it sometimes seemed that if all the customers should happen to get over on one side of the dance floor, the restaurant might capsize. The only small, nervous men in the place were the six waiters, all named Itzig, who kept down to skin and bones racing from the kitchen to the tables and back again. Nobody at Haimowitz's ever stopped eating. The patrons boldly subscribed to the notion that a large steak is as palatable at nine-thirty in the evening as at seven. They had never heard of an arbitrary division of darkness into dinner and supper hours with a conventional interim. They called dinner supper and they ate supper all night.

There was a woman singer who looked a little like Pola Negri, who sang Yiddish songs specially composed for her at five dollars each by a song writer who lived on a chair in a Roumanian tea shop. There was plenty of sacramental wine—free to reporters—and the place was pervaded by an atmosphere of well-bred enjoyment and meat broiled with garlic. The only ill-mannered persons I ever saw at Haimowitz's were a hockey player from Brown University and a novelist from the Deep South, both of whom were tossed out on their ears, because they butted in on women at other tables. "Friendship is all right," Haimowitz explained, "but not with the hands."

As a feature of the fall opening the musicians changed their shirts.

"People are getting married very much on the East Side," Haimowitz once said, "and we got booked every night weddings, the poor guys."

Abe was a member of the League of Neighborhood Mayors, a social organization of prominent men like himself and Mayor Rizzo, but the other societaires seldom attended his fall openings.

"Aren't you friends?" I once asked him.

"Until money," he replied.

All Star, Double Headed Wedding

The love of feasting is so deeply rooted in the Jewish character that a crowd will assemble for even a vicarious celebration. Working on this trait, a man named Samuel P. Mogelewsky, president of the World Clothing Exchange, 759 Broadway (suits from $8.95) invented an indoor sport that brought him thousands of customers. It was public weddings.

I saw Mr. Mogelewsky run what the typed announcements referred to as a "double-headed all-star Jewish wedding" at Cooper Union.

Two thousand persons, guests of Mr. Mogelewsky, and dressed in the neatest merchandise of the World Clothing Exchange, witnessed the marriage of Ida Chaiken, 19, and Gabriel Kimmelman, 21.

There was no room for another person, and to obtain

seats for a valued customer Mr. Mogelewsky had to buy back two tickets to his own party, at $1.50 each.

The same 2,000 remained to see Irving Cohen, 22, wed Audrey Schneider, 19, and while half the audience maintained that Cantor Yosele Schlisky, who officiated for the first couple, out-chanted Cantor Yosele Shapiro, who worked the second half of the double-header, there were as many of the opposite opinion.

Mr. Mogelewsky, in evening clothes which mutely advertised the World Clothing Exchange, an extra large size, explained that the evening's activities were entirely at his expense, including the schnapps, the three cantors, a choir of forty singers and "one ton of stuffed fish."

He ran a radio station in his store, and on every program appealed to young couples wishing a free de luxe marriage to telephone him. He promoted the weddings periodically, and anybody who bought a suit got a ticket for the next wedding.

"This is an opinion that I got from my father," he said, "that to help people that can't afford a wedding to get married is a good thing."

"And if they haven't any money to live on after they get married?"

"Well, but that was his idea," parried Mr. Mogelewsky. "I follow in his footsteps.

"I call out on the radio for young people that have been keeping company five years and can't get married. Sometimes they don't tell me the truth. Maybe they only been going together four years, but I can't help it. So I spend all that money"—

Here Joseph Cohen, the store manager, ventured an interjection.

"What it cost him tonight," he said, "I hope that you and I earn it every month."

Mr. Mogelewsky waved a deprecating hand.

"We fit them up from shoes on their feet the young couples," he said. "And the wedding you can see for yourself it's done up to perfection. If a millionaire would make it he couldn't do better."

A microphone was set up on the speaker's platform, near the chuppa, or canopy borne by four World Clothing salesmen in natty tuxedos fresh out of stock. Before the first wedding the audience listened to a number of singers, including Esther Field, the Yiddish Kate Smith, Francis Adler, the Yiddish Gypsy, and Cousine Friedele, the Female Rosenblatt.

Mr. Mogelewsky then marched up the centre aisle at the head of fifty bridesmaids, wearing sashes marked "World Military Bridesmaids." Twenty-five bridesmaids were dressed as George Washington, and twenty-five as Eddie Leonard. All carried Malacca walking sticks, and at their entrance the band played "The Stars and Stripes Forever" very softly, in slow time.

The bridesmaids formed two lines and crossed their walking sticks overhead, and Mr. and Mrs. Mogelewsky walked under the sticks, followed by Miss Chaiken and Mr. Kimmelman, both of whom took their places under the chuppa, where they remained during a lengthy recital by Cantor Schliski.

At length the cantor offered a glass of wine, both drank, and Mr. Kimmelman dropped the glass and stepped on it, completing the ceremony. The wedded pair and relatives then adjourned to a private chamber, where several hundred-weight of fish awaited them.

The new Mrs. Kimmelman, letting down after the strain, smoked a cigaret. All the relatives ate slowly, because they knew the Cohen-Schneider nuptials would last a long time, and the Cohen-Schneider relatives could not start eating until Cantor Shapiro finished his exercises of virtuosity.

Bierman Sits Cool-blooded

One of the proudest men I ever interviewed was Manuel Bierman, the winner of a citywide pinochle tournament.

"Bierman sits cool-blooded," Bierman narrated with overt admiration for his hero. "This fellow already has 1,184 points and Bierman has 836. We are playing 1,200 points. For myself I would say it is no use to play further. But I couldn't sell out the kibitzers, that had bet on me up to $500. So I played out a nine, so cool-blooded—I melded the dix, eighty kings and a pinochle—'Nu,' I said, 'the rest of the cards you can have—'".

A transcription, verbatim of Mr. Bierman's story would have taken pages, but, anyway, it ended like most of Mr. Bierman's stories, in the triumph of Mr. Bierman and the kibitzers who had had the good judgment to bet on him.

"They kitzeled (tickled) each other with pleasure," concluded the pinochle champion as he laced his morning coffee with a healthy charge of schnapps, "and they sent out to buy me a box of 25 cent cigars."

Mr. Bierman is a good pinochle player, and he would be the last to deny it.

Short, rotund, gray-haired, with a wide, jolly face and a gray mustache that tries to hide under his nose, he devoted himself to a breakfast of mush and milk and smoked whitefish in his apartment on Grand Concourse, and told of his epic struggle against Robert Nussman, of Paterson, in the final game of the New York district tourney, digressing to detail various interesting hands of a pinochle career that began forty years ago. Frequently he quoted P. Hal Sims, who had presided as referee.

" 'Bierman,' Mr. Sims says to me, 'you can play cards for my money any time.'

"This here Nussman melded big every time and I came in in back of him with the count, until finally I jumped over him. When I was finished with such a battle with such a shark I felt like a man drives a machine 100 miles an hours 100 hours—so dizzy.

"So I flopped in a taxi with my wife and drove home and took a cup of tea, hot, and even then I couldn't sleep the next day."

That victory netted Bierman a prize of $300.

Mr. Bierman's wife is a small, nervous woman. They have eight grownup children.

How did Bierman learn to play pinochle? From a book, from a teacher?

"I learned from watching bum players," he said. "So if you'll watching good players and bum players both, it is like learning good material and material which is no good, so you can choice out the playing which is good. Because pinochle is not a game like poker, which however way the cards fall you can't battle against it. Pinochle is a game for judgment."

As for learning from a book, even a book written by P. Hal Sims, Mr. Bierman, who is fond of parables, asked:—

"Which is the best doctor—or a young doctor who has learned in books with lectures, or a experienced doctor which has practiced in clinics with observations? The doctor that has learned from practice, from experience? So is answered your question.

"How soon I come to know I could play good pinochle? Listen, when a boy begins to walk you give him a hammer and chisel. If he don't drop them, you know he'll be a good carpenter."

During his long career of pinochle triumphs—the tournament was but a crowning episode, an opportunity to demonstrate publicly that virtuosity of which all his acquaintance were long aware—Mr. Bierman had on occasion overcome not only brilliant playing but chicanery.

There was a time, he remembered, when the proprietor of a cigar store in Eighth Avenue tried to take him with a deck on which the cigar store man had marked all the kings and aces. The wary Mr. Bierman put the same nail-marks on the nines and tens, which confused the cigar man terribly. Mr. Bierman won $30. "When I had his $30 I couldn't hold my water no longer," he told me. "So I threw him the cards in the face and said, 'Loafer, let this be a lesson.' "

FISH THEATRE

One of my favorite New York microcosms is inhabited by officers of the New York Zoological Society. These gentlemen are unperturbed by the anthropoid events that keep most of my friends in a continual state of gibbering anxiety. Their sole preoccupations are with captive fish, reptiles, birds and mammals. Most of them pursue entomology as an avocation. I do not think I would like to be so unperturbed myself as a regular thing. I would be afraid that some fascist might smack me behind the ear in 1947 while I was examining the sexual organs of a *urinophthalmus,* or perhaps the striation of a bird of paradise's tail. But it is restful to know where you can go when you want to get away from it all. You can go to the Administration Building at the Bronx Zoo, or to the Aquarium. Men who work around animals are almost always good company, whether the animals are racehorses or rhinoceroses. It is impossible to conceive of a zoologist who is a prude, or who is essentially mercenary. There never has been any real money in the business.

The archetype of an animal man was the late Dr. William Temple Hornaday, who was the director of the Zoo for the first thirty years of its existence. After he retired he moved up to Stamford, Conn., and edited a journal called "Plain Truth," in the interests of the American wild duck. I remember talking to him on his seventy-eighth birthday. He was mightily perturbed over the predicament of the Northern white rhinoceros.

"The Northern white rhinoceros is poised on the edge of a precipice, just about to take the plunge into oblivion," he said. A wind of indignation ruffled his white whiskers and an iron hard hand pounded his desk in a sleepy business building in Stamford.

"The natives are killing it off in the most unprincipled and devilish manner to sell the horns to Chinese apothecaries. The apothecaries grind them into powder for rich senile Chinese old men."

"But, Dr. Hornaday, why let a Northern white rhinoceros spoil your birthday?"

"It's the infernal injustice of it," Dr. Hornaday said. "Here is man, a completely unsatisfactory animal, bound to destroy all the other animals. What happened to the Labrador duck?"

"I don't know, Dr. Hornaday."

"Extinct. How about the Carolina parrakeet? The California vulture, I need hardly tell you, is pretty nearly a thing of the past."

Dr. Hornaday was not a vegetarian or a camera hunter. He had a great reputation as a big game hunter for museum specimens. But he believed that without longer and stricter closed seasons on most forms of American game extinction was inevitable by 1940.*

"Something can be done to avert the slaughter," he said. "Public opinion has been mobilized behind the pronghorn antelope. The fight we made for the fur seal was most successful. President Hoover never should have been defeated. He did a great deal for the wild duck."

Pastels of tigers, lithographs of Rocky Mountain sheep,

* Probably he was wrong.—Ed. Note

---

oil paintings of grizzly bears and a carved wooden penguin adorned the small room.

Dr. Hornaday wished to discuss no political issues.

"Just say a word for the grizzly bear," he enjoined. "There is an animal that has been grossly maligned.

I like the Aquarium better than the Zoo because it is more like a cathedral. The members of the Aquarium staff are younger, one might almost say sportier, than their colleagues uptown, but their charges are immensely sedate. The contemplation of fish has a sedative effect. I have seen a company of German tourists, frightened, harried, blustering people on a conducted trip to New York (they were allowed to spend four dollars a day) walk into the Aquarium and become instantly polite. One big slob stood in front of a tank of codfish for fifteen minutes. *"Die sorgen nicht,"* he said finally, which was a tipoff on life back where HE came from.

Behind the Tanks

The head man at the Aquarium is Charles M. Breder, Jr.

When Breder, Jr., orders sea trout (*Salmo trutta*) in a restaurant, he is frequently served a piece of weakfish (*Cynoscion regalis*). He discerns no difference in the taste of the two fish, but instantly detects the imposture because he recognizes the soft, spongy texture of *Cynoscion's* flesh. Filet of sole is apt to prove more amusing to Mr. Breder than sea trout; sole may turn out to be whiting (*Gadus merlangus*), young cod (*Gadus callarias*), flounder (*Flesus flesus*), or even occasionally dogfish (*Scylliorhinus canicula*). Mr. Breder is not an epicure but an ichthyologist. He is a narrow-shouldered man with a thin, youthful face, blue eyes, and light brown hair parted in the middle.

His skin is almost translucent. He usually looks preoccupied and slightly worried, and twirls two gold keys about his right forefinger whenever his hands are not employed with some specific task. The keys are emblems of Phi Beta Kappa and Beta Lambda Sigma, honorary fraternities. The impression of youth and fragility is exaggerated, for Breder is forty-one years old and tough enough to survive a tropical expedition that cost the lives of two associates.

Breder became Chief at the New York Aquarium last November, on the retirement of Dr. Charles Haskins Townsend, who had been Director for thirty-five years. For fourteen years before his promotion he had served as Aquarist and Assistant Director. In 1926 he won the annual Cressy Morrison medal of the Academy of Sciences for a magisterial work on "The Locomotion of Fishes." This carries with it a prize of two hundred and fifty dollars and a great amount of kudos. Dr. William K. Gregory of Columbia, a distinguished paleontologist, observed after reading Breder's paper that the young man was a genius.

The new chief of the Aquarium does not leave his profession behind him when he goes home at night. He lives in a rustic wood-and-stucco house at Mahwah, in the township of Hohokus, New Jersey. In the back yard of this house he has built a C-shaped fish pond. Last summer he brought to it from the Aquarium a number of *Gasteropelecus*, minute fresh-water flying fish from South America. *The Gasteropelecus* had never flown in the Aquarium; apparently they sensed the danger of crashing into glass. At Mahwah they soared through the air from five to six feet at a time, a great distance in relation to their length, which is two and a half inches. Breder wanted to study this "flight" to see how it differed from the aerial gliding of the oceanic flying fish.

The Breder home is comfortable enough, but hardly a model of decoration. When Breder bought the house two years ago he spent most of his available capital on the fish pond, an excellent darkroom in the basement, and the steel shelving in his study. Suitable furniture will be bought in due time, he says calmly. Breder and his wife own a battered Dodge, but the ichthyologist seldom drives it. When driving a car, he explains, he sometimes begins to meditate about fish; then he bumps something or lands in a ditch. Mrs. Breder often motors to New York and brings him home. She says she isn't interested in fish except for cooking purposes.

On six mornings a week Breder boards the 7:41 train at Mahwah, which is the station this side of Suffern on the Erie. The Erie runs through fairly rugged country within a short distance of New York. This makes the region a favorite with naturalists who have to commute. Gloria Hollister, Dr. William Beebe's assistant, lives at Suffern when she is not under water. Dr. Frank Lutz, the curator of insects at the American Museum of Natural History, gets on at Ramsey, the station after Mahwah on the way to town. Dr. Willis J. Gertsch, the Museum's spider expert, is another Ramsey man. Breder and Lutz generally play chess on a pocket board until the train reaches Jersey city. "A couple of fellows from the Planetarium live out this way too," Breder once remarked, "but of course I don't know any of that crowd."

Breder cannot remember a time in his life when he was not interested in fish. As a boy in Newark he filled the attic of his parents' house with tanks of goldfish, killies, and sticklebacks, and eventually with tropical fish. These last had a budding vogue between 1912 and 1914, but the World War destroyed the fish-importing business. The postwar fad is a revival. The present principal of the Newark Commercial and Technical High School remembers young Breder distinctly as the boy who always drew pictures of fish on the margins of his German compositions. Breder illustrates most of his ichthyological papers with competent sketches, but he has never felt moved to draw anything other than a fish.

There is a curious world behind the tanks of the New York Aquarium. The visitor in the centre of the cylindrical old building sees only the glass fronts of the fish tanks, apparently built into a solid wall. But behind the wall, a rather flimsy one, are two tiers of grated catwalks which make a three-quarter circuit of the building. From these catwalks one looks down, instead of forward, into the tanks. Passing along the lower walk, the Aquarium worker strolls over the dorsal fins of barracudas and sharks and the evil heads of morays. The walk has no railing and members of the staff occasionally slip and take a header into the shark tank, frightening the sharks. The upper catwalk circles above the upper tier of tanks, where zebra fish from West Africa and *Astyanax* from Venezuela pop to the surface to look up at the attendants, and blue puffers from Florida spit water a foot into the air. There are tanks on the first floor and the gallery. The executive offices are on the third floor.

Breder moves through this humid environment with a deep understanding of the other inhabitants. He knows the unfortunate penchant of black bass of the same size for trying to swallow each other, like competing corporations. After such an attempt one bass is partially swallowed and the other chokes to death. He understands also that while some fish are highly gregarious, others, like the *Galápagos Beau Gregory*, insist on plenty of room. Each Beau Gregory appropriates a beat like a policeman's and assaults any fish who gets in his way. The little stickleback, friendly enough while a bachelor, becomes a neighborhood terror during the hatching season, when it will not allow any other fish within yards of its nest. The one general diplomatic law among fish is based on priority. The first specimen in a tank will bully a later arrival, even when the second fish is decidedly the larger. The rule is valid even among fish of different species. If, for example, a number of harmless mullet are placed in a tank and a barracuda is later introduced into it, the barracuda will not touch them. It will even try to get away from the mullet, although in a wild state it preys on them.

No one ever adopted a career with less uncertainty than Breder. When he was twenty-one, he introduced himself to J. T. Nichols of the Department of Fishes in the American Museum of Natural History, announcing, "I want to get into ichthyology." (Nichols did not consider this bizarre; he says that every year two or three young men disclose the same ambition.) Nichols suggested the United States Bureau of Fisheries as a good starting point for an ichthyological career. Breder had never had any college training (shortly after graduation from high school he had taken a job as electrical draftsman at the Federal Shipbuilding Company in Jersey City), but he entered a competitive examination for the position of Biologist in the Division of Scientific Inquiry of the Fisheries Bureau. Most of his competitors were Ph.D.'s, but Breder landed the job. He afterward told one of the examiners that he had studied biology in the Newark Public Library. He came to the Aquarium after a couple of years divided between Washington routine and straining the waters of the Atlantic Coast for the eggs of weakfish. Breder and an associate in the Bureau were the first to identify these eggs. The post of Aquarist at the Aquarium carried with it a considerably better salary than his government job.

Breder did not inherit this urge to mess with fish. Charles M. Breder, Sr., who died last summer, was secretary of the Public Service Company of New Jersey, the corporation that controls virtually all Jersey light and power. The elder Breder was an electrical engineer. He had steered his son into the electrical drafting job in the shipyard, thinking that young Charles would eventually enter M.I.T.

When the younger Breder came to the Aquarium, he was entrusted with the duty of keeping the fish alive. The Director, like the captain of a ship, is responsible for the safety of his charges, but the chore itself falls on the Aquarist, who corresponds to a first officer. Fish of certain species were kept in non-flow tanks at that time, and they lived only a few weeks. This was because their secretions eventually turned the water acid and it killed them. Breder rigged a device that released minute quantities of bicarbonate of soda into the water at a rate that maintained a constant alkaline balance. It stopped mortality in the non-flow tanks while the Aquarium was building up its present complete set-up of separate circulatory systems. None of the fish on exhibition now are in stagnant water. The young man's ingenuity won him the respect of Dr. Townsend, the Director. As a reward, Townsend permitted

him to take a six-month leave of absence in 1924 to go
on an expedition into the unexplored interior of southern
Panama as a representative of the American Museum of
Natural History.

The primary purpose of the expedition was commercial
rather than scientific. A man named Richard Oglesby
Marsh had been employed by the Firestones and Henry
Ford to search for suitable rubber lands in Central America.
When these industrialists gave up Central America and
turned their attention to Liberia for rubber land, Marsh
got backing from the du Ponts. He believed there were
great tracts suitable for rubber cultivation in Darien, in
the southeastern part of Panama. Darien, although lying
within a hundred miles of the Canal Zone, had never been
explored because it was the home of hostile Indians. Since
Marsh did not want the Panamanian officials to know he
was looking for rubber land, he called his quest a search
for the White Indians of Darien. He invited scientific
institutions to send representatives with him at his backer's
expense. The Smithsonian Institution and the University
of Rochester sent an ethnologist and a geologist respec-
tively. Breder was the expedition's fish-and-reptile man.
The party left the Pacific coast of Panama in February
and came out on the shore of the Gulf of Darien, on the
other side of the Isthmus, three months later.

Dr. J. L. Baer, the ethnologist, died of infected insect
bites. Dr. Raoul Brin, a botanist sent with the party by
the Panamanian government, succumbed to blackwater
fever. Breder was carried aboard a fruit boat on a stretcher,
suffering from malaria, but he brought out notes for a
scholarly paper on "The fishes of the Rio Chucunaque
Drainage, Eastern Panama." Breder is expert at the ar-

rangement of beasts by class, sub-class, order, sub-order, family, genus, and species, a pursuit technically known as taxonomy. The discoverer of a new species, when he has placed it in relation to all other known animals, has the privilege of naming it. His own name is then tagged onto the title he has inflicted on his prey; for example, *Rivulus chucunaque chucunaque Breder*, a designation a quarter of an inch longer than the minnow involved. On the Darien expedition Breder added five species to the twenty-two thousand already known to ichthyologists.

The White Indians, the most publicized quarry of the expedition, turned out to be partial albinos. They were strange creatures with light-brown hair, fish-belly skins, and fluttery eyelids. These whites appear as sports in families of red Indians. The offspring of two White Indians is invariably red. Marsh brought a couple of his White Indians back to the United States to meet President Coolidge. Breder says he saw one of them about six months ago, riding a bicycle near the New York approach to the George Washington Bridge. He didn't get a chance to talk to him, but he says the Indian looked pretty much at home. There is, incidentally, a compact colony of San Blas Indians in Brooklyn. The White Indians belong to the San Blas nation.

Most laymen believe that a fish swims by means of its fins, as a bird flies with its wings or a man swims with his arms and legs. They seldom give much thought to the subject. Breder, observing his charges in the Aquarium, found that fish deprived of some or all of their fins showed no appreciable loss of speed, although they maneuvered awkwardly in turning, rising, or diving. The vertical, unpaired fins on the backs and bellies were evidently used as keels for balance, the paired breast fins as ailerons in changing depth and direction or for slow locomotion in close quarters. Only in a few specialized sorts, such as the sea horse, do the fins provide the chief motive power. Breder then felt a need to know what did push fish through the water. He determined finally that the swimming of most fish was a combination of two movements: a tail swing from side to side and a contraction of the muscle flakes, or muscular casing of the fish's body. Fast-swimming fish like the mackerel perform these movements so rapidly that they seem one continuous motion. To the human eye it appears that the fish darts forward in a straight line, but in fact it swings from side to side in a short arc as it advances.

Breder later became preoccupied with some fish of a marine species that he had found living in fresh water on Andros Island in the Bahamas. The water, although devoid of salt, had a high chalk content because Andros is a coral island. Breder placed sea fish of the same species in his sea-water tanks at the Aquarium and gradually drew off sea water, replacing it with fresh water containing calcium. Finally he had his subjects living in fresh water. It was hard water, however like that in parts of the central United States. In these hardwater regions fish survive which are closely related to prehistoric marine species. Relatives isolated in softwater lakes and river systems at the emergence of the land mass must have disappeared several hundreds of thousands of years ago. Breder's modern fish on Andros helped explain the anachronistic fish of Arkansas.

This apparently undirected curiosity of Breder's has at times been a little hard to explain to the trustees of the

New York Zoological Society, the conservative organization which operates the Aquarium and the Bronx Zoo and contributes about twenty-five per cent of their support. The Society, as stated on the title page of its annual report, was "founded in 1895 for the establishment of the Zoological Park; conservation of the animal life of the world—fishes, mammals, birds; promotion of zoology through exploration and publication; and in 1900 the direction of the New York Aquarium in Battery Park." While "publication" certainly implies at least some preliminary observation, the amateur animal lovers who constitute most of the Society's membership are more apt to be impressed by adventures in a bathysphere or *safaris* in Africa than by experiments on the renal tissues of lungfish.

Dr. Townsend always believed that the primary purpose of the Aquarium was to edify the public with plenty of sea lions and alligators. But his Aquarist showed such unremitting diligence in routine work that Townsend first tolerated Breder's researches and then protected them.

Breder arrives at the Aquarium at 8:55 every morning nowadays and goes to his office on the third floor. The vast Director's office, the shape of half a pie, dwarfs him. Surrounded by its mahogany furniture and portraits in oil of eminent defunct zoologists, he appears like a minnow in a strange tank. He escapes as soon as he can to the Aquarist's room on the same floor, a sunny place filled with jars of deceased fish pickled in formaldehyde. There he consults with his subordinates, Christopher W. Coates, the new Aquarist, and Dr. Ross Nigrelli. Coates for seven years before his and Breder's promotion had charge of the tropical-fish collection on the second floor. After his

talk with Coates and Nigrelli, Breder starts on his tour
of the tanks.

The Aquarium has three main circulatory systems. One
carries pure sea water, which has been brought from beyond Ambrose Channel in a tank boat. This water is stored
under the Aquarium lawn. A second system uses harbor
water pumped from under the Battery sea wall for the less
fastidious salt-water creatures. The third has New York
City water. In each system there are several loops of
pipes, each serving a group of tanks with inhabitants who
need water at the same temperature. The sea turtles in
their floor pool swim in tepid bay water; the horseshoe
crabs and killifish take bay water *au naturel;* the alligators
and penguins have warm fresh water; and the pelicans
have cold Croton. Other exhibits need temperatures of
from forty degrees, for the brook trout, to ninety for the
lungfish. The highly publicized electric eel must have his
water at not less than eighty degrees or more than eighty-
five. A fish in too cold water falls a speedy victim to
parasites. Electric pumps drive the water through the
loops, and each loop has its own electric heater and its own
filter system. Temperature is regulated by thermostats.
If the power should fail, a supplementary system of pneu-
matic pumps would shoot air through the water, main-
taining the oxygen supply but not the temperature. Some
exhibits might last twenty-four hours under such conditions.
Others would die in three or four. Most of the Aquarium's
small tropical fish swim in water imported with them,
which is guarded like good wine. Within the Aquarium
are fish living in Ganges, Nile, and Amazon water. As
there is barely enough for the fish in one or two minuscular
tanks, each brand is kept constantly flowing through minia-

ture filter. Clogging must be detected instantly if the fish are to survive.

Problems of feeding are complex, but seldom so urgent as those of circulation. If a fish will eat only live tubifex worms and none are immediately available, it usually can get along for a few days without eating. The African lungfish can go without food for four or five years, and frequently does.

His tour of inspection finished, Breder goes to pursue his ichthyological investigations at lunch. Usually he eats in the basement of the Whitehall Building. Since his interest is not limited strictly to vertebrates, he sometimes orders scallops. If the scallop flesh has a vertical grain he knows it is a scallop. If the grain runs perpendicular to the axis of the cylinder, he knows that the scallop has been punched from the wing of a skate. Although it is sometimes said that scallops are made from shark meat, Breder has never found any that were.

Afternoons vary more than mornings. Often Breder receives foreign ichthyologists from the aquaria in London, Paris, or Göteborg, the Marine Institute at Tel-Aviv, or the Australian Museum at Sydney. He must be a diplomat, since there may be an opportunity to swap two shark suckers for a scorpion fish, or a batch of horseshoe crabs (common here but unknown in Europe) for some luminous sea anemones. The late Prince of Monaco, a renowned aquarist, was a passionate amateur of horseshoe crabs. Breder also is asked to criticize plans for projected aquaria in other cities. One is now building at Colombo, in Ceylon.

The business of getting new specimens takes up considerable time. The Aquarium buys in the open market only as a resort. Its funds for the purchase of new fish are limited to the receipts from the sale of mounted seahorses, picture postcards, and books of photographs, never more than a couple of thousand dollars a year. To this is added an annuity of five hundred dollars from an endowment fund. To get cheap fish, Coates and Breder cultivate relations with wireless operators on freighters. They pay these operators a few dollars for transporting specimens. The operators carry trade goods for the natives who catch the fish. An old man in Beira, Mozambique, receives a fifth of Scotch every time one American ship touches there. He provides magnificent zebra fish. The radio men also carry bundles of Breder's, Coates', and Nigrelli's castoff clothes and trade them to St. Helena boys for live fish.

During Breder's evenings at Mahwah he works on two books. One is a definitive treatise on oceanic flying fish. The other is an encyclopedia of the reproduction of fish. Breder is not a fluent writer like Beebe or Ditmars, but his thoughts have considerable sweep. In the first part of the book on reproduction he says, "What an animal does is equally as important as what it has." He says he means that in the survival of a species, reproductive methods may be as significant as anatomic details. The dinosaur may have been a languid lover. The uxorious stickleback is a good bet to outlast man.

The Lecherous Leaf Fish

The head funny man at the Aquarium is Christopher W. Coates, the Aquarist. A tall, friendly Canadian with a mildly British manner, he has a genius for publicizing fish. He will speak of a fish three-quarters of an inch long as a "surly beast" or a "cheerful beggar," or stroke a dogfish's back with unaffected cordiality. Under the spell of Coates's gentle voice, newspapermen begin to detect personal traits of fish which are extremely difficult to set down on paper for people who have never met Coates. Some reporters sink into a Coatesian hypnosis and become unable to write about anything *but* fish. Despatched in the general direction of a four-alarm fire, they come back with a description of an electric catfish. A case of ichthyomania, if detected early, can sometimes be cured. The sufferer is allowed to taper off on stories about snakes which are found by policemen along Broadway (the snakes have escaped from sideshows), stories about cats which fall into chimneys and have to be extracted by the emergency squad, stories about circus press agents, the annual Butlers' Ball under the auspices of Mrs. James Field, and finally Columbia commencements and interviews with politicians on what is wrong with the Republican party. After four or five years the convalescent is about ready to work on human beings again when he meets Coates at a bar, is induced to re-visit the Aquarium, and on the morrow comes steaming into the city room with another red hot story about a sea anemone. I remember one affair Coates got me into that threatened to engulf my journalistic career. It all started with a couple of leaf fish. The leaf fish had children—about 150 black dots the size of fleas. It was the first time that leaf fish had been bred in captivity.

"Why, a fellow from Florida offered me a Madagascar lace plant for a breeding pair," Coates, told me.

"The only trouble is that it would cost about $40,000 to feed the leaf fish until they grew up, leaving a net deficit of $36,250 if everything went smoothly."

The mature leaf fish (*Monocyrrhus polyacanthus*), is a creature exactly resembling a pointed and slightly irregular green leaf floating in the water. It has a profile like a public utility executive and an appetite to match.

It will eat only living fish and each leaflet demands seven meals a day.

"Experiments we conducted a year ago indicated that a female guppy produces twenty-one offspring in a month," Mr. Coates said. "A guppy is about the cheapest and most prolific aquarium fish. The female guppy requires approximately seventy-two cubic inches, or about four gallons of water in which to produce her brood.

"It would therefore take the efforts of one guppy, batting 1,000 for a month, to feed one leaf fish for three days. It would take ten guppies, hitting on all cylinders, to feed it for a month. To feed 150 young leaf fish you would need 2,000 female guppies, each in a four-gallon tank. I say 2,000 rather than 1,500, because even among guppies there is incompatibility, and of 2,000 guppies wed you couldn't count on more than 1,500 producing.

"Well, you would need 200 male guppies to start breeding operations, so that would mean a total of 2,200 tanks with 8,800-gallon tank capacity and I do not know where we could place that many fish unless they built a penthouse on the building, which would run to money.

"The combined efforts of our 2,200 breeders would produce 31,500 eating guppies for the leaf fish every month. You follow me, of course. But it must be remembered that each mature guppy eats ten worms a day and each young fish an average of two.

"That would call for, roughly, 80,000 worms a day. You can't breed worms as fast as guppies. That would mean the employment of two full-time worm diggers. At forty cents an hour that's in item of $32 a week. These are very minute white worms which are found in great clusters. On angle worms, of course, the cost would be prohibitive.

"In four months the leaf fish would be ready for the market—not fullgrown, but large enough to ship. Four 31,500 is—let's see—126,000 guppies they would have eaten by that time. Guppies now retail at $10 or $15 a hundred. A fair retail valuation on the hypothetical guppies eaten would be $15,000.

"One hundred and fifty leaf fish at $50 a pair, which is about the market price for adults, would bring $3,750, leaving a clear loss on the score of guppy consumption alone, of $11,250. To this we must add," and here Mr. Coates brought out a chart on which he had evidently been working for a long time.

2,200 breeding guppies at 5 cents (wholesale) . . . $110
Wages two worm diggers 4 months (17 weeks) at
   $16 a week (40 hours) each   544
Cost of erecting penthouse on Aquarium to house
   2,200 guppy tanks of 72 cu. in. capacity 25,000

TOTAL $25,654

"Plus the loss already accounted for, this would make a deficit of $36,804. The society could not stand the loss.

"So, we will leave them all in the same tank until their appetites develop," Coates said. "They will eat each other until we get down to a few particularly rugged specimens, and then maybe I will get my Madagascar lace plant."

This wouldn't have been so bad, but about a week later the leaf fish, probably in collusion with their boss, produced a second edition of 100 leaflets. Right after the publication of the first story the Aquarium had been besieged by small boys, each begging the chance to rear one leaf fish. I went rushing down to the Aquarium, like Dr. Dafoe, to see the second batch. Although he saw no imminent prospect of a $100,000 appropriation to feed leaf fish, Coates had placed the second lot in a separate tank. He is subject to a kind of Hippocratic oath never to give up a fish.

Emulous of the leaf fish, the snakeheads, a pair of ugly beasts from the Euphrates region, also had kicked through with fifty wiggling black dots.

The snakeheads would receive less consideration than the leaf fish, Coates said, because, while not exactly common in this country, they are fish of uninteresting habits and very plain faces.

Right in the middle of his troubles a woman asked him why the trigger fish continually picks up sand from the bottom of his tank, swims upward and then blows the sand out of his mouth.

"I think he gargles with sand because of minute forms of animal life in his gills," said Coates. "Or maybe it is an early form of sandblasting. Or maybe he just does it for fun."

"I ask," said the woman severely, "because my 4-year-old boy tried to imitate him, and swallowed a lot of gravel. I don't think such a fish should be on exhibition."

"What I would really like to have for our collection," he said to me, "is a couple of Egyptian *mormyridae*. The mormyridae is a fish with a long snout like a miniature elephant—one might say a schnozzle fish. It has the largest brain in proportion to its bodyweight of any animal except man."

"And is it very smart?" I asked.

"Well, they very seldom catch any," he replied laughing merrily.

As if two stories about his ichthyological Jukes family hadn't been enough, Coates gave me an exclusive tip a few days later—on the birth of another 150 leaf fish. I went to the Aquarium to tell him firmly that the World-Telegram was not interested. He told me about *Astronotus ocellatus*, which was unable to obtain a hot bath. Astronotus, which looked rather like a butterfish with a bullseye on its tail, had just arrived from Brazil. The water in its tank was chilly. The heating system was not yet working— this was early in September. He got me worried about the silly fish. I suggested giving it a hot water bottle. I thought this so comical that I found myself taking notes for another story about the Aquarium.

They had got a specimen that Coates called *Pinelodus* question mark, a foul-visaged catfish, also from Brazil, of a species which could not be identified by any of the staff. Pinelodus is a genus. His temper was as ugly as his face, which was saying a lot, and he had eaten a *Chalcinus elongatus*.

They also had young *Protopteri ethiopici*, lung fish of the species noted for curling up into mudballs and going into a deep trance for a couple of years at a time.

From the appetites they exhibited,—beef heart is their favorite scoff—Coates said he had high hopes that at least one would eclipse the record of Public Opinion, the champion protopterus of North America, a ward of the Bellevue

Medical College, who had snoozed for four years without intermission.

"They call him Public Opinion because he evidently cannot be aroused," Coates said.

My boss was by now beginning to call me Friday Liebling, because every day for me seemed to be fish day. But Coates got me again. "It's not about fish," he said loftily. "It's about turtles."

No Hurry

In a square wire cage under an elaborate sun-ray lamp he had an experiment in progress, one which I must confess it was a delight to contemplate. Three tortoises, affectionately known as Shanty Hogan, Equipoise and Harold Ickes, were growing. Fabulous ages have been ascribed to tortoises, particularly those of the Galápagos Islands, and the Aquarium had set out to raise three from the cradle and check on their rate of growth, the number of rings added to the plates of their shells (one ring a year is the tradition) and the age they attain under the most favorable conditions.

The tortoises, particularly Shanty Hogan, the biggest, put away an astonishing quantity of lettuce and tomato salad and overripe fruit every day, but they did not know they were in a cage. They had never moved far enough to find out.

"It is very restful to work on this experiment," said Coates. "The best method, I find, is to sit down and read the Encyclopedia Brittannica. I am up to volume 'Cz-Dr' now, and by the time my direct lineal descendants take over the experiment there will be several new editions for them to read. With luck, this thing may last us into the twenty-eighth century."

By now he is probably up to Mu-Nu.